# RUSSIAN MILITARY THOUGHT

# RUSSIAN MILITARY THOUGHT

THE EVOLUTION
OF STRATEGY
SINCE THE
CRIMEAN WAR

GUDRUN PERSSON

GEORGETOWN UNIVERSITY PRESS / WASHINGTON, DC

© 2025 Gudrun Persson. All rights reserved. No part of this book may be reproduced or utilized in any form or by any means, electronic or mechanical, including photocopying and recording, or by any information storage and retrieval system, without permission in writing from the publisher.

The publisher is not responsible for third-party websites or their content. URL links were active at time of publication.

Library of Congress Cataloging-in-Publication Data

Names: Persson, Gudrun, 1962– author.
Title: Russian military thought : the evolution of strategy since the Crimean War / Gudrun Persson.
Description: Washington, DC : Georgetown University Press, 2025. | Includes bibliographical references.
Identifiers: LCCN 2024056799 | ISBN 9781647126377 (hardcover) | ISBN 9781647126384 (paperback) | ISBN 9781647126391 (ebook)
Subjects: LCSH: Strategy. | Russia—Military policy. | Soviet Union—Military policy. | Russia (Federation)—Military policy.
Classification: LCC UA770 .P384 2025 | DDC 355.020947—dc23/eng/20250209
LC record available at https://lccn.loc.gov/2024056799

♾ This paper meets the requirements of ANSI/NISO Z39.48-1992 (Permanence of Paper).

EU GPSR authorized representative Logos Europe, 9 rue Nicolas Poussin, 17000, La Rochelle, France. E-mail: Contact@logoseurope.eu.

26 25      9 8 7 6 5 4 3 2  First printing

Printed in the United States of America

Cover design by TG Design
Interior design by BookComp, Inc.

*To Lars Erik Blomqvist*

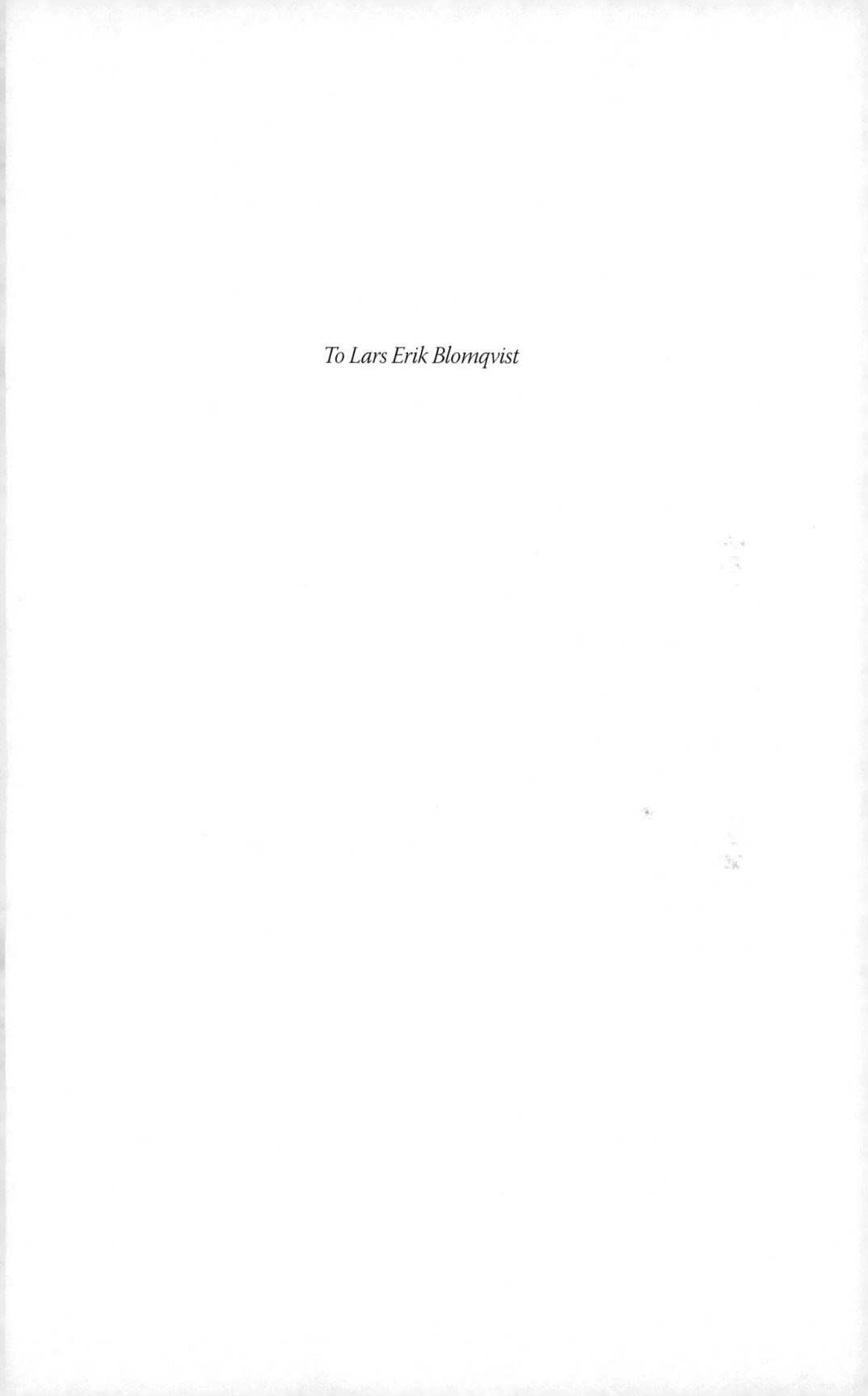

# CONTENTS

*Preface* ix
*Acknowledgments* xi

    Introduction: Why Study Russian Strategic Thought and How?    1

1   A Brief History of Early Russian Strategic Thought    16
2   A Time for Change in the Wake of the Crimean War    29
3   Forming a Soviet Strategy from the Ashes of World War I    59
4   The Legacy of World War II    82
5   In Search of a Strategy beyond Nuclear Weapons    103
6   In Search of a Strategy from the Breakup of the Soviet Union to the Full-Scale Invasion of Ukraine    122
7   Conclusions and Thoughts on the Art of Winning    167

*Selected Bibliography*    181
*Index*    193
*About the Author*    207

# PREFACE

Transliteration follows a modified version of the system of the Library of Congress. I have also omitted the ´ for soft signs. In a few cases, I have kept the spelling of well-known names, such as Trotsky rather than Trotskii and Vasily Sokolovsky rather than Vasilii Sokolovskii. For Sokolovsky in the references, I use Sokolovskiy since that is how it was transliterated when *Soviet Military Strategy* was published. In some cases, most notably surnames of foreign origin, I have chosen their original form—for instance, Goethe rather than Gëte.

All translations are my own unless otherwise noted.

# ACKNOWLEDGMENTS

I could not have written this book without the support of many people. Above all, I would like to thank Magnus Petersson, who has provided intellectual and practical support throughout the process. In addition, Beatrice Heuser read a large part of the manuscript and gave constructive and encouraging suggestions at a crucial stage.

Importantly, I am very grateful to the Axel and Margaret Ax:son Johnson Foundation for Public Benefit and Olle Engkvists Stiftelse, who provided generous financial support. The Swedish Defence Research Agency (FOI) provided me with a leave of absence when this project began in earnest in 2021.

I am grateful to the two anonymous readers for Georgetown University Press for their helpful suggestions. The patience and support by Donald Jacobs, senior acquisitions editor, has been vital.

I have benefited greatly from inspirational discussions with my academic colleagues throughout the years. In particular, Roy Allison, Ann-Sofie Dahl, Petteri Lalu, Andrew Monaghan, Katri Pynnöniemi, and Bettina Renz have been helpful, as well as my colleagues in Slavic studies at Stockholm University. Richard Langlais helped me with language editing as well as offered advice along the way. The staffs at the Stockholm University Library, the library at FOI, and particularly Johan Andersson at the Anna Lindh Library deserve special thanks.

I would also like to thank my friends Niklas Rossbach and Julie Hansen, who never stopped believing in me. There are many others to whom I am very grateful for advice and stimulation—too many, in fact, to be listed here. But this does not diminish my gratitude to them.

# INTRODUCTION

## Why Study Russian Strategic Thought and How?

> *The security of the Russian system is uppermost in the Russian official mind; it is not a question of frontier security but something more intangible.*
> ISAIAH BERLIN, 1946

Russia is again using armed force to achieve its political objectives. To understand why, Russian strategic thought cannot be ignored, yet for a long time the West has done precisely that. As a result, Russian strategic thought has often confused Western politicians and analysts, who have at times characterized it as "backward." Western reactions to the strategic thought underpinning Russia's use of military force reveal the persistence of ignorance and misunderstanding. There are thus several crucial reasons for studying the long evolution of Russian strategic thought.

First, writings on strategy and doctrine reveal how Russia has managed the connection between policy and strategy, the organization of the armed forces, education, and how they have been used as a tool of change. The debates on strategy influence how the armed forces are organized and how they train. In brief, the ideas and concepts expressed in the literature on strategy reveal a framework of thought and therefore shape future possibilities for Russia. It is vital that the West understand this in order to avoid mirror-imaging and be able to develop a sustainable strategic relationship with Russia.

Second, military strategic thought is closely linked to Russia's very existence as a state. Its strategic thought encompasses the broader context of foreign and domestic policy as well as the army's ties to the country's leadership. Considering the importance that the armed forces have had in the Russian Empire, the Soviet Union, and the Russian Federation, strategic thought goes to the heart of the Russian state. It sheds light on Russia's self-image and search for a national identity, which in turn has fundamental consequences for Russia and, not least, for its neighbors.

Third, Russian strategic thought is insufficiently studied, which frequently results in Western surprise when Russia engages in confrontation and deploys its armed forces. This has been illustrated most recently by Russia's annexation of Crimea in 2014 and again by the full-scale invasion of Ukraine in 2022.

Fourth, the Russian view of strategy is broader and more encompassing than recognized in the West, which, again, often leads to the latter's bewilderment.

In this study of the evolution of military strategic thought in Russia, I sometimes use "strategic thought," and "military thought" as shorthand. Russian military strategic thinking, as we shall see, is not limited to the strictly military realm of strategy.

This book traces the influential drivers of Russian military strategic thought and uncovers not only continuity but also reform efforts over a period of 160 years, from the mid-nineteenth century up to the 2022 invasion. As we shall see, the constants are more prevalent than the changes. The focus lies on the periods after either defeat in war or state collapse, although the legacy of World War II and the advent of nuclear weapons are also considered. The reason for this is obvious. In times of catastrophe, the necessity to rethink strategy and doctrine becomes imperative and the opportunity for change arises. For too long, Western understandings of Russian strategic thought have focused narrowly on Soviet concepts, without taking into account the imperial legacy. It is an often overlooked fact that the great military theorist Carl von Clausewitz (1780–1831) at one point served briefly in the Russian army, as did Baron Antoine-Henri Jomini (1779–1869) and Henry Lloyd (ca. 1720–83).

This book offers a deeper and more nuanced qualitative analysis, arguing that without understanding the past evolution of thought it is not possible to grasp the mindset of the current Russian leadership. I show how the study of military thought on strategy and doctrine can reveal possible directions for change.

Russia has a long history of wars and an equally long tradition of military thinkers, yet in many Western works on military strategic thought Russian thinkers are often mentioned only in passing, if at all. Walter Pintner found not even one Russian military thinker worthy of a deeper study.[1] And yet the military has been, and still is, an important part of the Russian state and its history. The Russian debates on strategy and doctrine are much richer than sometimes believed. In her book on how we have been shaped by war, Margaret MacMillan argued that we do not take war as seriously as it deserves.[2] The same could be said about Russian strategic thought.

Adapting to new thoughts and theories is mainly an intellectual exercise, with far-reaching consequences for the armed forces and defense of the country.

The French historian Marc Bloch reflected in his analysis of the French defeat by Germany in 1940 that it was above all an intellectual defeat: "Our leaders, or those who acted for them, were incapable of thinking in terms of a new war. In other words, the German triumph was, essentially a triumph of intellect—and it is that which makes it so peculiarly serious."[3] Many years later, Andrew Marshall, director of the Pentagon's Office of Net Assessment, observed, "The main challenge in the Revolution of Military Affairs is an intellectual and not a technological one."[4] When there is no solid vision of a future war or no coherent military doctrine and concepts of operations, it is highly probable that the way military organizations will build and equip their forces will not be in compliance with the demands of the strategic environment.[5]

So, what factors influence the development of Russian military thought on strategy and doctrine? Drawing on Beatrice Heuser's book on strategy,[6] I focus on the following questions in examining the writings of some of the most influential Russian military thinkers during the selected period of 160 years:

- Is war seen as an inevitable part of human life, a legitimate activity, or something to be contained and avoided?
- Who is the adversary, and how is the adversary seen—as a hated enemy or an equal?
- What role does technology play in relation to the morale of the soldier and the armed forces?
- What role does geography play?
- How is the enemy to be defeated—by offensive or defensive actions?
- What is the view of future war?

Russian thinking about strategy and doctrine evolves in response to international (mainly Western) military thought and experiences from Russia's past and more recent wars. Therefore, this book will examine several factors and their impact on military strategic thought: domestic and foreign policy, history, technology, geography, and the influence of foreign theorists. These can in turn be divided into hard factors (technology and geography) and soft factors (policy, history, and foreign influence).

Subsequent to the dissolution of the Soviet Union, Russian military thinkers have been rediscovering their own legacy. Many of the leading military theorists of the 1920s and 1930s had been persecuted because of the repressive Bolshevik system and—if not forgotten—were prevented from assuming their place in Russian military thought, with disastrous consequences for the country.[7] Now, theorists from both czarist and Soviet times are being republished and reevaluated. Therefore, the time is ripe for a longer-term study of Russian strategic thought.

## HOW TO STUDY RUSSIAN STRATEGIC THOUGHT

Studying military thought is inevitably, according to Harald Høiback, "an elusive undertaking."[8] It is a complex exercise, full of pitfalls. This book, unlike many contemporary Western analyses, which commit the error of mirror-imaging, explains Russian concepts by taking Russian theories, terms, and contexts as its starting point. It relies on Russian debates, theories, and doctrines in tracing continuities and change over time. Although these debates and other aspects do not allow us to predict Russia's policy choices in a future crisis, they do reveal a framework of thought and therefore shape future possibilities. In order to prepare for the future, these thoughts should be analyzed and put into context.

Given the complexity of the subject, I approach it from a multidisciplinary perspective, drawing on theoretical insights from history and political science. The structure is largely chronological, while the chapters consist of an analytical/descriptive part followed by an interpretive one, as well as a section where I discuss the impact—that is, the relevance today—of the debates analyzed.

My qualitative analysis shows how specific concepts take on additional meaning when they are interpreted as a part of a greater context. In other words, this study deals with military thought as the conscious, scientific, professional, and intellectual scholarship on war, conflict, and national security in Russia.[9]

In analyzing Russian military thought, Peter von Wahlde distinguished between nationalists and academics—that is, he applied the Slavophile-Westernizer controversy to military thinking.[10] In brief, the nationalists tried to show the superiority of Russian military art over Western, whereas the academics argued that Russian nationalism in military affairs hindered military progress.[11]

Finding this distinction inadequate, William Fuller divided the two groups into "magicians" and "technicians," arguing that his division allows a broader interpretation, wherein a technician simultaneously can be a Slavophile.[12] Soviet scholars have drawn the line between academics and representatives of the national Russian school.[13] Later, Tor Bukkvoll drew the distinction between three categories of Russian military thinkers: "traditionalists," "modernists," and "revolutionaries."[14] According to Valerii Konyshev and Aleksandr Sergunin, there are two main schools of thought: traditionalists and nontraditionalists.[15] These categorizations must not be exaggerated. The ensuing controversies have sometimes been overstated, creating artificial contradictions.[16] That does not mean that the different schools are unimportant. The consequences of choosing one or the other side have a direct impact on strategy and doctrine, as we shall see.

Because of the long time span, I have chosen the writings of a few of the leading military theorists from each period using the following criteria: (1) they were prominent during their lifetimes and recognized as such by their contemporaries, and (2) in contemporary Russia they are considered to be leading military thinkers.

## KEY CONCEPTS

"Strategy" is an ambiguous term and needs to be defined. Its meaning has changed considerably over the centuries.[17] Since Clausewitz's definition "the use of engagements for the object of the war," the word has developed to include a broader meaning, sometimes called "grand strategy" or "major strategy." Jomini, who had a huge influence on Russian military thought in the nineteenth century, spelled out in his *Summary of the Art of War* the relationship between war and politics or, in other words, why a government goes to war, in the following nine points:

- to reclaim certain rights or to defend them;
- to protect and maintain the great interests of the state, as commerce, manufactures, or agriculture;
- to uphold neighbouring states whose existence is necessary either for the safety of the government or the balance of power;
- to fulfil the obligations of offensive and defensive alliances;
- to propagate political or religious theories, to crush them out, or to defend them;
- to increase the influence and power of the state by acquisitions of territory;
- to defend the threatened independence of the state;
- to avenge insulted honour;
- or from a mania of conquest.[18]

This is a more inclusive interpretation of strategy than its narrower, operational meaning. It involves both intellectual capabilities and the utilization of all of the state's resources.[19] Richard Betts has defined it as a plan for using military means to achieve political ends,[20] and Lawrence Freedman summarized it in a succinct way: "Strategy is about the relationship between (political) ends and (military, economic, political, etc.) means. It is the art of creating power."[21]

In the 1870s Genrikh Leer (1829–1904) noted that strategy in the broadest sense is a "synthesis of all military affairs, its generalisation, its philosophy."[22] Aleksandr Svechin observed in the 1920s that strategy decides issues related to the use of armed forces as well as to the use of all the country's resources to achieve the final military goals.[23]

In the following chapters, I use "strategy" in this broader sense, which also corresponds well with how the term has been used in Russian military thought—that is, it has a holistic, all-encompassing meaning. This is consistent with the writings of many scholars of Russia from various disciplines, who argue that an inclination to holism is characteristic throughout the Russian intellectual tradition in literature, religious philosophy, and the sciences.[24]

"Doctrine" is an equally undefined term in need of some qualification. There is no commonly recognized definition,[25] and it can also be interpreted in both formal and informal terms. For the purposes of this book, I find the Russian thinking of the early 1920s on the topic of a unified military doctrine particularly useful. This debate is analyzed in greater detail in chapter 3. Suffice it here to say that the definition used by the then head of the General Staff Academy, Andrei Snesarev (1865–1937), is close to what became the official one and also encapsulates earlier perceptions of military doctrine in Russia: "It is a set of military-state achievements and military foundations, practical techniques and skills of the people, which the country considers to be the best for a given historical moment and with which the military system of the state is permeated from top to bottom."[26]

This suggests a broad, holistic view, where the strategic objectives of the state, military science, technology, and the morale of the people should be systematically combined with the framework of the military doctrine. This means that the military doctrine had a political side and a technical one, which is precisely what Mikhail Frunze (1885–1925) used in 1921 as an argument in favor of a written doctrine.[27] As noted many years after these debates in *Soviet Military Strategy*, edited by Marshal Vasily Sokolovsky (1897–1968), "military doctrine depends directly on the social structure, the state problems with regard to domestic and foreign policy, and the economic, political, and cultural state of a country."[28] The idea and use of a doctrine was to become established in the Soviet Union and has continued up until today.

Importantly, Western doctrines tend to focus on the method of war; Russia is describing the superstructure surrounding it. The Russian approach to doctrine is extensive, political, and deductive.[29] This is often misunderstood or ignored in the West, contributing to Western bewilderment regarding Russian strategic thought.

Moreover, there is a distinction to be made between "doctrine" and "military thought." The doctrine establishes the official position, whereas the debate between military theorists might sometimes be fierce. However, some theories from the debate may find their way into the doctrines. In fact, the early 1920s discussions and debates on a unified military doctrine eventually materialized into such a doctrine. A more recent example is Andrei Kokoshin's writings. He argued for years about the need for a formula of nonnuclear deterrence to be conceptualized in Russia's military doctrine and in other plans regulating the armed forces.[30] Eventually, a paragraph on nonnuclear deterrence was included in the Military Doctrine of 2014.[31]

This book examines some of the key issues discussed over time: man (morale) and technology, offensive/defensive warfare, threats, and views about future wars. All these questions touch on the relationship between strategy and doctrine. Exploring as it does this aspect of intellectual life in Russia, this book contributes to our knowledge of the development of strategy and doctrine in Russia.

## SOURCES

This book is mainly based on Russian-language sources. Parts of the data came from archival research. One chapter (2) is to a large extent based on my research in the main archives of the Russian Military History Archive (RGVIA) and the State Archive of the Russian Federation (GARF). Included here are the war plans of 1870 and 1873. Furthermore, a major portion of the sources consists of original writings by some of the most influential Russian writers of each period. Compared to past studies of the Soviet period, the present study benefited from access to what is now plenty of core material in military periodicals that were not previously available: *Voennaia mysl* (Military thought), *Nezavisimoe voennoe obozrenie* (Independent military review), *Vestnik Akademii voennykh nauk* (Bulletin of the Academy of Military Sciences), and *Voenno-promyshlennyi kurier* (Military-industrial courier). The debate in military journals, both old and new, provided a rich source material that is too seldom used. Raymond Garthoff, in his seminal book *Deterrence and the Revolution in Soviet Military Doctrine* (1990), made extensive use of the previously confidential journal *Voennaia mysl*, which had only then just been made available to the outside world. He discovered that there were no substantial differences between the confidential writings and what was discussed in the open military journals. I used these journals extensively, including *Voennaia mysl* (or its equivalent), from 1918 to the present. The multi-volume work *Rossiiskii voennyi sbornik* (Russian military collection), edited by A. E. Savinkin from the 1990s and onward, was also a valuable source.

The various editions of the Russian/Soviet military encyclopedias were also used, as were numerous memoirs of key individuals.

## PREVIOUS RESEARCH

Several Russian works have served as an inspiration. Andrei Kokoshin's book, *Soviet Strategic Thought, 1917–91* (1998), is an abbreviated version of his *Armiia i politika* (Army and politics) (1995). This is an in-depth, seminal study of Soviet military thought, written at a time of fundamental change. Kokoshin, at the time, was both an academic and held public office as secretary of the Defense Council of the Russian Federation and secretary of the Security Council of the Russian Federation. His book on Svechin was published in 2013. Several other of Kokoshin's works, such as *Politologiia i sotsiologiia voennoi strategii* (The political science and sociology of military strategy; 2018), have been useful. Moreover, Vladimir Zolotarev has edited a useful anthology, *Istoriia voennoi strategii Rossii* (A history of Russia's military strategy; 2000). Its authors trace the long-term development of Russian military strategy, with the explicit aim to "show its regular patterns of development."

In addition, I have benefited from several Soviet works on military thought. A few works stand out. P. A. Zaionchkovskii's *Voennye reformy 1860–70 godov v Rossii* (Military reforms of the 1860–70s in Russia; 1952) is indispensable for anyone working on the military reforms during the reign of Alexander II. L. G. Beskrovnyi's *Russkaia voenno-teoreticheskaia mysl XIX i nachala XX vekov* (Russian military-theoretical thought in the nineteenth and the beginning of the twentieth centuries; 1960) is useful for its inclusion of some of the core texts of the nineteenth and early twentieth centuries. G. P. Meshcheriakov's *Russkaia voennaia mysl v XIX-om veke* (Russian military thought in the nineteenth century) (1973), and P. A. Zhilin's edited volume, *Russkaia voennaia mysl konets XIX-nachalo XX v.* (Russian military thought at the end of the nineteenth and the beginning of the twentieth centuries; 1982) provide useful details, as does I. A. Korotkov's *Istoriia sovetskoi voennoi mysli: Kratkii ocherk; 1917–iiun 1941* (History of Soviet military thought: A short essay; 1917–June 1941; 1980).

Military thought on strategy and doctrine over a longer period has been largely neglected by Western scholarship of the Russian army. Yet there are a few exceptionally well-researched works that inspired my book, such as William Fuller's *Strategy and Power in Russia 1640–1914* (1992), David Rich's *The Tsar's Colonels: Professionalism, Strategy, and Subversion in Late Imperial Russia* (1998), and William Odom's *The Collapse of the Soviet Military* (1998). Although all three studies touch on military thought, relying mainly on Russian sources, they do not focus on it as this book does. Pavel Baev's work *The Russian Army in a Time of Troubles* (1996) is a useful contribution, although his focus is primarily on the post-Soviet period.

Roy Allison's *Russia, the West and Military Intervention* (2013) delves into more current issues. Dominic Lieven has made important research, not least in *Empire: The Russian Empire and Its Rivals* (2000) and *The End of Tsarist Russia* (2015).

Recently, three valuable books on Russian military thought have been published in English. In *Strategiya: The Foundations of the Russian Art of Strategy*

(2021), Ofer Fridman has translated and commented on several key texts by Russian/Soviet military strategic thinkers, including some of those in exile after 1917. Oscar Jonsson has advanced the field by analyzing military thought on war from the Soviet era, with a narrow focus on information warfare, in *The Russian Understanding of War: Blurring the Lines between War and Peace* (2019). Ofer Fridman's *Russian "Hybrid Warfare": Resurgence and Politicization* (2018) examines the Western and Russian debates on hybrid warfare and explores the nature of the confrontation between the two.

Another significant contribution is Norbert Eitelhuber's book on Russian strategic culture, *Russland im 21. Jahrhundert: Reif für eine multipolare Welt?* (Russia in the twenty-first century: Ripe for a multipolar world?; 2015). Dimitri Minic's recent study *Pensée et culture stratégiques russes: Du contournement de la lutte armée à la guerre en Ukraine* (Russian strategic thought and culture: From bypassing armed struggle to war in Ukraine; 2023) reveals deep insights into current Russian military thought.

During the Soviet period, there were various Western studies on Soviet military thinking, mostly focusing on doctrine but also on the Red Army during World War II. Here I have profited particularly from Garthoff's book on the Soviet doctrine and Dale Herspring's works on the high command, both the Soviet Union's (1990) and the Russian Federation's (2006). David Glantz's *The Military Strategy of the Soviet Union: A History* (1992) touches on some of the questions in the present work, although he did not have access to much of the material that is now available. In addition, Edward Luttwak's *The Grand Strategy of the Soviet Union* (1983) is a good read but does not contain a single Russian source.

Brian Taylor is one of the few scholars who treats the period from imperial Russia up to contemporary Russia. He does this in his *Politics and the Russian Army: Civil-Military Relations, 1689–2000* (2003), although his book analyzes the role of the army in domestic political struggles—that is, civil-military relations. David R. Stone examines the development of the Russian army in his work *A Military History of Russia: From Ivan the Terrible to the War in Chechnya* (2006).

Frederick Kagan and Robin Higham edited two volumes, *The Military History of Tsarist Russia* (2002) and *The Military History of the Soviet Union* (2002), that deal mainly with the development of the armed forces and how the Russian army performed in battle but do not examine military thought specifically. Dima Adamsky explores the impact of cultural factors on the revolution in Soviet military affairs in *The Culture of Military Innovation: The Impact of Cultural Factors on the Revolutions in Military Affairs in Russia, the US, and Israel* (2010). In his *Russian Nuclear Orthodoxy: Religion, Politics, and Strategy* (2019), he uncovers the Russian Orthodox Church's role in strategic deterrence.

He develops the theme of deterrence in his *The Russian Way of Deterrence: Strategic Culture, Coercion, and War* (2023).

Several recent books have appeared analyzing Russia's ongoing war against Ukraine and previous wars during the 1990s and 2000s. Serhii Plokhy's *The Russo-Ukrainian War* (2023) is useful, as are Mark Galeotti's *Putin's Wars: From Chechnya to Ukraine* (2022) and Owen Matthews's *Overreach: The Inside Story of Putin's War against Ukraine* (2022).

All these works stop short of covering the longer period, from imperial Russian and Soviet to contemporary strategic thought.

Regarding the general development of military thought, Azar Gat's books are modern classics. His *A History of Military Thought: From the Enlightenment to the Cold War* (2001) brings together his trilogy on modern military thought (1989, 1992, 1998) and is a fundamental work for any student of the subject. His books serve as an inspiration, although his cultural and philosophical outlook is significantly broader than this book's. Heuser's book *The Evolution of Strategy: Thinking War from Antiquity to the Present* (2010) is likewise a modern classic on the topic. Martin van Creveld writes about military thought and military theory in *The Art of War: War and Military Thought* (2000). He covers the period from ancient China to the war in Yugoslavia in a very broad, but not in-depth, study.

This book builds on and engages with the findings of the above-listed studies. However, repeating old clichés does not add sufficient insight to Russian strategic thought. Consequently, this book assumes a longer time perspective and explores the variety of factors influencing military thought, including policy, history, technology, and geography. It also examines continuity and change in Russian military thought and challenges the view that Russia was "backward" in this area. In these ways, I hope it makes an original and timely contribution to the field of Russian military history.

## LIMITATIONS

A necessary limitation is that this book does not analyze the impact of Russian military strategic thought on operations and tactical behavior. Nor does it attempt to trace developments in each branch of the armed forces.

Military capability can be assessed on three different levels: the conceptual (in other words, doctrines and military thinking), the structural (i.e., the organization), and that of the personnel (which refers to education, motivation, and the social situation). This book focuses on the conceptual level. Furthermore, Russia was and is primarily a land power, so the "land-centric" outlook predominates; the naval, air, and other aspects of doctrine and strategy are only touched upon when necessary. The reason for this is the simple fact that the Russian military was traditionally driven by the perception that wars are decided on land.[32]

In addition, a few words of clarification are needed. Thinking about war inevitably touches on strategic culture, which has developed into an entire research field within security studies since the term was briefly introduced by Jack Snyder in a 1977 RAND Corporation report.[33] The term covers the topics of strategy and culture and contains various schools of thought.

There is a major disagreement about the extent to which culture can be isolated as an explanatory factor. Common for most of the literature on strategic culture so far are two main arguments.[34] First, due to cultural differences across security communities, different communities will make different strategic choices when faced with the same security environment. Second, existing strategic culture theory also suggests that particular communities are likely to exhibit consistent and persistent strategic preferences over time. In other words, the situation is static. Any appreciation of the role of agency in producing security structures is absent.[35]

The scholarship on strategic culture has mostly been developed in the Western world, but recently Russian academics and researchers have started to explore the concept more thoroughly in relation to security studies.[36] Kokoshin notes that every country has its own strategic culture that reflects how the armed forces are organized and how military force is applied.[37] He defines it as "a set of stereotypes of sustainable behavior of the relevant subject during the large-scale use of military force in terms of its political tasks and military goals, including preparing, taking, and implementing strategic decisions."

However, in spite of many efforts, the study of strategic culture still does not have a coherent methodological design. There is no consensus in the discipline on how this could be achieved. Høiback carefully examines the challenges in defining culture and determining its possible impact. According to him, doctrine rests on "authority," "rationality," and "a-rationality." He concludes that when "all attempts to explain a political decision or a particular military outcome have failed, culture may be of some help."[38]

To be clear, it lies beyond the scope of this book to analyze "Russian strategic culture" in great detail. Nevertheless, this study sheds some light on some of the most urgent questions within this field, to the possible benefit of specialists of strategic culture.

## OUTLINE

Following this introduction, a brief historic survey of the development of early Russian thought on military strategy is provided. This chapter is intended as a short general background. Chapter 2 examines the consequences of the defeat in the Crimean War (1853–56). It forced Russia to rethink its strategy and doctrine, and as a consequence fundamental military reforms were launched under the then war minister, Dmitrii Miliutin (1816–1912). It is also during this period that the study of military science and theory became more systematic and professionalized.

Some of the contentious debates of the mid-nineteenth century are examined. This provides a background leading up to the vibrant debates regarding strategy and doctrine following the defeat in the Russo-Japanese War (1904–5) and the Russian Revolution of 1905. One question was especially vital: Should Russia prepare for a future offensive war or a defensive one? Several military thinkers argued for a defensive posture, but the czar, Nicholas II (1868–1918), opted for an offensive strategy, due to policy concerns both domestic and foreign. The question of a unified military doctrine was now being raised and discussed in a serious manner. However, it was not resolved before 1914. Some radical military thinkers argued that the ethos of the armed forces should be to fight for the country rather than for the czar.

The next chapter explores the developments after the collapse of the empire, the defeat in World War I, and the Civil War. The young Bolshevik state was trying to work out a strategy and doctrine for the future, with a keen eye on the latest wars. The focus is on the debates in the early 1920s, centered on a unified military doctrine, the role of new technologies (airplanes and tanks), as well as the offensive/defensive strategy discussions. The experiences from the world war only partly colored the discussions, since the Civil War dominated the debate among the young Bolshevik thinkers. Wars of the future, according to several military theorists of the 1920s, would become increasingly large-scale and ever more complex. The chapter also introduces Andrei Snesarev's texts. His thought is less known in the West, but it is being rediscovered and quoted in the current development of Russian military thought. He examines wars not only from a historical and economic perspective but, importantly, also from a moral one and the role of the state. The contributions of Aleksandr Svechin (1878–1938) are also examined, as are the roles of Boris Shaposhnikov (1882–1945) and Mikhail Tukhachevskii (1893–1937). The importance of these debates cannot be overstated; they play a crucial role today when Russia is developing its military strategy for the future.

Chapter 4 examines the legacy of World War II. In the years following the Soviet victory, the debate on strategy and doctrine was completely dictated by Joseph Stalin. The main enemy was considered to be "American-British imperialism," which was described as having similarities with German fascism. Stalin's concept of "permanently operating factors" of war was the official military theory.[39] The introduction of nuclear weapons did not immediately change the Soviet view of future wars, and it was only in the 1960s that this issue could be discussed in depth. The result was Sokolovsky's *Soviet Military Strategy*. The works by Adm. Sergei Gorshkov (1910–88) are also analyzed in chapter 4, since he played a key role in making the Soviet navy oceangoing. Furthermore, Soviet military policy, both before and long after World War II, stressed the importance of an offensive strategy. It was not until the mid-1980s that Russian strategists drew on the lessons of the war and seriously challenged the offensive strategy.[40]

Chapter 5 analyzes Soviet military thought at its highpoint, namely during the career of Nikolai Ogarkov (1917–94), chief of the General Staff from 1977 to 1984, who stands out as the most prominent military thinker of the time. Furthermore, his legacy serves as a bridge to current military thought. He understood the interrelationship between political and military factors and that their management could benefit the national security of the country. His contribution to developing the thinking on the "military-technical revolution" still has its value today. His thoughts on the future battlefield remain far-reaching.

In the next chapter, contemporary issues are outlined against the backdrop of the dissolution of the Soviet Union and the experiences of Afghanistan and Chechnya. The war in Georgia in 2008 gave impetus to a major, and well-financed, military reform. What impact did it have on military thought on strategy and doctrine? Special attention is given to geography, domestic and external policies, and offensive/defensive strategy. The thinking of prominent theorists such as Nikolai Makarov (1949–), Makhmut Gareev (1923–2019), Andrei Kokoshin (1945–), and Valerii Gerasimov (1955–) are examined. The current Russo-Ukrainian War is put into context.

The final chapter explores the essence of the strategic debates on the development of strategy and doctrine in contemporary Russia. What are the continuities, and what are the significant changes? What are the implications for Russia and its neighbors? I argue that Russian strategic thought is not "backward." The Russian Federation does have a strategy that is continuously developing. The crucial point for Russian strategic theorists is to find the right balance between military thought, Russia's resources, and political choices, between lessons from history and adapting to future technological demands, and between domestic and foreign threats.

## NOTES

*Epigraph:* Isaiah Berlin, *The Soviet Mind: Russian Culture under Communism*, ed. Henry Hardy (Washington, DC: Brookings Institution Press, 2003), 92.
1. Walter Pintner, "Russian Military Thought: The Western Model and the Shadow of Suvorov," in *Makers of Modern Strategy from Machiavelli to the Nuclear Age*, ed. Peter Paret, 354–75 (1994; repr., Oxford: Oxford University Press, 1986).
2. Margaret MacMillan, *War: How Conflict Shaped Us* (London: Profile Books, 2020), 3.
3. Marc Bloch, *Strange Defeat: A Statement of Evidence Written in 1940* (London: W. W. Norton, 1999), 36.

4. Quoted in Dima Adamsky, *The Culture of Military Innovation: The Impact of Cultural Factors on the Revolution in Military Affairs in Russia, the US, and Israel* (Stanford, CA: Stanford Security Studies, 2010), 1–2.
5. Adamsky, 146.
6. Beatrice Heuser, *The Evolution of Strategy: Thinking War from Antiquity to the Present* (Cambridge: Cambridge University Press, 2010), 29–30.
7. Andrei Kokoshin, *Soviet Strategic Thought 1917–1991* (Cambridge, MA: MIT Press, 1998), 40–44.
8. Harald Høiback, *Understanding Military Doctrine: A Multidisciplinary Approach* (London: Routledge, 2013), 5, 55–66.
9. Peter von Wahlde, "Military Thought in Imperial Russia" (unpublished PhD diss., Indiana University, 1966), viii.
10. Von Wahlde, 95–116.
11. For an introduction to the Slavophile-Westernizer debate, see, e.g., Tibor Szamuely, *The Russian Tradition* (London: Fontana Press, 1974), 254–71, and Iver Neumann, *Russia and the Idea of Europe*, 2nd ed. (London: Routledge, 2017), 28–38.
12. William C. Fuller Jr., *Strategy and Power in Russia 1600–1914* (New York: Free Press, 1992), 303–5, 514.
13. L. G. Beskrovnyi, *Ocherki voennoi istoriografii Rossii* [Essays on the military historiography of Russia] (Moscow: Izdatelstvo Akademii nauk SSSR, 1962); P. A. Zhilin, ed., *Russkaia voennaia mysl konets XIX–nachalo XX v.* [Russian military thought at the end of the 19th century and beginning of the 20th century] (Moscow: Nauka, 1982).
14. Tor Bukkvoll, "Iron Cannot Fight: The Role of Technology in Current Russian Military Theory," *Journal of Strategic Studies* 34, no. 5 (2011): 681–706.
15. V. N. Konyshev and A. A. Sergunin, *Sovremennaia voennaia strategiia* [Contemporary military strategy] (Moscow: Aspekt Press, 2014), 85–105.
16. Gudrun Persson, *Learning from Foreign Wars: Russian Military Thinking 1859–1873* (Solihull, UK: Helion, 2010), 77.
17. Heuser, *Evolution of Strategy*, 3–28.
18. Antoine Henri de Jomini, *The Art of War: Restored Edition* (Kingston, Ontario: Legacy Books, 2008), 2.
19. Paret, *Makers of Modern Strategy*, 3.
20. Richard K. Betts, "Is Strategy an Illusion?," *International Security* 25, no. 2 (2000): 5–50.
21. Quoted in Heuser, *Evolution of Strategy*, 27.
22. G. A. Leer, *Zapiski strategii* [Notes on strategy] (Saint Petersburg: Obshchestvennaia Polza), 1.
23. A. Svechin, *Strategiia* [Strategy] (Moscow: Voennyi vestnik, 1927), 15.
24. Dmitry (Dima) Adamsky, "From Moscow with Coercion: Russian: Deterrence Theory and Strategic Culture," *Journal of Strategic Studies* 41, nos. 1–2 (2018): 33–60.
25. Høiback, *Understanding*, 1–2.
26. A. E. Snesarev, "Edinaia voennaia doktrina" [A unified military doctrine], *Voennoe delo*, no. 8 (April 26, 1920): 225–33.
27. M. V. Frunze, *Edinaia voennaia doktrina i Krasnoi Armii* [Unified military doctrine and the Red Army] (Moscow: Voennoe izdatelstvo, 1941), 6–7.

28. V. D. Sokolovskiy, *Soviet Military Strategy*, 3rd ed., edited with an analysis and commentary by Harriet Fast Scott (London: Macdonald & Jane's, 1968), 38.
29. Høiback, *Understanding*, 45.
30. A. A. Kokoshin, *O sisteme neiadernogo (prediadernogo) sderzhivaniia v oboronnoi politike Rossii* [About the system of nonnuclear (prenuclear) deterrence in Russia's defense policy] (Moscow: Izdatelstvo Moskovskogo universiteta, 2012).
31. *Voennaia doktrina Rossiiskoi Federatsii* [The Military Doctrine of the Russian Federation], December 25, 2014, http://www.scrf.gov.ru/. Versions of this series of documents are referred to as "Military Doctrine" in the main text.
32. Makhmut Akhmetovich Gareev, *M. V. Frunze, Military Theorist* (Washington, DC: Pergamon-Brassey's, 1988), 246. See also Norman Cigar, "The Soviet/Russian Sea Power, Land Power Debate in the Era of Perestroyka," *Journal of Slavic Military Studies* 22, no. 4 (2009): 459–84. For a useful analysis of the czarist navy, see Jacob Kipp, "The Imperial Russian Navy 1696–1900," in *The Military History of Tsarist Russia*, ed. Frederick W. Kagan and Robin Higham, 151–77 (New York: Palgrave, 2002).
33. Jack Snyder, *The Soviet Strategic Culture: Implications for Limited Nuclear Operations* (Santa Monica, CA: RAND Corp., 1977).
34. Edward Lock, "Refining Strategic Culture: Return of the Second Generation," *Review of International Studies* 36, no. 3 (2010): 689.
35. Lock, 692.
36. T. A. Alekseeva, "Strategicheskaia kultura: Evoliutsiia kontseptsii" [Strategic culture: Evolution of the concept], *Polis*, no. 5 (2012): 130–47; A. A. Kokoshin, *Voporosy prikladnoi teorii voiny* [Questions of an applied theory of war] (Moscow: Izd. dom Vysshei shkoly ekonomiki, 2018), 160–61; A. A. Bartosh. "Strategicheskaia kultura kak instrument voenno-politicheskogo analiza," [Strategic culture as an instrument of military-political analysis], *Voennaia mysl*, no. 7 (2020): 6–21.
37. Kokoshin, *Voporosy prikladnoi*, 160–61.
38. Høiback, *Understanding*, 56, 182.
39. Kokoshin, *Soviet Strategic Thought*, 111–13.
40. Gareev, *M. V. Frunze*, 207–10.

# 1
# A BRIEF HISTORY OF EARLY RUSSIAN STRATEGIC THOUGHT

*We are Russians, God is with us!*
ALEKSANDR SUVOROV

"The origins of military thought are unknown," Martin van Creveld noted.[1] But if one is to trace any of the origins of Russian military thought as informed by practice, it would be to Peter the Great (1672–1725), Field Marshal Petr Aleksandrovich Rumiantsev (1725–96), and Generalissimo Aleksandr Vasilevich Suvorov (1730–1800). Their imprint on Russian thinking about war and conflicts was and still is profound. In the early nineteenth century, strategic studies was introduced at the newly created Imperial Military Academy (renamed in 1855 the Nicholas General Staff Academy in commemoration of Czar Nicholas I).

## FROM THE STEPPE TOWARD PROFESSIONALIZATION: A BACKGROUND

During the time when Russia consisted of little but Muscovy, the army was an integral part of the state and the ruling elites. The obsession with foreign supremacy and invaders became an early dominating thought in the rulers' strategy, dating back to the Teutonic knights and the Mongol invasions. It was through the army that the czars could expand their territory over the centuries and finally call it an empire.

Raids and counterraids remained the basic strategy of the Muscovite steppe army.[2] In this, they had adopted some of the Mongols' military strategies and structures. Foreign interventions during the so-called Time of Troubles (*smutnoe vremia*) did not prevent Muscovy from expanding. During that time, both the Poles and the Swedes entered Moscow. For instance, on March 12, 1610, Swedish field marshal Jacob Pontusson De la Gardie (1583–1652) arrived in Moscow, together with the czar's troops under the command of Mikhail Skopin-Shuisky (1586–1610), in an effort to prevent Polish forces from getting to the capital in the succession chaos that had broken out since the last czar of the Rurikids had died.

Domestic political consolidation, assisted by the army's reliability and loyalty, was key to the expansion.[3] For the initial three centuries, the focus of Muscovy's military activities was concentrated on the steppe, but toward the mid-sixteenth century, confrontation in the West became more and more intense. Both the Polish-Lithuanian Commonwealth and Sweden were increasingly challenging.

From the 1650s, a grand strategy began to crystallize until Muscovy eventually was declared an empire by Peter I. The civil and military elites were combined in mobilizing the economic and human resources to achieve the status of a great power.[4] During the seventeenth century, Muscovy doubled in size. From the end of the fifteenth century to the end of the nineteenth century, Muscovy/Russia grew by 130 square kilometers a day.[5]

During the reign of Peter I, major reforms were introduced that affected the entire Russian state. Peter took the title "emperor" and thus has been described as the "father" of the Russian Empire. Warfare, according to many scholars, was ultimately the most significant driver in Peter's transformation of Russia.[6] His strategy, which underpinned his reforms, was to create an efficient military force. Particularly important in his strategic outlook were his efforts to coordinate military action and diplomacy. He established military councils (variously called *voennye sovety*, *konsilii*, or *konsiliumy*), where strategy was debated among the principal generals and foreign-policy experts until the final decision was taken by the czar. They took place ten to twenty times a year.[7]

Peter laid the foundations of a standing regular army and established a Russian navy. In devising a recruitment system, he was to a large degree inspired by Sweden. The new field regulations, also borrowed from Sweden, had a strategic view of operations.[8] The extent to which Peter's reforms fully succeeded is disputable, but some of them are relevant for the topic of this book. He opened Russia's first secular schools for training specialists. He set up a few military establishments based on the Western model—for instance, the School of Mathematics and Navigation, the two Moscow artillery schools, and two engineering schools, one in Moscow, the other in Saint Petersburg.

Moscow University was founded only later, in 1755; in 1786 Catherine II (1729–96) introduced a regular system of primary and secondary education. Before the nineteenth century, there were only a few specialized military academies and no specialized military journals or military newspapers in Russia.[9] It should be noted that Petr Shuvalov (1711–62) had already proposed the establishment of a higher military academy in the 1750s, but those plans came to nothing. Shuvalov was convinced that a young officer must acquire a sound knowledge of the principles of war. "Leadership is not enough," he maintained.[10] It was not until 1832 that a higher military academy was established in Saint Petersburg, at the suggestion of Antoine-Henri Jomini, who was an adviser to Nicholas I (1796–1855).

Early modern Russian military thought, however, was much more sophisticated than sometimes believed, as Eugene Miakinkov has shown.[11] The successes of the Russian army in the eighteenth century were underpinned by advanced strategic thought.

From Peter the Great and onward, the offensive was the preferred military strategy, although this was not unique to Russia. In the 1890s Nikolai Nikolaevich Sukhotin (1847–1918), then head of the General Staff Academy, conducted a study of Russia's wars since 1700 and concluded that Russia had been at war for a total of 106 years, in thirty-eight campaigns.[12] Of those, thirty-six were proudly described as "offensive." According to the study, Muscovy's warfare was mostly defensive; only with Peter did offensive wars prevail. The study also found that on only two occasions since Peter 1—in 1812, during the Napoleonic Wars, and in the Crimean War (1854–56)—had Russia conducted mainly defensive wars. Russia had been at war for 353 years, or two-thirds of its existence, during the more than 500 years of its history up until 1898.[13]

As would be expected, Sukhotin conveyed a traditional Great Russian view of the expansions and the subordination of other peoples under Russian rule. Moreover, he emphasized that Russia's war against Napoleon (1799–1814) had saved Austria and Prussia, "the entire German world, entire Europe." He stated that Russian military history testified to the fact that for Russia, "war had always and throughout all times been, spontaneously and consciously, a sacred, great, and important act in the life of the state. War was always for us a matter of the people: war was always a war for 'Faith, Tsar, and Fatherland.'" Finally, he stressed that the most important strength throughout Russian military history was the spirit, based on a "selfless sacrifice by an individual for the benefit of the common cause."[14]

This echoes, if we omit the czar, Russia's official rhetoric around its current large-scale invasion of Ukraine. Furthermore, this was made even more concrete when the idea of the individual's willingness to sacrifice was encouraged by Patriarch Kirill and received the blessing of the Russian Orthodox Church.[15]

During the eighteenth century, Russia was almost constantly in a state of war. The Great Northern War against Sweden lasted from 1700 to 1721. The following year, Russia launched military offensives against Persia (1722–32) that lasted for a decade. This was followed by the War of Polish Succession (1733–35), the war against the Ottomans (1736–39), and four campaigns against the Crimean Tatars (1735–38). After that, Russia fought another war against Sweden, from 1741 to 1743.

In the latter part of the eighteenth century, Russia fought eight wars: the Seven Years' War, 1756–63; the Russo-Swedish War of 1788–90; two wars against the Ottoman Empire, 1768–74 and 1787–91; three wars against Poland, 1768–72, 1792, and 1794; and one against France, in the second anti-French coalition, 1799–1800.

During this period, in 1783, Crimea was finally incorporated into the Russian Empire. According to Sukhotin, it had taken Russia eight wars and thirty-seven years to seize the peninsula from the Ottomans.

## STRATEGY AND POLICY

Rumiantsev was born in the Kiev region, in modern-day Ukraine. Educated in the Preobrazhensky Life Guards Regiment, he served with distinction in the Seven Years' War and was promoted to governor-general in Ukraine by Catherine II. He was tasked with integrating the territory into the Russian fiscal and administrative system, and during his time serfdom was established, in 1783. He never left his military career and later commanded the Second Army and fought several campaigns against the Turks and Poland. He was well-read and acquainted with the Western military thought of the time.[16]

Rumiantsev had a significant impact in his time, mainly because of the manual, *Obriad Sluzhby* (Customs of military service), that he wrote for his troops in 1770.[17] It is in twelve parts, about the everyday life of the troops, detailing everything from force formations and marching rules to camp management and hospitals. It was so successful that in 1776 it was adopted as a manual for the entire army, thereby contributing to the development of Russian military doctrine. The foundations of this doctrine lay both in understanding the basic principles of war and applying them to exploit Russian strength, while minimizing Russian weakness.[18] Important for this analysis are Rumiantsev's thoughts on the army and its relations to the state, as well as his thoughts on the relationship between war and policy. As Heuser has shown, strategic thought and practice existed long before the word "strategy" was coined.[19]

In 1777 Rumiantsev wrote a memorandum to Catherine II titled *Thought*, consisting of sixteen articles.[20] Its purpose was to secure sufficient means for the army, given the territorial expansion of the empire; it reveals that Rumiantsev had thought deeply about his profession. Initially, he underlined that the military institution is different from all others but that all armies could not be similar:

> The military institution, which is different from all others, has become simultaneously indispensable to all states, according to some European views; however, due to the inequalities in a physical and moral sense, they could not have been in either quantity or quality similar to one another, and as governments have discovered that the army is a burden on all other components of the state, they are now striving to employ all means to improve the connections among them, an endeavor in which some countries have done better than the rest.[21]

His differentiation between the civilian and military worlds was in line with a prominent discussion during the Military Enlightenment.[22]

Rumiantsev emphasized that the Russian military was not like any other because of "our great vastness, diverse and mostly wicked neighborhood." Regarding foreign influence, he recommended with great insight that Russia, therefore, should "imitate others only to the extent that it suits our needs."[23] This question of foreign influence, and how to relate to it, is one of the issues that has been debated in Russia for centuries. This military debate, thus, preceded the discussions between the Slavophiles and the Westerners in the nineteenth century.[24]

Rumiantsev was acutely aware that external security was linked to the internal and economic security of the empire. In a letter to Nikita Panin, minister of foreign affairs from 1762 to 1780, he wrote, "A man who simply looks at what lies immediately before his eyes will be unable to see what advantages may derive from the perception of the less obvious attendant circumstances. I could easily go astray if I left myself in ignorance of the political side of affairs, for this lays down the guidelines for the military aspect." Christopher Duffy called this a Clausewitzian statement.[25]

Laying out his thoughts on the military councils, he recognized that the sovereign decided its membership, although he advised against choosing members who were without any war experience. At the same time, he emphasized that it was the government who made the ultimate decisions regarding new legislation within this area.[26] Rumiantsev was not simply paying lip service to his sovereign but expressed the core of Russian strategic thought and military doctrine: the primacy of politics in affairs concerning war and peace.

Even while at war with the Turks in 1774, he asked Catherine to provide him with the "intentions of the allies and other monarchies, and the tasks that will be assigned to your other land forces and the navy." He needed this to be in order because "my actions here, without doubt, should coincide with all the others, and it easier to achieve this when the general picture is known."[27] This demonstrates an insight that the responsible military commander must be aware of the political objectives of the war in order to be able to achieve them.

Furthermore, he realized that to be able to sustain the Russian army (and navy) with educated officers, specialized military schools were needed. It was no longer enough to rely on the skills of foreigners, he maintained. And foreign specialists were expensive. It would be much more reasonable to establish "military scientific, arts and craft schools on the basis of the best schools," he argued. This way, the Russian army would secure over a long time the supply of "quartermasters, auditors, doctors, oboists, locksmiths, turners, and others."[28] This would later become reality in various specialized military institutions.

Taking a larger view of modern military thinking, Rumiantsev was very skeptical of general and universal rules for military art. This "scientific" view had been proposed by the French count Jacques Antoine Hippolyte Guibert (1743–91), Lloyd, and others.[29] In 1769 he wrote another letter to Nikita Panin:

> Our trade has its rules, but they are in many cases indeterminate, and devoid of concrete substance and precision, for they proceed essentially from the judgement of the commander. What the whole art of war comes down to is this . . . to hold the main objective of the war constantly in view, to be aware of what proved useful or damaging in similar cases in past times (giving due weight to the lie of the ground and the associated advances and difficulties), and to evaluate the enemy by working out what we might do if we were in his place.[30]

Rumiantsev had early insights into some of the most pressing strategic issues that Russian military theorists would explore, analyze, and argue about in the coming centuries: whether the art of war is a science or not, the relationship between policy and war, the individual commander's and soldier's roles on the battlefield, and the importance of military history and intelligence about the enemy. In that sense, he could rightly be called "the father of Russian military thought."[31]

Rumiantsev made an important contribution to Russian strategic thought, which was later recognized by Soviet theorists. But he was not so exclusively Russian as claimed but also well-read on contemporary military thought in the West, which he then could criticize or voice approval of in the manner of any intellectual. He found inspiration in the Prussian army, for which Aleksandr Svechin criticized him much later, calling him a "blind admirer of Frederick the Great."[32] During the second campaign against the Ottomans, 1787–91, he commanded the Second Army, but after a conflict with Catherine's new favorite, Count Grigorii Potemkin (1739–91), he was removed from command, in 1789. Rumiantsev spent the rest of his days in loneliness on his estate in Ukraine. This is not an unusual fate for an important strategic thinker in the history of Russian strategic thought.

## THE SCIENCE OF WINNING

Suvorov became known during his lifetime as the general who never lost a battle. He was bestowed with many honorary titles, among them "generalissimo"—a title never previously or afterward bestowed on anyone in czarist Russia. (The only one after him to receive this rank was Joseph Vissarionovich Stalin [1878–1953].) Suvorov was highly educated, well-read, and spoke several languages, including Turkish and Finnish.[33]

Suvorov's *Nauka pobezhdat* (The art of victory; also translated as "The science of victory" and "The science of winning") was completed in 1795 and is probably the most important book in Russian military thought.[34] It continues to be the standard work in higher military education in today's Russia. Suvorov claimed to walk in the footsteps of Rumiantsev.[35]

In this short book, he laid down the foundation for Russian military thought on the battlefield. Although he was the most successful commander of the century in Russia, he never had responsibility for overall strategy, which is hardly surprising. That was the realm of the czars.

However, in his ability to formulate succinct sentences, his impact on Russian military thought was profound. It is Suvorov who most clearly formulated the thought that wars are decided by the superiority of the spiritual over the material. Phrases such as his "train hard, fight easy," "theory without practice is dead," and "the bullet is a fool, the bayonet is a fine chap," have entered Russian military vocabulary. Today, in the Russian Armed Forces, he is considered to be the father of "Russian national military doctrine."[36]

Despite the attempts by subsequent generations of Russian military thinkers to make Suvorov uniquely Russian and national, he was very knowledgeable about the leading military theorists of his time. Suvorov's father, Vasilii Ivanovich, had translated into Russian the works of Sébastien Le Prestre de Vauban (1633–1707), a military engineer and master of fortifications during the reign of Louis XIV; Suvorov later claimed that they had read the translations carefully together and compared them to the French originals.[37] Furthermore, in a letter in French to his three-year-old godson, in 1793, he gave the following advice on necessary future reading: "As a military man, study carefully Vauban, Coehoorn, Curas, Hübner, a bit of theology, a bit of physical exercise and morale. Read Eugene, Turenne, commentaries by Caesar, Frederick II, the first volumes of Rollin, and "Rêveries" by Count de Saxe. Languages are for the literature. Dance, mount, and turn the weapons around."[38] In other words, Suvorov encouraged his godson to study the works by Vauban; Menno van Coehoorn (1641–1704), a Dutch engineer; Hilmar Curas (1673–n.d.), a German historian and scholar, whose *Einleitung zur Universalhistorie* (Introduction to universal history; 1723) was translated into Russian; Johann Hübner

(1668–1731), a German geographer and scholar who wrote an early textbook on geography, *Kurze Fragen aus der alten und neuen Geographie* (Brief questions from old and new geography; 1693), which was translated into Russian in 1719; Prince Eugene of Savoy (1663–1736), an Austrian field marshal; and Henri de La Tour d'Auvergne de Turenne (1611–75), a French marshal general. In addition, Suvorov's mention of "the first volumes of Rollin" refers to the French historian Charles Rollin (1661–1741), whose *Histoire romaine depuis la fondation de Rome jusqu'à la bataille d'Actium* (Roman history from the foundation of Rome to the Battle of Actium) came out in five of the nine volumes planned. The mention of "Rêveries" is to Maurice de Saxe (1696–1750), famous for his *Mes rêveries* (My reveries), published after his death, in 1757. Works by Julius Caesar and Frederick II were evidently part of the curriculum. Suvorov was well acquainted with the standard literature of the Military Enlightenment, which had a great impact on Russian military thought. The role of officers was to educate soldiers about the nature of the military world, rather than to instruct them in simple drills.[39]

Suvorov's doctrine could be summarized as speed, assessment, attack (*bystrota, glazomer, natisk*). Training was the very foundation of military art, and Suvorov exemplified the ability to view the art of war in its essentials. The application of these essentials with the material at hand required a fundamental understanding of the characteristics and capabilities of the Russian peasant soldier and his gentry officers.[40] He ended his book with the following words, to be repeated in chorus by the troops after a public reading of the text: "Subordination, Exercise, Obedience, Education, Discipline, Military Order, Cleanliness, Health, Neatness, Sobriety, Courage, Bravery, Victory! Glory! Glory! Glory!" Thus, Suvorov set the ideal of Russian soldiers and officers that would have a great impact on the Russian army's self-image.

In line with most of his contemporaries, he was convinced that the offensive was the only way to wage war. Retreat, he thought, was equal to weakness. "A step backward is death," he said.[41] He did not develop any deeper thought on strategy and policy or on the relationship between the political and military leaders. Napoleon allegedly said about Suvorov, "He had the soul of a great commander, but he did not have his head."[42]

On the battlefield, however, he knew how to act. Ahead of the war against France, he summarized the war plan to Paul I (1754–1801) in 1798 as follows.

1. Only offensive actions.
2. Speed on the march, attack with fury, cold steel.
3. Do not debate—assess and decide.
4. All the power to the commander in chief.
5. Attack and beat the enemy on the field.

6. Do not waste time in sieges. . . .
7. Never disperse forces to guard various points. . . .
8. Never overburden yourself with fruitless maneuvers, countermarches, or so-called tricks of war, which are only suitable for poor academics.[43]

The closest he came to strategic insight was formulated in his much-quoted sentence "One minute can decide the outcome of the battle, one hour the outcome of the campaign, and one day the fate of empires."[44]

Despite his successes, Suvorov died in disgrace because of a whim of Paul I, which, according to Soviet writers, contributed to his death.[45] But he was not forgotten, and the literature on Suvorov is enormous. His legacy has been the inspiration for such military thinkers as Dmitrii Miliutin, Mikhail Ivanovich Dragomirov (1830–1905), and Makhmut Akhmetovich Gareev. Vladimir Ilich Lenin (1870–1924) introduced parts of Suvorov's *Nauka pobezhdat* into the curriculum of the newly created Red Army in 1918. During World War II, Stalin created a decoration in his honor, and military schools today carry his name. In recent years, the chief of the General Staff, Valerii Vasilevich Gerasimov, quoted Suvorov's "Theory without practice is dead."[46]

## DEVELOPING STRATEGIC THOUGHT

The first professor of strategy at the Imperial Military Academy was Baron Nikolai Vasilevich Medem (1796–1870).[47] He had a background as an artillery officer and had participated in the war against Napoleon in 1813–14. Medem laid the ground for formal strategic study in Russia. At the academy, his lectures on strategy fostered a new generation of military reformers and strategic theorists, which is examined in chapter 2. Miliutin, who would become war minister under Alexander II (1818–81), attended the academy in 1835–36 and remembered Medem's lectures fondly: "Despite the apparent dryness of the subject, despite the shortcomings of the lecturer's voice and cough, they were so entertaining, one might say captivating, that we, the listeners, were sometimes thrilled and found it difficult to restrain ourselves from expressing it straight to him."[48]

Medem's book on strategy in Russia, for which he was awarded the prestigious Demidov Prize, was published in 1836.[49] Medem also wrote a prize-winning book on tactics, but he wrote his book on strategy in the stifling era of Nicholas I. In the aftermath of the Napoleonic Wars, the Decembrists demanded a constitution and the abolishment of serfdom, but their uprising failed and unrestrained authoritarianism became the hallmark of Nicholas's reign. The military sphere was characterized by formal regulations, with an unreasonable focus on marches and parades.

Given the general circumstances, Medem's work, *Obozrenie izvestneishikh pravil i sistem strategii* (An overview of the most famous rules and systems of strategy), is remarkably clarifying. Without reservation, he noted political objectives as being a vital part of strategy. The purpose of his book was to provide a comprehensive overview of strategic literature in Russian, "to avoid unnecessary repetitions of what foreigners have already discovered long ago."[50]

Medem started with an overview of strategic thought by the leading Western strategists of his day, from Lloyd to Clausewitz, including Frederick II and Jomini. He was most appreciative of Jomini and Clausewitz, although he argued that not all of Clausewitz's thoughts were completely lucid or even tenable.[51] He particularly mentioned Clausewitz's thoughts on the relationship between policy and war and on the objectives of war but did not elaborate. This is understandable, given the overall constraints of Nicholas I's Russia. Incidentally, in a Soviet 1960s edition of texts by the leading Russian military theorists of the nineteenth and early twentieth centuries, which includes Medem's *Obozrenie*, the section on Clausewitz was omitted.[52]

The main argument of *Obozrenie* was that there cannot be immutable laws in strategy that can guide the actions of the commander in war. Medem was in complete agreement with Clausewitz on this issue and in disagreement with Jomini. Medem emphasized the importance of taking all factors into account. This was in essence a thinly veiled criticism against the way strategy had been taught in Russia. He turned against the hitherto common practice of studying only one of the leading strategists and memorizing the "immutable laws." To do that was not only superficial and one-sided but also potentially dangerous, Medem wrote.[53]

He defined strategy as a combination of many different factors and means. Strategy is a much broader field of study than most other sciences, and Medem compared it to medicine. But it was also an art and could be compared with chess—that is, one must learn how to move the figures, but that alone does not make you a great chess player. The basis for studying strategy was "the knowledge of the characteristics of all strategic elements and means, the assessment of their mutual influence, and the study of the importance of each individual element in relation to the actual military actions."[54] This holistic view of strategy has remained one of the constants of Russian strategic thought.

To study geography alone or to focus solely on the material side or the operational and communication lines was important but not enough. Since wars have a political goal, this was a vital part of the study of strategy, as were the enemies' strengths and weaknesses and one's own. The talented commander, according to Medem, ultimately had a decisive role in carrying out a successful strategy. During the Soviet period, Medem's importance was acknowledged, although he was criticized for this latter point and for not being able to see the laws of military art.⁵⁵

After the publication of Medem's book, Russian strategic thought started to develop rapidly. Russian military theorists had a growing sense of self-confidence and felt a need to emphasize Russian uniqueness. Medem had hoped that his text would lead his countrymen to engage in strategic literature together with the foreigners rather than feel obligated to catch up with them.

## NOTES

*Epigraph:* V. Domnin, ed., *Ne chislom, a umeniem: Voennaia sistema A. V. Suvorova* [Not by numbers but by skills: The military system of A. V. Suvorov]," in *Rossiiskii voennyi sbornik* [Russian military collection], ed. A. E. Savinkin, vol. 18 (Moscow, Voennyi universitet, Russkii put, 2001), 432–33.

1. Martin van Creveld, *The Art of War: War and Military Thought* (London: Cassel, 2000), 14.
2. Carol Belkin Stevens, *Soldiers on the Steppe: Army Reform and Social Change in Early Modern Russia* (DeKalb: Northern Illinois University Press, 1995).
3. Carol Belkin Stevens, *Russia's Wars of Emergence, 1460–1730* (London: Routledge, 2013), 31.
4. John LeDonne, *The Grand Strategy of the Russian Empire, 1650–1831* (Oxford: Oxford University Press, 2004), 6.
5. Richard Pipes, *The Formation of the Soviet Union: Communism and Nationalism 1917–1923* (Cambridge, MA: Harvard University Press, 1964), 1; Orlando Figes, *The Story of Russia* (London: Bloomsbury, 2022), 93–94.
6. Vasilii Kliuchevskii, cited in Aleksandr Golts, *Voennaia reforma i rossiiskii militarizm* [Military reform and Russian militarism] (Uppsala: Acta Universitatis Upsaliensis, 2017), 259–60. On Peter's strategy, see Fuller, *Strategy and Policy*, 36–37, 71–81.
7. Fuller, *Strategy and Policy*, 71–75.
8. Claes Peterson, *Peter the Great's Administrative and Judicial Reforms: Swedish Antecedents and the Process of Reception* (Stockholm: Nordiska bokhandeln, 1979), 394–409; A. A. Kokoshin, *Vydaiushchiisia otechestvennyi voennyi teoretik i voenachalnik Aleksandr Andreevich Svechin* [The outstanding Russian military theorist and military commander Aleksandr Andreevich Svechin] (Moscow: Izd. Moskovoskogo universiteta, 2013), 362.
9. Peter von Wahlde, "Military Thought in Imperial Russia" (PhD thesis, Indiana University, 1966), chap. 1.
10. Quoted in Christopher Duffy, *Russia's Military Way to the West* (1981; facsimile ed., Knighton, Wales: Terence Wise, 1994), 60, 142ff.
11. Eugene Miakinkov, *War and Enlightenment: Military Culture in the Age of Catherine II* (Toronto: University of Toronto Press, 2020).
12. N. N. Sukhotin, *Voina v istorii Russkago mira* [War in the history of the Russian world] (Saint Petersburg: Trenke i Fiusno, 1898), 13–14, 31–32.
13. Sukhotin, 30–31.
14. Sukhotin, 35.

15. "Russian Patriarch Kirill Says Dying in Ukraine 'Washes Away All Sins,'" Radio Free Europe / Radio Liberty, September 26, 2022, https://www.rferl.org/a/russia-patriarch-kirill-dying-ukraine-sins/32052380.html.
16. Duffy, *Russia's Military Way*, 168–73.
17. Petr Rumiantsev, "Obriad Sluzhby" [Customs of military service], in *Russkaia voennaia mysl XVIII vek* [Russian military thought in the eighteenth century], ed. V. Goncharov, ed., 118–38 (Moscow: Terra Fantastica, 2003).
18. Bruce Menning, "The Imperial Russian Army, 1725–1796," in Kagan and Higham, *Military History of Tsarist Russia*, 70.
19. Beatrice Heuser, *Strategy before Clausewitz: Linking Warfare and Statecraft* (Oxford: Routledge, 2018).
20. Petr Rumiantsev, "Mysl" [Thought], in Goncharov, *Russkaia voennaia*, 99–117.
21. Rumiantsev in Goncharov, *Russkaia voennaia*, 99.
22. Miakinkov, *War and Enlightenment*, 119.
23. Rumiantsev in Goncharov, *Russkaia voennaia*, 99–100.
24. Miakinkov, *War and Enlightenment*, 233.
25. Duffy, *Russia's Military Way*, 169.
26. Goncharov, *Russkaia voennaia*, 117.
27. Quoted in Eugene Miakinkov, "A Russian Way of War? Westernization of Russian Military Thought, 1757–1800" (master's thesis in history, University of Waterloo, Ontario, 2009), 62.
28. Goncharov, *Russkaia voennaia*, 103–4.
29. Miakinkov, "Russian Way of War," 61.
30. Quoted in Duffy, *Russia's Military Way*, 169.
31. Miakinkov, "Russian Way of War," 45–75.
32. A. Svechin, *Evoliutsiia voennogo iskusstva* [The evolution of the art of war], vol. 1 (Moscow: Gos. Izd. Otdel Voennoi Literatury, 1927), 290–91.
33. Fuller, *Strategy and Power*, 157.
34. Aleksandr Suvorov, *Nauka pobezhdat* [The art of victory], in Goncharov, *Russkaia voennaia*, 302–16.
35. Duffy, *Russia's Military Way*, 173.
36. Savinkin, "Ne chislom," 14. Hereafter, "Russian Armed Forces" (or "Soviet Armed Forces") means the armed forces subordinated to the Ministry of Defense.
37. Philip Longworth, *The Art of Victory: The Life and Achievements of Generalissimo Suvorov 1729–1800* (London: Constable, 1965), 19.
38. V. S. Lopatin (ed.), *A. V. Suvorov: Pisma* [A. V. Suvorov: Letters] (Moscow: Nauka, 1986), 253–54.
39. Miakinkov, *War and Enlightenment*, 109.
40. Menning, "Imperial Russian Army," 70.
41. Savinkin, "Ne chislom," 299.
42. Savinkin, 175.
43. Savinkin, 73–74.
44. Savinkin, 166.
45. "Suvorov," in N. V. Ogarkov, ed., *Sovetskaia voennaia entsiklopediia* [Soviet military encyclopedia], vol. 7 (Moscow: Voenizdat, 1980), 586–88.
46. Valerii Gerasimov, "Razvitie voennoi strategii v sovremennykh usloviiakh: Zadachi voennoi nauki" [The development of military strategy under modern conditions: Tasks of military science], *Vestnik Akademii Voennykh Nauk*, no. 2 (2019): 8.

47. For biographical details, see G. A. Leer, ed., *Entsiklopediia voennykh i morskikh nauk* [Encyclopedia of military and naval sciences], vol. 5 (Saint Petersburg: V. Bezobrazova i komp, 1891), 116–17. See also Olaf Rose, *Carl von Clausewitz: Wirkungsgeschichte seines Werkes in Russland und der Sowjetunion* [Carl von Clausewitz: History of the impact of his work in Russia and the Soviet Union] (Munich: R. Oldenbourg Verlag, 1995), 32–38.
48. D. A. Miliutin, *Vospominaniia 1816–1843* [Memoirs 1816–1843], ed. L. G. Zakharova (Moscow: Rossiiskii arkhiv, 1997), 147.
49. Nikolai Medem, *Obozrenie izvestneishikh pravil i sistem strategii* [An overview of the most famous rules and systems of strategy] (Saint Petersburg: II Otdeleniia Sobstevennoi E. I. V. Kantseliarii, 1836).
50. Medem, v–vi.
51. Medem, 162, 190.
52. L. G. Beskrovnyi, ed., *Russkaia voenno-teoreticheskaia mysl XIX i nachala XX vekov* [Russian military-theoretical thought in the nineteenth century and the beginning of the twentieth century] (Moscow: Voennoe izdatelstvo Ministerstva Oborony Soiuza SSR, 1960), 98–125.
53. Medem, *Obozrenie*, 208–10.
54. Medem, 169, 177, 186–87.
55. Beskrovnyi, *Russkaia voenno-teoreticheskaia*, 11.

# 2

# A TIME FOR CHANGE IN THE WAKE OF THE CRIMEAN WAR

> *You will witness these horrible, heart-rending scenes; you will see war without the brilliant and accurate alignment of troops, without music, without the drum-roll, without standards flying in the wind, without galloping generals—you will see it as it is, in blood, in suffering, and in death!... We must at least take consolation in the thought that we did not begin the war, that we are only defending our country, our native land.*
>
> LEO TOLSTOY

The previous chapter analyzed early Russian military strategic thought. That thought was informed by practice and the study of Western/European military strategists. The Crimean War forced Russian strategists to rethink strategy and doctrine. The role of technology, growing nationalism in Europe, and the changes in warfare relating to strategy and doctrine were all issues of major concern for the Russian strategists. This chapter focuses on the thought of Alexander II's war minister, Dmitrii Alekseevich Miliutin, the early war plans of the 1870s, and the writings of Mikhail Dragomirov and Genrikh Antonovich Leer.[1] Closer to World War I, one of the most influential military strategic thinkers was Gen. Nikolai Petrovich Mikhnevich (1849–1927), whose thought is also analyzed.

## "FOR THE FIRST TIME, I CAN BREATHE EASILY"

The Crimean War broke a period of forty years of peace in Europe. The war was only the first in a series of wars that would transform not only the map of Europe but also the armies and, consequently, the societies that fought them.[2] The traditional standing, professional army was replaced by mass forces, citizen armies recruited through conscription. At the time of the Crimean War (1853–56), none of the European powers, except Prussia, had a recruiting system based on universal conscription. After the Franco-Prussian War, in 1870–71, conscription was the dominant recruiting system in Europe. This was the period when modern, industrialized nation-states took shape, while both nationalism and demands for liberalism in the political sphere grew. In science, positivism, with its roots in the Enlightenment, was the current trend.[3] Charles Darwin published *On the Origin of Species* in 1859, and Karl Marx's first volume of *Das Kapital* appeared in 1867. In the arts, realism gained power over romanticism. In Russia, Fyodor Dostoevsky wrote *Crime and Punishment* (1866), and Leo Tolstoy completed *War and Peace* (1865–69).

Russia's defeat in the Crimean War had a profound effect on its strategic military thought. Although it may be true in general that "after the Crimean War debacle the Russian officer corps experienced a loss of confidence and prestige,"[4] this despondency did not influence those officers involved in developing the armed forces. On the contrary, it seems the death of Nicholas I rather invigorated some of them—for instance, the future head of the General Staff, Nikolai Nikolaevich Obruchev (1830–1904), who allegedly said when he learned the news, "For the first time, I can breathe easily."[5] The future war minister, Miliutin, noted:

> I, and the larger part of the contemporary younger generation, did not sympathize with the old regime, which was built on administrative arbitrariness, police repression, and strict formalism. . . . Even in the military sphere . . . the same concern for order and discipline prevailed: they were not striving for essential improvement of the troops . . . but only for . . . the splendid view of parades . . . which killed the true fighting spirit.[6]

The repressive rule of Nicholas I had contributed to a sense of insecurity and hopelessness—the very opposite of the emperor's rationale for conducting it.

During this period, the study of military science and theory became more systematic and professionalized. In fact, in the decades to come, Russian military thought flourished, touching on and contributing to the most important issues of the time, not shrinking from pushing reforms that would ultimately bring changes not only in the army and fleet but also in Russia's system of government. This development culminated in 1874, when universal conscription was introduced.

On the European political scene, Russia turned to domestic political reform in the famous phrase of Foreign Minister Aleksandr Mikhailovich Gorchakov (1798–1883), "*La Russie ne boude pas, mais se recueille*" (Russia does not sulk but composes itself). Plans to form an alliance with France, the former enemy, came to a halt when France sided with the Poles in the rebellion of 1863. Meanwhile, four wars dramatically altered the European balance of power that had been established in 1815 in Vienna. The war of 1859 between Piedmont (part of the Kingdom of Sardinia), which was supported by French troops, and Austria was the second war on the road to Italian unification. France was indisputably at the height of its status as a great power when the war was over. Nevertheless, within eleven years, Napoleon III would see his empire crumble and find himself a prisoner of war of the Germans.

German unification was accomplished with the political skill of Otto von Bismarck (1815–98) and the military power of the Prussian army. Three wars completed German unification. First, after a formal dispute over succession, Austria and Prussia invaded Denmark in 1864, and Denmark was forced to give up its duchies to the joint rule of Austria and Prussia. According to the agreement reached in Gastein in 1865, Prussia was to rule Schleswig and Austria Holstein, but this arrangement did not last long. Second, the Austro-Prussian War of 1866 established Prussian supremacy in Germany. Finally, in 1870 in the Franco-Prussian War, all of the German forces were united under Prussian command. Within a month of the start of the war, eighty-three thousand men surrendered to Prussia at the Battle of Sedan, and Napoleon III became a prisoner of war of the Prussian king. France, however, continued to fight for another five months, under the leadership of the newly declared Third Republic. As a result of the German victory, Alsace and Lorraine were occupied by German forces. On January 18, 1871, at Versailles, King Wilhelm I of Prussia was proclaimed emperor of Germany.

In addition to these events, other changes were also reshaping Europe. Italy secured the annexation of Venetia as a result of the war in 1866, in spite of the military failure against the Austrian army. The Austrian Empire was shaken, and in 1867 the Austrian-Hungarian dual monarchy was created. Italian unification was completed in 1870 when the Italians seized the opportunity to occupy the papal state of Rome. On October 2, 1870, the people of Rome voted for a union with the Kingdom of Italy.

Neither Russia nor Britain intervened during this process, mainly because the threat from a united Germany was not perceived as very great. The danger to peace and stability in Europe appeared to come from France under Napoleon III. However, in 1870 Russia took the chance to denounce the clauses of the Treaty of Paris, which prohibited Russia from keeping warships in the Black Sea. At that time, it was largely a symbolic gesture, and when the Russo-Turkish War broke out, in 1877, Russia had not yet built up a navy in the Black Sea.

## CHANGES IN WARFARE

If events on the political scene were eventful, the military development was no less significant. The 1860s was the period when—according to most military historians—warfare became "modern"—that is, technological and industrial. Three factors are particularly important: (1) the appearance of conscript armies and trained reserves, (2) the growing importance of officer education and the rise of general staffs, and (3) the technological development, including the military application of the steam railway, the electromagnetic telegraph, and the rifling of muskets and cannons.[7] Deciding which of these factors should be emphasized as most important in determining the "modernity" of warfare varies somewhat. Nevertheless, one feature that made this period distinct from the Napoleonic era was the unprecedented peacetime involvement of all sectors of society in military efforts.

In the mid-nineteenth century, technological and scientific advances, in conjunction with political, economic, and social change, affected the armed forces. Industrialization and technological development led to specialization and division of labor.[8] New machinery in the factories, steam-driven trains, and new production methods increasingly required specialists. Larger than ever and with a growing sophistication in weaponry and command, control, and supply systems, the armies of the mid-nineteenth century became increasingly complex organizations, in need of specifically trained specialists. A growing armaments industry took shape, spurred by the wars and scientific discoveries, such as the Bessemer steel-making process and modern manufacturing systems producing metal cartridges. The days when the soldier was responsible for making his paper cartridges were over. Armories faced increasing difficulties in keeping up with the latest developments in rifle and cannon models and production methods.

The social and military implications were far-reaching. Soldiers as well as officers needed to be educated, and officers needed skills to educate civilians in a comparatively short period of time. At the same time, shorter mobilization times—through the use of railways—made detailed, advance war planning more important.

Furthermore, the period saw several international agreements related to the conduct of war. They were designed to protect both soldiers and civilians by imposing limitations on the use of military force. The Red Cross was brought into existence by the twenty-six-nation agreement signed in Geneva in 1864. The Declaration of Saint Petersburg, in 1868, prohibited the use of explosive charges in projectiles under fourteen ounces. The intent was to prevent the development of an explosive bullet following that of the cannon shell. A prohibition on the bombardment of cities was agreed to at the 1874 conference in Brussels, following the Prussian siege of Paris in 1870–71.[9]

The conscript army was not a new phenomenon in Western warfare. Large-scale use of conscripted soldiers had been practiced at the beginning of the century when the armies of Napoleon fought on the battlefields of Europe. During the French Revolutionary and Napoleonic Wars, masses of people were put under arms, but these were temporary situations, and the practice was largely abandoned after those wars. The prospect of arming and training large parts of the population for military service was not only expensive but could prove to be politically dangerous.

There were also a number of reasons for the military establishments to be skeptical of conscript armies. The professional, long-service armies functioned well and allowed for plenty of time to train the troops and cultivate an esprit de corps. There were doubts about the effectiveness of civilians in arms. For instance, how could civilians—with only a relatively short period of service—be trusted to stay in a battle and fight? After all, desertion was a big enough problem in the long-service armies. During the Revolutionary Wars of the mid-1790s, the French army had suffered yearly desertions of around eight percent of its total strength. In the war of 1859, it has been estimated that around fifteen thousand Austrian troops deserted.[10] In Russia the rates of desertion were lower than in other European armies, although the official figures are not very reliable.[11]

As the armies increasingly consisted of amateurs, the officer corps became more professional—that is, more specially trained. Larger armies and faster mobilization times increasingly required educated (rather than well-connected) officers. At the same time, the aristocratic percentage of the officer corps in the European armies started to decline. The Russian army was no exception, and from the time after the Crimean War to 1911, the nobility's share of the officer corps shrank from around 90 percent to about 50.[12] This is not to suggest that aristocratic officers were not educated—quite the contrary was often the case— but it is clear that connections through patronage and birth gradually became less influential.

The rise of the general staff, as the brain of the army, and a more specialized, educated body of officers was a process underpinned by several factors. The increasing pace of technological invention and the growing complexity of warfare played an important role. The military use of trains made advance planning both necessary and feasible. Trains ran on certain tracks, at certain times, with certain amounts of men and supplies—all which could be planned. The electric telegraph facilitated quick communication between headquarters. If mobilization and the concentration of large armies and their supply were to work in the case of war, the planning and organization had to take place before its outbreak. Moreover, all this greatly increased the demand for more detailed intelligence about foreign armies. During the second half of the nineteenth century, the use of military attachés became more widespread. Whereas the major European powers had two to five military attachés in 1860, their numbers had grown to between fifteen and twenty in 1913. In Russia in the mid-1860s, the numbers of military attachés abroad were around twelve, along with eleven other officers.

The close-order infantry column seems to have become obsolete in view of larger forces and vastly improved firepower. In other words, the two- or three-lines-deep close-order formation of the infantry battalion was suicidal against the new weapons, with their greater firepower and accuracy. A more flexible formation was required, where every man used his initiative, which would have direct implications for military education. Consequently, the technological development did not diminish the role of the noncommissioned officer or of the soldier on the battlefield; it increased it. The troops needed motivation to advance and endure on the battlefield in spite of the firestorms.

The improved firepower seemed to have strengthened the importance of defensive over offensive action. The role of the most traditional and prestigious arm of all, the cavalry, changed. In the American Civil War, the cavalry had been used for raiding and reconnaissance and had fought on foot as "mounted infantry." This was fundamentally different from the traditional cavalry shock attacks, which had become increasingly difficult to conduct in face of the intense nineteenth-century fire.

## LESSONS FROM CRIMEA

After the Crimean War, a period dominated by domestic reforms prevailed in Russia. The reforms during the reign of Alexander II are popularly called "the Great Reforms." Perhaps the most fundamental reform took place in 1861, with the emancipation of the serfs. This reform preceded the abolishment of slavery in the United States and was underpinned by the army's need to recruit ever more soldiers. It would also enable the introduction of universal conscription. Other important reforms, apart from the military ones, involved local government and the judicial system. However painful the defeat of the Russian army in the Crimean War may have been, Sevastopol was no Jena that triggered immediate and radical reforms. It was a humiliating defeat but not fatal. Russia did not have to surrender to the complete will of a foreign power.

The military reforms were underpinned by the views of the man who was war minister from 1861 to 1881, Miliutin. He came from an impoverished noble family and had made a name for himself through the publication of several works on military statistics and military history. Miliutin surrounded himself with reform-willing officers and had the ear of Alexander II. He was a firm supporter of the autocracy and viewed the reforms as necessary to preserve it but disliked hereditary privileges and believed that merit and knowledge should be the sole criteria for promotion. In the mid-1860s, he summarized his views:

> In our view, there are two fundamental, essential conditions [that are] the sine qua non without which every political theory in application to Russia ought to be considered worthless. The first is the unity and integrity of the state; the second is the equality of all its members. For the first condition, a strong central power and a decisive predominance of the Russian element

(we are talking about the empire...) are necessary. For the second condition, it is essential to cast away all outdated outlived privileges, to take leave, once and for all, of the rights of one social group (*kasta*) over another. But a strong central power precludes neither personal freedom of the citizens, nor does it preclude self-government; neither does the predominance of the Russian element mean the oppression and destruction of other nationalities. Rather, it means the elimination of ancient privileges.[13]

Miliutin was convinced that only by creating a nation of equal citizens would the autocracy survive; he firmly supported the emancipation of the serfs. In a memo in 1856, he explicitly stated that serfdom hindered the shortening of the time of service.[14] His main argument was based on the firm conviction that only by creating equal citizens could the unity of the state be preserved. By educating soldiers and officers, the nation would benefit in two ways: the men would not only become better, from a military point of view—they would also become better citizens.[15]

The Crimean War had highlighted the need for educated officers. The introduction of rifles was changing the way battles were fought, and officers needed a good military education. The fact that Miliutin, at the beginning of his twenty-year term as war minister, concentrated on educational reforms, rather than immediately pursuing the issue of a conscript army with uneducated soldiers suggests that he was both a realist and well aware of the requirements of modern warfare. Miliutin's reforms created a new system for military education, based primarily on talent and merit rather than on birth and patronage.

In 1867 mandatory courses in literacy were introduced for all soldiers. By 1868 the War Ministry began to provide a small sum of money for the necessary educational supplies. Under Alexander III (1845–94), teaching the soldiers literacy was no longer obligatory but nevertheless continued throughout the 1880s. At the beginning of the 1890s, only one military district maintained literacy courses. This was Kiev Military District, under the command of Dragomirov, whose thoughts we return to below.

The military districts were created in 1864–65. Initially, there were ten, which by 1871 had grown to fourteen. As they were created, army and corps organization was abolished, and the division became the largest unit within the district. This was controversial among some of the generals. The military districts enjoyed considerable autonomy, not only in such matters as supply and military logistics but also in threat analysis and even defense planning.[16]

Universal military conscription was introduced in 1874, stipulating obligatory service for all males for fifteen years: six in the line, nine in the reserves. Universal conscription encompassed the idea of the citizen-soldier—the patriotic, educated man with close ties to the army unit and to the fatherland. The law of 1874 specified that "the strength of the state does not depend exclusively on the number of its troops but is based chiefly on the moral and intellectual qualities of the army, which can be fully developed only on condition that the defense of the country has become the common task of the people and when all, without distinction of rank or class, unite in that sacred cause."[17]

Nationalism was growing in strength in Europe, most notably with the unifications of Germany and Italy. At the same time, the distinction between the military and civilian life of nations became less apparent. War correspondents used the telegraph to send their reports from the war. Soldiers on leave could travel home and back, and the wounded could be treated at home.

The wars of the 1860s and 1870s had demonstrated that the war effort increasingly became the concern of the entire nation. Mobilization and deployment of large armies had become more dependent on the systems that raised them. The ability of a country to train, arm, and deploy a large army involved larger sections of society than ever before in the history of warfare. This is not to suggest an absolute link between economic power and military power. An economically poor country can choose to organize society in such a way as to give it military power, and an economically strong state can choose not to create a strong military system. Nevertheless, the link between economic and military power was becoming stronger.

Even if Russia's focus lay on domestic reforms, it did not remain idle on the international scene. Expansion in Central Asia continued throughout the reign of Alexander II. The cities of Turkistan and Chimkent fell in 1864, Tashkent in 1865, and Samarkand in 1868. The khanates of Khiva and Bukhara became Russian protectorates in 1871, and Kokand was annexed in 1876. The main reason for these advances was largely motivated by the search for defensible borders rather than economic or geopolitical motivations.[18] In addition, as will be shown below, it was framed as a "civilizing mission."

## STRATEGIC THOUGHT DEVELOPS

Military thought on strategy and doctrine progressed in the decades following the Crimean War.[19] Early on, one of the most significant measures during this period was the creation of a new military journal, *Voennyi sbornik* (Military collection), in 1858, initially with the radical Nikolai Gavrilovich Chernyshevskii (1828–89) as the editor for a brief period. The journal proved to be an important base for military debate. In general, *Voennyi sbornik* and the military newspaper *Russkii invalid* (The Russian invalid) played important roles in shaping and reflecting the military attitudes of the Russian army. The most influential institution apart from the War Ministry and the Main Staff was the General Staff Academy.[20] Paramount in decision-making was the czar.

The role of technology, growing nationalism, and the changes in warfare relating to strategy and doctrine were all issues of major concern for Russian strategists. In this section, I focus on the early war plans of the 1870s and the writings of two of the most influential military theorists of the period, Mikhail Dragomirov and Genrikh Leer. They were not only influential at the time but are also being rediscovered in today's Russia. But, to begin, the first proper war plans are taken into account.

## FRIENDS AND FOES IN THE WAKE OF CRIMEA

One of the first, if not the first, strategic document in Russian war planning to approach the contemporary requirements was produced in the War Ministry in 1870. The document "Dannyia dlia otsenki Vooruzhennykh sil Rossii" (Facts for the evaluation of the armed forces of Russia) consists of 204 pages, handwritten by a clerk.[21] The author is unknown, but a qualified guess is that it was written by the chief of the Military-Scientific Committee, Nikolai Obruchev, during the first half of 1870, before or just at the outset of the Franco-Prussian War.

Not surprisingly, the author noted that neutrality had been the only possible policy for Russia after the Crimean defeat, but in view of European developments, Russia needed to change. Russia was forced to respond since Europe had begun to view Russia as no longer being a purely solitary state: Europe began to see Russia not only as the land of powerful Russian people, full of life, receiving freedom, using a system of land organization (*zemelnoe ustroistvo*) unthinkable in the feudal West, and rich both in economic and moral terms but also, more importantly, as a state with racial (*plemennye*) connections to Slavic peoples that extended far beyond its political borders, reaching to the Elbe and the Adriatic. Russia would be a leader for all Slavic peoples, reflecting an influence not only on the future fate of Europe but also on the whole world. The strategic document depicted Russia as a victim of circumstances, surrounded by ever more powerful adversaries, and growing nationalism in Europe was seen with trepidation. Changing national interests in European politics now meant that Russia had a few new friends but, above all, more enemies. Neither France nor Prussia could be trusted any longer. In other words, as far as Russian strategic planners were concerned, an alliance with France in 1870, a reality twenty-two years later, was very remote.[22]

Who, then, was Russia's potential enemy, and was the Russian army prepared to fight? In answering these questions, the memorandum described military developments in Europe during the last ten years. If the single most important event in European political relations was the growing strength of nationalism, the equivalent on the military side was the introduction of "armed masses."

It was not likely that a single country would embark on an offensive campaign against Russia. Consequently, Russia had to prepare for an attack by a coalition of forces. This coalition was likely to consist of three different constellations: (1) Austria and Prussia (including the states of northern Germany), (2) Austria, Prussia, Turkey, and Sweden, or (3) states mostly interested in the political and economic instability of the Ottoman Empire (the so-called Eastern Question): Austria, Turkey, France, Italy, and England.

Thus, in practice the Russian strategic analysis in 1870 excluded any offensive action and was very pessimistic about Russia's chances in resisting an attack by coalition forces. The underlying assumption was that an offensive could only succeed if Russia had a coalition partner or at least a friend who would refrain from attacking. In 1870 that friend was undoubtedly Prussia, which did not mean that Russia saw it as an ally. At the outbreak of the Franco-Prussian War, Miliutin described both Austria-Hungary and England as "unreliable."[23] Austria was present in all the three scenarios. Conspicuously absent in the strategic analysis is any evaluation about which scenario was most likely. The Russian army was simply preparing for everything. Within only three years this had changed.

## GERMANY/AUSTRIA: THE MAIN THREAT

The work on a strategic survey of Russia began in 1872. The military districts were instructed to provide the War Ministry with surveys of the possible theaters of war in their districts. The military attachés were also involved in providing estimates of the size and mobilization times of the foreign armies. This material was then compiled in two strategic surveys: one of the European frontier districts and the other of the Caucasus. Obruchev was responsible for the former, Grand Duke Mikhail Nikolaevich for the latter.

Obruchev's plan, "Considerations on the Defense of Russia," was, no doubt, the more significant document.[24] In effect, it was the first Russian war plan that laid the basis for all of the war plans up to 1909.[25] Although it does not contain all the details for mobilization and deployment as the plan of 1880 and subsequent plans did, the strategic concept outlined in 1873 remained the same.[26] Obruchev's plan was defensive in thought and action. It was a defense based on three pillars: mass of men, railways, and fortresses, all in the western parts of Russia.

The threat to Russia in 1873 was perceived as coming from the west, above all from Germany and Austria-Hungary. England was mentioned only in passing as a threat to Russian interests in the south—the Caucasus and Central Asia. The German army seemed invincible on the battlefield, and in a unified Germany a great military power had suddenly appeared at the Russian borders.

Obruchev's view in the war plan was that Russia was more or less isolated in the European arena and therefore had to cope alone. He felt that neither Germany nor Austria was to be trusted in the diplomatic sphere.

The basic thought in Obruchev's plan was that Russia had to prepare for a war against a coalition since the reasons for war were not likely to be personal quarrels among the European sovereigns but would instead be based on significant political differences:

> In preserving peace, all prepare for war. . . . The art of diplomacy can provide us with allies and equalize our chances in a fight with the enemy. Strategic considerations cannot venture into the diplomatic domain, but must consider the defense system of the State from the situation where we have to—not attack—but defend ourselves, which means [preparations] for a war with a first-rate opponent.[27]

The transition from peace to war had become instantaneous, according to Obruchev. The army had to reflect the geographic and political situation of the empire and its history, not merely the current political situation. Looking westward, he saw two powers bound by common interests joining against Russia and being able to raise sixty divisions, supported by reserves. He concluded, "Here is our main danger (*opasnost*). In order to avert it we must be able to stand up against these neighbors with equal power."

The idea behind Obruchev's calculations was to stand firmly in the west and not retreat from Poland. There was no question of withdrawing into the depths of the empire. Historically, the vastness of the territory and the distance of governmental centers from the borders had undeniably been an asset, but to pursue such a strategy in 1873 would be mortally dangerous, Obruchev maintained. To retreat from Poland, even for a short period, could lead to the loss of Poland. It would look like a defeat and have implications that were dangerous. In addition, the position on the Vistula was the only really good one from which to mount an offensive.

The thought that a future war in Europe would take place on Polish territory remained in the subsequent, more elaborate war plans of 1880, 1883, 1887, and 1890. All of them also provided for initial cavalry raids to thwart German and Austrian concentration at the borders of Russia. However, from 1887 onward, Russian plans started to provide options for offensive action against Austria, even at the beginning of the war. One of the reasons for this was that the Russian war planners became convinced that the very lack of roads and railways, the size of the country, and its poverty—that is, all of the things that were seen in 1873 to work against Russia—could work to its advantage. In 1880 Obruchev thought that they were factors "about which an invading army must think twice and which could possibly free more of our troops for an offensive."[28] These strategic thoughts are colored on the one hand by fears of foreign invasion and on the other by fears of internal uprising. The events of 1863 in Poland were still vivid in the memory of the Russian strategic planners and would remain there for a long time. The fear of an uprising in Poland explains both the conviction that it was impossible to retreat into the interior and the reluctance to undertake offensive action. In the case of an offensive, in 1873 the Russian army did not have enough reserves to leave behind to secure internal order.

The Russian generals were deeply affected by the growing strength of nationalism in Europe. Miliutin held up Germany as an example of a "homogeneous" state. Obruchev pointed at the growing strength of "nationalism" and the need for Russia to respond to this development. Both expressed fears about the "unreliability" of the population in the border areas. At the same time, the army was seen as a unifying instrument in Russia, as something that society as a whole should gather around. The Great Russians were seen as the leading nationality of the empire.

## THE ARMY AND THE STATE

Particularly noteworthy in developing Russian military strategic thought are the writings of Genrikh Leer, professor of strategy at the General Staff Academy.[29] Leer was one of the most significant Russian military theorists and later served as commandant of the General Staff Academy from 1889 to 1898. At the time, he was also highly regarded internationally and was appointed an honorary member of the Swedish Academy of War Sciences. He was firmly based in the positivist school of thought, not least inspired by Jomini and Lloyd, both of whom he frequently refers to in his writings. Jomini was a Swiss general who had left Napoleon and transferred his services to the czar and in 1832 helped create the Imperial Military Academy. Jomini's systematic writings on Napoleonic warfare were influential at the international level and continue to be today, not least in discussions on Clausewitz versus Jomini—that is, the positivist outlook rooted in the Enlightenment in contrast to German romanticism.[30] Lloyd was a Welsh officer and military writer whose thoughts on strategy were influential much later. His books influenced several Western military thinkers in the twentieth century.[31]

Leer was appointed chair of strategy in 1865 and proceeded to develop his thinking about the connection between the political system of a state and the organization of its armed forces. He noted that the military system was "only a reflection of the political system."[32] In the case of Prussia, he traced the reasons for the success of its army to the general political development there. It was Prussia's strength that in times of need it was able to achieve radical political and military reform. He recognized that Prussia had achieved its political goal by using force: "War, in certain respects, is *the political bayonet*, whereas all the other means, such as science ... are only *preparations*. War, however, *finally determines* the most important political issues."[33]

Importantly, Leer also tried to explore the connection between the military and the political organization of a state and to link the political system of a state to the kinds of war it was likely to conduct.[34] The military organization of a state was influenced both by foreign policy and domestic political conditions. Consequently, despotic regimes, characterized by centralization of power in the hands of one ruler and the absence of civil rights, were most likely to conduct offensive wars. Referring to Lloyd's *Analyse militaire des différentes frontières en Europe* (Military analysis of the different borders in Europe), Leer took the example of Turkey in the eighteenth century. Democratic republics (e.g., the ancient Greek republics) were the very opposite of despotic regimes and embodied equality for all in political and civic affairs. This system was generally unable to conduct offensive wars, while it was unusually strong in the defense. Monarchies, combining centralization with a certain amount of freedom and rights, were accordingly good for both offensive and defensive warfare.[35]

Leer saw the introduction of universal military service as a direct consequence of the tendency toward a public life (*obshchestvennoe ustroistvo*) based on equal rights under the law. This had led to larger armies on the battlefield and to an increase in the quality of the troops because the "best elements of the society" had begun to enter military service. The tactical formation of the armies had also changed as a consequence of the introduction of conscription. Tactics began to be based on *trust*, in contrast to the tactics of the eighteenth century, which were based on *mistrust*. Such trust led to more flexibility, wherein the initiative of the individual officers and use of the terrain both played a greater role. All this stood in sharp contrast to the old linear tactics, where the entire army was used as a machine under one commander on a flat battlefield.

Foreign policy also affected the military organization of the state. In Leer's opinion, foreign policy and military force complemented each other. It was the task of foreign policy to enter into coalitions or to remain neutral, thus influencing the question of securing the flanks and the rear—that is, the operational lines. He stressed that it was both easier and more convenient to secure the operational lines through foreign policy than to rely on military force alone.[36]

Finally, he formulated a military policy for Russia. Russia had already fulfilled its political mission in serving as a bastion for Europe against the Tatars. Since it was Russia's political mission to bring Western European civilization, adopted and reworked by Russia, to the Asiatic peoples, Leer felt the military policy of Russia should continue to be the traditional policy of Peter I—namely, defense in the west and offense in the east. Insofar as the Russian army had conducted offensive campaigns in the west, these had been offensive only from a military point of view but had remained defensive from a political point of view, according to Leer.

The thought that Russia served as the defender of Europe against the invasions from the east, to which Leer subscribed, is frequently heard in the political rhetoric of the 2020s. In addition, Leer obviously defined an offensive war as one with civilizing missions, and he did not count Peter I's challenge to Sweden's hold on the Baltic, for instance, as one of these.

Leer has been accused of relating contemporary warfare to the experience of the Napoleonic Wars and of failing, therefore, to appreciate the changes that had emerged. Although it is true that Leer related and compared the latest events on the battlefield with the experience of the Napoleonic Wars, this did not necessarily mean that he did not see or value the new dimensions in warfare. His preoccupation with theory, according to one historian, led him to concentrate on the wrong trees while the entire forest around him was changing.[37] In my view, however, by connecting political and military reform in an effort to achieve a strong army, he was hardly focusing on the wrong trees but instead provided formidable support to the war minister, who was in the midst of planning the introduction of universal military service.

Another influential military theorist during this period was Mikhail Dragomirov. He had graduated from the General Staff Academy in 1856 and soon gained a reputation as one of the most perceptive military thinkers. After being wounded in the Russo-Turkish War, he was appointed commandant of the General Staff Academy, in which post he served from 1878 to 1889. He can also be found in the famous 1891 painting by Ilya Repin *Reply of the Zoporozhian Cossacks to Sultan Mehmed IV of Turkey*. He was internationally renowned militarily and an honorary member of the Swedish Academy of War Sciences. Several of his writings were translated into French.

Dragomirov was outspoken in his view that the outcome of the wars in 1859 and 1866 could be ascribed to national factors. His thoughts on the influence of national factors on warfare deserve attention. In his articles on the war in 1859, Dragomirov interpreted the war as a struggle between the "Latin and German races."[38] He viewed the Italian efforts to obtain independence as a natural consequence of the fact that the Austrian Empire was inherently flawed: "Austria, put together from different parts which do not have anything organic in common, at an early stage engendered mistrust among the people, forcing together those who do not have any common interests."

He mocked the Austrian government's investments in roads and railways, as it seemed that the Austrians had thought that roads would bring together the different people, "not noticing that no railway can provide a relationship among those who cannot stand each other." He was full of admiration for the Italians, who fought bravely in spite of meager military means and who had set a clear goal for themselves: Italian unification and independence. Dragomirov stressed that the material side of warfare was useful only if morale was sound. It is worth noticing that Dragomirov had already formulated one of the basic principles in his military thinking, a principle he would not shrink from regardless of the technical developments throughout the century.

The Prussian success in 1866 was also ascribed to national factors. According to Dragomirov, it was both the political system and the characteristics of the Prussian "race" (*prusskaia rasa*) that constituted the recipe for Prussian victory.[39] Moreover, he remarked that respect for the law was widespread, recognized by every Prussian regardless of class. As a consequence of this "lawfulness" (*zakonnost*), everyone in Prussia accepted their military duty.

In summary, the Russian officers saw the national unity of Prussia and the internal unity of the society (where all sectors were gathered behind the army) as two of the most important explanations for the Prussian victories. Dragomirov was far from alone in stressing this. In analyzing Prussia, Leer made a distinction between the military spirit of an army and the national spirit (*narodnyi dukh*), which stemmed from the historical development of the nation. It was necessary for a successful army to have both.

Dragomirov's insistence on the moral element in warfare, which led him to talk more about the traditional bayonet attack than firepower, has given him a bad reputation in view of the Russian defeats in 1904–5 and in World War I. As a consequence, his ideas and the rationale for his conclusions have been somewhat obscured, as we see below.

## VIEWS ON STRATEGY

It is no exaggeration to say that the importance of military history grew during the 1860s to such an extent that by the 1870s it was the cornerstone of Russian military science. Two institutions were instrumental in this development: the General Staff Academy and the Consultative Committee—later renamed the Military-Scientific Committee—within the Main Staff. Military history was important for two reasons. On one hand, it served as a tool for comparing the current developments with those of the past. On the other, it was intended to encourage coherent thinking on strategic and tactical issues. It is this reasoning that lay behind the substantial changes in the military history and the strategy courses offered at the General Staff Academy in 1865. These courses had not changed in any significant way since the establishment of the academy in 1832.

One hotly debated question was about military science and military theory. Leer is described as the founder of the "critical-historical" school in Russian military thought. He published a fundamental work on this in 1869, *Opyt kritiko-istoricheskogo issledovaniia zakonov iskusstva vedeniia voiny (polozhitelnaia strategiia)* (The experience of historical-critical research into the laws of military art [positive strategy]).[40] The essence of his critical-historical method was to search for the eternal laws of warfare by choosing appropriate examples from military history. It was important to choose facts closest in time to the period studied. The view that military science could be studied through the prism of military history was essentially the same approach advocated by the Prussian general Gerhard von Scharnhorst (1755–1813) half a century earlier in Berlin. However, Leer criticized the War Academy in Berlin for not having a course in strategy, although "a theory of strategy is entirely possible."[41] In his search for this theory, he clearly preferred Lloyd and Jomini over Clausewitz. In Leer's *Entsiklopediia voennykh i morskikh nauk* (Encyclopedia of military and naval sciences), only two pages were devoted to Clausewitz, whereas Jomini had four pages.[42] Lloyd also had two pages but in general was described much more favorably. It seems clear that Leer's analysis of Clausewitz was superficial, although he read his works in German.[43] This could hardly be explained by superficial reading but rather as an illustrative example of Leer adhering to positivism and being critical of Clausewitz for thinking too elusively.

Leer saw war as a natural phenomenon and argued against those who found war something evil and burdensome for the state. He wrote that "destruction and killing form only one side of war; the other side shows that *war is one of the most rapid and most powerful civilizers of societies.*"[44] In other words, war was seen as a natural phenomenon—a part of human life.

He defined strategy, in the broad sense, as a synthesis of all military affairs.[45] He equated the "theory of military art" with military science, the purpose of which was to assemble and elucidate laws that constitute military art and to investigate the characteristics of their elements and the relations between them in infinitely changing situations. Strategy hence was a synthesis of a moral element (the heart and the mind of the army and the nation in war, military psychology), a material one (technology, geography, fortification, tactics, administration), and a political element (domestic and foreign) as well as military politics and an element of chance.[46] "Therefore, the goal of strategy is to grasp the question of waging war at a given moment in all its aspects and solve it according to the prevailing situation—that is, to define a reasonable goal and direct all forces and means toward its achievement in the shortest time and with the fewest sacrifices."

Incidentally, Jomini, Clausewitz, and Lloyd had been in Russian service, albeit the latter two only for a short period. Jomini's insistence on the eternal principles of war corresponds very well with Leer's thoughts. In fact, Jomini was so influential at the academy, at the expense of Clausewitz, that Andrei Evgenevich Snesarev, who translated Clausewitz's *On War* in the 1920s, did not mince his words: "Jomini closed the door firmly and for a long time on his scientific rival. Leer was the successor to the strategic concept of Jomini and assimilated well this sectarian attitude toward the German military theorist, and Clausewitz became silenced.... The Academy of the General Staff, and after it Russian military thought, followed the path of strategic geometry and immutable rules."[47]

This was not quite true, as Dragomirov for one was influenced by Clausewitz. He tried to introduce Clausewitz in the academy and translated *On War* from French in 1888. Admittedly, it was not until 1902 that a more complete translation was published.[48] Snesarev, however, did not think very highly of the translation skills of Karl Voide, the translator of the 1902 version.

Dragomirov wrote mostly on tactics and training, but occasionally he developed his thoughts on war and conflict. The purpose of the military estate is to beat the enemy with a minimum of effort and losses, Dragomirov claimed.[49] He found such a close connection between tactics and strategy that it was hard to draw a definite line between them. "In all military undertakings there are two elements: strategic, or an element of showing the objectives, and tactical, or an element of execution to achieve the goals."[50]

Regarding the question of military science and military theory and the search for eternal laws of warfare, Dragomirov and Leer were not in agreement. In fact, Dragomirov emphatically denied the existence of a military science. Dragomirov claimed that military theory alone can be applied to military art and that science is unthinkable. In an often-quoted passage, he wrote, "At the present time, nobody would assert that there could be a military science; that is as unthinkable as a science of poetry, art, and music."[51] This has been used by Soviet scholars to criticize Dragomirov for a lack of understanding of the existing laws and consistent patterns of military affairs.[52] However, his elaborations are often ignored. According to him, science and theory are not the same thing, and therefore "every science has a theory, but every theory cannot be a science." He maintained that military theory was useful but not a recipe for creating an Austerlitz or a Königgrätz. Military theory did not help in those or other battles. But they should be studied and analyzed by the military "just as a painter or a composer studies masterpieces—not to copy them, but to be inspired by them." Military theory, according to Dragomirov, should be firmly based on the study of military history, but, even so, theory could never be used as a guide to actions. "Theory is the arsenal where you can find all kinds of weapons," he wrote, "but which one to pick is the choice of the one picking."[53] He emphasized the role of chance in war (which was indefinite), and therefore "in order to reach the set goals [*tseli*] it is necessary to trust one's own view and sound thought."[54]

Leer has traditionally been said to belong to the "academics," whereas Dragomirov has been labeled as belonging to the "nationalist school." Therefore, it is worth noticing that Dragomirov and Leer did agree on the purpose of war (to win with the fewest losses) and the view of war as a natural phenomenon.

Dragomirov, in three articles analyzing *War and Peace* from a military point of view, argued against Tolstoy's pacifist views on war.[55] Dragomirov disputed his view that war is against human nature and reason. In nature, Dragomirov noted, everything is based on "struggle" (*borba*), and a human being cannot be above the laws of nature. He quoted the famous dictum "Perpetual peace is only possible in the graveyard."[56] Dragomirov maintained that war is not against parts of human nature but only one side of that nature and that this side has to do with human survival instincts.[57] Also, Dragomirov insisted, war was not necessarily against reason; it depended on the *purpose* for which war is fought. "War is a phenomenon, independent of human will: not without reason Pirogov called it a 'traumatic epidemic.'" Nikolai Ivanovich Pirogov (1810–81) was a prominent medical doctor who organized the Russian medical service in the Crimean War and the Russo-Turkish War.

We see how their views differed, but it is important to note that the main difference was in the focus of their writings. Leer was a firm believer in positivism and the systematic study of military affairs, as was Dragomirov. In his preface to a textbook on tactics, Dragomirov noted, "That captures, to our mind, the rationality and fruitfulness of Baron Medem's view that one should pay attention to the positive, and not creative, side of military affairs, which are always and in everything activities of living personalities and not of a theory."[58]

## MEN AGAINST FIRE: MORALE VERSUS TECHNOLOGY

One of the most topical questions discussed by military thinkers in Miliutin's time involved the consequences of increased firepower. The developments in this area raised many questions: about possible changes in the tactical formations and entrenchment tactics and about ways to boost morale and prepare the troops for the storm of bullets and shells on the battlefield of the future. Ultimately, how could the soldiers be trained to survive in the coming storm of steel?

What did Dragomirov say that made such an impression on his contemporaries? His basic ideas can be summarized in three principles:

- Teach the soldier only what was necessary in war.
- Treat the soldier with respect.
- Emphasize the bayonet attack in training, not because firing is not important but because the bayonet attack requires more psychological strength, which is more difficult to train and takes longer to acquire.

These thoughts stood in sharp contrast to the traditional view in Russia on how to create an effective army. The first point was one of Suvorov's principles, but after the Crimean War it also encompassed an indirect criticism of the army of Nicholas I, where the emphasis on training lay on the parade ground. The second point related to the efforts to create a more humane environment for the soldier, which was linked to a more restrictive use of corporal punishment. The third point essentially subscribed to the Napoleonic principle that war was largely a moral exercise.

Dragomirov not only translated Clausewitz; he also reedited Suvorov's *Nauka pobezhdat* and was known in his time through the oft-repeated Suvorov dictum "The bullet is a fool, but the bayonet is a fine fellow." He defended this view throughout his life, for which he has received much criticism. Therefore, what was his argument?

A debate in the pages of *Voennyi sbornik* in 1872 is revealing. L. M. Baikov, a young General Staff graduate, started the debate.[59] Baikov claimed that the lessons of the Battle of Königgrätz had not been properly appreciated. He acknowledged, in accordance with Dragomirov and others, that Königgrätz had shown the need to create a national (*narodnaia*) army and had demonstrated the need for national education and universal military service. However, he challenged Dragomirov in the tactical field by claiming that the traditional infantry attack in close-order column had become almost impossible. An observer with the Prussian army in 1870–71, Loggin Logginovich Zeddeler (1831–99), expressed similar views in an article where he summarized his impressions from the war.[60] More cautiously than Baikov, he noted the growing importance of fire on the battlefield and wondered whether Suvorov would have trained his troops to attack in close-order formation. He pointed out that the war had shown that the frontal attack had become very difficult to conduct and led to enormous losses. He argued that firearms had gained strength on the battlefield to the degree that "at least in this war, they have replaced the bayonet attack."

Dragomirov replied to both articles.[61] He accused Baikov of being incapable of an objective analysis and of being a "knight of the bullet." Dragomirov did not see anything that changed the established truth that fire prepared the way for the bayonet attack. He stressed that the bullet and the bayonet did not exclude, but rather complemented, each other; consequently, the dispersed order was a complement to the close-order formation. The purpose in war was not to kill and wound as many as possible but "to force the enemy to surrender to us." The morale of the troops, displayed in the bayonet attack, is the determining factor on the battlefield, and it made little sense to talk about "tactics of fire" and "tactics of the bayonet" since the only tactics worth the name were "sound tactics."

In response to Zeddeler's doubts about Suvorov's training methods, Dragomirov coldly replied that this issue was irrelevant: "A change of weapons might lead to a change in training methods in how to handle this weapon, but it hardly has anything to do with the moral strength of people."

Why were Dragomirov and others so reluctant to diminish the emphasis on the bayonet in favor of fire? It was not, as sometimes believed, that the Russian military thinkers were unaware of, or underestimated, the increased importance of fire on the battlefield. One reason was the conviction that diminishing the emphasis on the bayonet would negatively affect the soldier's will to fight. It could potentially lead the soldier to be more concerned for his own safety than to concentrate on the task, which was to move forward in spite of the rain of bullets. In other words, firepower was seen as something that potentially could paralyze the troops.

Finally, the 1870–71 war could be seen as a confirmation of the opinion that technology alone is not sufficient to win wars. In this war, the Prussian needle gun was technically inferior to the French chassepot, yet Prussia had won.

## DEBATES ON STRATEGY AND DOCTRINE PRIOR TO WORLD WAR I

Russian military thought on strategy and doctrine developed quickly during the remaining years of the century and the beginning of the new one, especially after the defeat in the Russo-Japanese War (1904–5). The domestic changes following the Russian Revolution of 1905, together with the continued professionalization of the officer corps, further sparked debates about strategy and doctrine.

A few years before the war broke out, Russia had taken the initiative of calling the first international conference on peace and disarmament, at The Hague in 1899, which led to the banning of expanding bullets (a.k.a. dumdum bullets) in war. After the war a second conference was held, in 1907.

The defeat in the Russo-Japanese War was, again, a blow to Russia's international prestige. What had seemed necessary to uphold Russia's standing in the world led to the opposite. Within the General Staff, Obruchev had argued against the use of military means to further Russian interests in the Far East. "Russia has enough enemies in Europe and Central Asia to create new ones in the Far East," he wrote in 1895 and advocated a diplomatic solution to the mounting tensions.[62] In strictly military terms the war was not lost, but fears of an uprising at home caused Nicholas II to make for peace.[63] The army had been used at home to put down the massive workers' demonstrations in January 1905 on "Bloody Sunday."

The Russo-Japanese War resulted in administrative changes, albeit short-lived. Two new institutions were created: the State Defense Council, chaired by Grand Duke Nikolai Nikolaevich. Another change was that the General Staff was made independent from both the War Ministry and the old Main Staff, in a move clearly inspired by the Prussian model. This meant that all strategic planning for war was made independent of the war minister. The State Defense Council was expected to coordinate military and naval policy but failed, not least due to political infighting, and the council was abolished in 1909. Following this failure, the General Staff was again subordinated to the war minister.

Miliutin was not amused. In 1909, at the age of ninety-four, he wrote an article on the state of Russia's military situation, which was published in 1912.[64] He drew lessons from the war and developed his thoughts on future warfare and the consequences for the Russian armed forces. It is worth examining his article, not least since the former chief of the General Staff, Nikolai Egorovich Makarov, considered it to be highly relevant in our present day and age.[65]

Most importantly, Miliutin criticized his contemporaries for not paying enough attention to the fact that the way wars were being fought had changed dramatically. "We had no one who understood the complexity." In order to cope with future challenges, he suggested several measures. First, he was very critical of the decision to make the General Staff independent, which he characterized as "harmful." He noted that wars break out suddenly, regardless of international alliances and Hague conventions and that Russia must focus on securing a successful beginning of the war (*nachalo voennykh deistvii*). This is a central concept further examined in chapter 4.

Miliutin observed that the current changes in warfare led to two requirements: (1) to strengthen the personal *initiative*, from the top all the way through to the individual soldier, and (2) to secure greater independence for armies, corps, and divisions. In addition, he stressed the importance of "getting rid of a great evil, our customary way to wage all our wars—namely the excessive overflow in our headquarters of incompetents (*tuneiadtsy*) with no responsibilities, constituting a terrible burden on the army."

In view of the increasing specialization of the various branches of arms, the importance of more specialist education was emphasized. "Encyclopedic knowledge brings little benefit in practice." He reflected on the state of Russia's military development through the centuries:

> Just as we in the past, in Rus' were forced to organize our troops after the example of Western states with the help of invited foreign masters, generals and sailors, now and in the future we must observe what is going on abroad, order and buy from foreign lands various samples of new discovered curiosities. . . . Our enormous mother Russia moves forward for two centuries behind the leading peoples of Western Europe and will hardly surpass them anytime in the future. This appears mainly at the technical and economic level.[66]

Miliutin concluded his article with a prediction that the role of cars and machines would change the battlefield, where mobile armored batteries would dominate, and that land battle would become more like naval battles.

By referring to the need for practice rather than encyclopedic knowledge, Miliutin wittingly or unwittingly supported a group of reform-minded officers on the General Staff, often called the Young Turks, informally led by Nikolai Nikolaevich Golovin (1875–1944). One of their arguments in the wake of the Russo-Japanese War was that Russia had failed because it did not have a unified military doctrine. It was a question touching on the identity crisis of the armed forces, and the empire, in the aftermath of the defeat. The lack of such a set of guiding principles in war and peace had led to the disaster in the Far East. The opponents of having a doctrine argued that a doctrine could be harmful, threatening the thinking and initiative of the military leadership. At the core of the debates was the thorny issue of which wars to study in order to find the best sources for drawing up a military doctrine. Two main schools developed: the Academic School followed Leer's thoughts on identifying the eternal principles and laws through military history, and the Russian Nationalist School focused on Russia's glorious past, emphasizing the victories during the reign of Peter the Great, Suvorov's successes, and the training of Dragomirov.[67]

In the end, these vivid discussions came to nothing. A decree in 1912 simply prohibited any further debates on this issue, which shows precisely how sensitive this issue was, as it touched on the core of the empire. Czar Nicholas II bluntly stated, in an order in 1912 to the head of the General Staff Academy, Gen. Nikolai Nikolaevich Yanushkevich (1868–1918), "Military doctrine is what I say it is. I ask you to convey to Neznamov that it should no longer be discussed."[68]

One of the most influential military strategic thinkers in the years up to the beginning of World War I, in 1914, was Gen. Nikolai Mikhnevich. From 1904, he was head of the General Staff Academy and then head of the Main Staff from 1911 to 1917. He tried to justify the existence of various schools of thought. In his studies of the relationship between domestic and foreign policy and military affairs, he was also a predecessor to Aleksandr Andreevich Svechin, whom we meet in the next chapter.

In Mikhnevich's *Osnovy strategii* (The foundations of strategy), the impact of the wars of the 1860s and 1870s is evident. Mikhnevich further developed Leer's thought. War, according to Mikhnevich, was a phenomenon in the life of civilized societies that consisted of material, economic, and spiritual dimensions. The aims of contemporary wars (1913) were either *ideological (idealnye)*—for example, *national unification* or *national unity*—or *economic*—to conquer markets, capitals, or trade routes or conduct wars in the colonies. He noted that "these clear goals can be characterised by a desire *to weaken the power of neighbours* (e.g., the Crimean War in 1853–56), in anticipation of a possible struggle in the future."[69] Due to the impact of railways, wars will break out suddenly, and the initial confrontations will become more important. But they will not be decisive since war might become more protracted. Therefore, he argued, the national economic activities of the nation are becoming more important.

Mikhnevich traced important factors influencing the ways of waging war, partly in the economic and technological resources of the state, partly in domestic politics, and partly in the morale of the armed forces and the entire nation. He argued that success in war "depends on the complete agreement between the foreign politics and military leadership, which in fact also depends on the internal organisation of the state." In a phrase that echoes to this day and age, he added, "Knowledge of the weaknesses of the internal politics can direct the blows of a skillful and innovative enemy to the right places."[70]

Geography also played an important role. Mikhnevich pointed to the fact that the Russian military had to know how to wage war on its western border, which required large armies "equipped with all the technological means of contemporary civilisation. On the other hand, it also has to be capable of conducting extended campaigns by small units in the deserts and half-civilised states of Central Asia." While this complicated the work of the Russian military, according to Mikhnevich, it also expanded its experience and outlook, thus offering a fullness and comprehensiveness to its lessons.[71]

In laying out the essence of a war plan, Mikhnevich noted that the character of future wars could be either offensive or defensive. The latter could be either actively defensive or passively defensive. As is shown below, the concept of active defense would be elaborated during the Soviet period and is currently being adapted to contemporary Russian military strategy.

Importantly, Mikhnevich noted, the character of future war is decided by "the desired *political goals* and only after that by various *military considerations*."[72] Politics, he maintained, sets the stage (*"mise en scène"*) for war. It also defines relations with other states that are not involved in the war but are interested in its outcome. "Their sympathy, or lack of it, can be of great significance in retarding or supporting the activities of war. Moreover, politics has a great work to do during the whole period of war, helping the military and using its successes to create a political situation unfavourable to the enemy." Mikhnevich wrote, "After some successes on the battlefield, diplomacy can initiate *peace negotiations*. In this case, military activities should not stop under any circumstances as decisive victory over the enemy has not yet been achieved. If military actions on the battlefield turn out to be unsuccessful, the successful intervention of diplomacy can save the day."[73]

He noted that the Russian armed forces were still too small per capita compared to other European competitors. According to him, Germany, with only half of the population of Russia, had an army almost as large as Russia's.[74] To find allies and build coalitions would be a solution; however, Mikhnevich was skeptical of waging war with coalition partners. "The private interests of each ally will take the lead, sometimes even overriding the common goal defined at the beginning of the war."[75] Interestingly, he was very clear when it came to ways of fighting against a coalition. In that case, *"it is important to find its weak side from the political as well as military point of view* and direct your blows against them. Under such circumstances, the political aspects frequently have significantly bigger potential than the military ones." Mikhnevich emphasized that time was the best ally of the Russian armed forces and *"therefore it is not dangerous for us to apply the strategy of attrition and exhaustion, as long as we avoid decisive clashes with the enemy at the border, where superiority of forces may be on his side."*[76] At the beginning of World War I, a year later, the latter part of this sentence would ring like an early warning. Gumbinnen was a success; Tannenberg was not.

## RELEVANCE TODAY

Armies are large organizations, and therefore one could expect them to show a certain reluctance to jump too quickly in adjusting to change. On the other hand, a general wait-and-see attitude is potentially dangerous and can lead to devastating results. Much of the problem consists of finding a balance in peacetime between adjusting to change and determining the actual value of innovations for war. There is a balance to be found here between novelty and tradition, between jumping to conclusions and resisting change. The fact that its position is directly linked to the security of the state does not make the army's situation an easy one. It is hardly surprising, therefore, that armies are often described as being marked by a curious contradiction. On one hand, they are oriented toward the present and future in their efforts to make the most rational use of their means and to be as efficient as possible. On the other, they are often perceived by both insiders and outsiders as the carriers of traditional values, represented by ceremonies that should be preserved at all cost.[77]

This balancing act between the past and prospects becomes more evident in times of radical change. In tactics, a balance needs to be found between technology and morale. The pre-1914 European armies were later accused of disregarding technology and of putting too much emphasis on morale. The experience of World War I certainly seems to vindicate this criticism. Nevertheless, many wars of the twentieth century have demonstrated time and time again that an army with poor morale, regardless of its technological superiority, does not win wars.

Why are some cultures ready to import entire systems straight from abroad, whereas others are not? Without attempting to address this complex question in its entirety, the following points can be made. No doubt, it has much to do with self-perception. Both Dragomirov and Leer wrote on this issue and made it clear that copying from abroad, without making adaptations to Russia, was seen as something negative and degrading. It would have been perceived as admitting that Russia did not have its destiny in its own hands.

History, or rather the interpretation of history, may have played a role here. The military reforms by Paul I, which included copying from Prussia, were widely seen among Russian officers as a failure and an embarrassment. It is also true that there was a tradition in Russian society of resentment against Germans, due largely to their success and affluence in Russia.[78] In addition, the issue of importing Western models was linked to nationalism and a growing conviction that foreign practices could not be copied. They would not work because a certain system had been developed for a specific nationality.

The view of the West as a source of inspiration rather than of imitation, and balanced by a firm belief in the Russian autocracy, would underpin the military reforms and the entire reform period. In connection with this, it is important to stress that the view of Russia as "backward" or "exceptional" was only invoked by Miliutin and Obruchev when they thought it would strengthen their case in the political debate. In general, it became popular among Western and Soviet scholars to apply the term "backward" to Russia. This, in my view, should not be overemphasized since it tends to mislead and obscure more than it explains. Implicit in this view is that Russia was exceptional or at least fundamentally different from other states. Although all nations differ from each other in some respects, we can conclude that the Russian army's impressions of foreign wars were neither backward nor particularly exceptional.

The development under Miliutin points toward an emerging professional attitude among officers. The Russian army had created a system that placed the emphasis on talent when educating its officers. Miliutin had not only understood the Prussian system but also shared the basic underlying views held by such reformers as Scharnhorst and August von Gneisenau (1760–1831).

In addition, why did the efforts to create an intellectual officer corps, so central for the Russian army in the 1860s and 1870s, seem to have been completely forgotten forty years later? Miliutin wanted a more self-confident army, with officers and soldiers united in professionalism and patriotism. Yet the general picture of the Russian army before 1914 is that of a deeply divided entity: the high command was plagued by personal rivalries, the officer corps was characterized by narrow group interests, the cavalry despised the infantry, and the artillery thought itself superior to both the infantry and the cavalry, while the Imperial Guards saw themselves as the only true military elite. In 1912 a senior general remarked that "there will never be unselfish cooperation amongst the higher leaders as in the German army."[79] One may only speculate on the reasons for this or, indeed, whether or not the situation was very much different from other armies. But two points can be made: intellectual development cannot be ordered by decree, and the changes introduced by Miliutin did not have enough time to mature. Military establishments, like other state institutions, are characterized by a corporate identity that develops over time, influenced by a number of factors. Miliutin pointed to the paramount role of the czar in this respect and even criticized Alexander II for not entirely appreciating the importance of intellectual development within the army.

To sum up, we have seen how the military strategists struggled with change and how both domestic and foreign policy influenced strategic thought. Geography does have a role, not least because of Russia's largely indefensible borders and, importantly, the fear of domestic unrest. The fixation with Poland and the Caucasus—that is, Russia's national interest—had a fundamental impact on Russian military strategic thought. A sense of insecurity is visible, possibly strengthened by historical experiences. During the Patriotic War of 1812, Napoleon did at one point reside in the Kremlin.

Following the wars of German unification, Russian military thinkers realized that wars break out suddenly, often without warning. The war plans after the alliance with France subscribed to an offensive strategy, despite calls from some military thinkers for a more defensive one. The "cult of the offensive" had reached Russia too, in line with the thinking in the other great powers at the time.

The need of a modern army for educated officers, able to think for themselves, had also been understood. The Russian officer corps had been professionalized and was moving in the direction of meritocracy. Russia planned for a short war, but so did everybody else. The view that Russia was the bastion of Europe and had protected it from the Mongols had firmly taken root.

The next chapter examines how the military theorists dealt with strategy and doctrine in the wake of the profound transformations following World War I: the fall of the empire and the rise of the Bolshevik Soviet Union.

## NOTES

*Epigraph:* Leo Tolstoï, *Sebastopol*, trans. Frank D. Millet (New York: Harper Brothers, 1887), https://www.gutenberg.org/files/61388/61388-h/61388-h.htm#FNanchor_H_8.
1. This chapter is partly based on Persson, *Learning from Foreign Wars*, parts of chaps. 2 and 5.
2. Michael Howard, *War in European History* (Oxford: Oxford University Press, 1976); Paul Kennedy, *The Rise and Fall of the Great Powers: Economic Change and Military Conflict from 1550 to 2000* (London: Fontana Press, 1988).
3. Azar Gat, *The Origins of Military Thought: From the Enlightenment to Clausewitz* (Oxford: Clarendon Press, 1989); Miakinkov, *War and Enlightenment*.
4. Brian D. Taylor, *Politics and the Russian Army, Civil-Military Relations, 1689–2000* (Cambridge: Cambridge University Press, 2003), 57.

5. Oleg Airapetov, *Zabytaia karera "russkogo Moltke" Nikolai Nikolaevich Obruchev (1830–1904)* [The forgotten career of the "Russian Moltke" Nikolai Nikolaevich Obruchev (1830–1904)] (Saint Petersburg: Aleteia, 1998), 52–53.
6. D. A. Miliutin, *Vospominaniia 1843–1856* [Memoirs 1843–56] (Moscow: Rossiiskii arkhiv, 2000), 325–26.
7. Persson, *Learning from Foreign Wars*, 11–23.
8. For a good survey of this development, see William H. McNeill, *The Pursuit of Power: Technology, Armed Force, and Society since A.D. 1000* (Oxford: Basil Blackwell, 1982), 206–61. Also useful is Kennedy, *Rise and Fall*, 183–93, and Samuel P. Huntington, *The Soldier and the State: The Theory and Politics of Civil-Military Relations* (1957; repr., Cambridge, MA: Belknap Press of Harvard University Press, 1995), 32.
9. R. A. Preston, S. F. Wise, and H. O. Werner, *Men in Arms: A History of Warfare and Its Interrelationships with Western Society* (London: Atlantic Press, 1956), 207–15.
10. Hew Strachan, *European Armies and the Conduct of War* (London: Unwin Hyman, 1983), 39; Gunther Rothenberg, *The Army of Francis Joseph* (West Lafayette, IN: Purdue University Press, 1976), 54–55.
11. Elise Kimerling Wirtschafter, *From Serf to Russian Soldier* (Princeton, NJ: Princeton University Press, 1990), 110–15. See also Duffy, *Russia's Military Way*, 46, 133; Fuller, *Strategy and Power*, 48–49, 167–68; and John H. Keep, *Soldiers of the Tsar: Army and Society in Russia 1462–1874* (Oxford: Clarendon Press, 1985), 222–23.
12. P. A. Zaionchkovskii, *Samoderzhavie i russkaia armiia na rubezhe XIX–XX stoletii, 1881–1903* [Autocracy and the Russian army at the turn of the twentieth century, 1881–1903] (Moscow: Mysl, 1973), 203–14.
13. P. A. Zaionchkovskii, "D. A. Miliutin: Biograficheskii ocherk" [D. A. Miliutin: A biographical essay], in *Dnevnik D. A. Miliutina* [D. A. Miliutin's diary], ed. P. A. Zaionchkovskii, vol. 1 (Moscow: Gosudarstvennaia ordena Lenina Biblioteka SSSR imeni V. I. Lenina. Otdel rukopisei, 1947), 32.
14. "Mysli o nevygodakh sushchestvuiushchei v Rossii voennoi sistemy i o sredstvakh k ustraneniiu onykh" [Thoughts on the existing disadvantages in the Russian military system and on the measures for their elimination"], March 29, 1856, quoted in Persson, *Learning from Foreign Wars*, 26, 86.
15. Zaionchkovskii, "D. A. Miliutin: Biograficheskii ocherk," 32
16. P. A. Zaionchkovskii, *Voennye reformy 1860–70 godov v Rossii* [Military reforms of 1860–70 in Russia] (Moscow: Izdatelstvo Moskovskogo Universiteta, 1952), 84–85, 95.
17. *Polnoe sobranie zakonov Rossiiskoi Imperii* [Complete collection of the laws of the Russian Empire], 2nd series, vol. 49, Law No. 52982, January 1, 1874, https://nlr.ru/e-res/law_r/search.php.
18. Fuller, *Strategy and Power*, 290.
19. Frederick W. Kagan and Robin Higham, "Introduction," in Kagan and Higham, *Military History of Tsarist Russia*, 6.
20. In 1869 the Main Staff consisted of seven branches: the General Staff, the Military-Topographical Section, the Committee for the Movement of Troops and Military Cargoes by Railway (created in 1868), the Committee for Preparing Data on the Mobilization of Troops, the Military-Scientific Committee, the Asiatic Section, and the Military Historical Commission. From 1866 the head of the Main Staff was also chief of the General Staff.

21. "Dannyia dlia otsenki Vooruzhennykh sil Rossii" [Facts for the evaluation of the armed forces of Russia], quoted in Persson, *Learning from Foreign Wars*, 110–16. Zaionchkovskii only commented very briefly on the contents of this document. See Zaionchkovskii, *Voennye reformy*, 258, 364.
22. On the military agreements in the Franco-Russian alliance, see Airapetov, *Zabytaia karera*, 263–69; Fuller, *Strategy and Power*, 350–62; and George F. Kennan, *The Fateful Alliance: France, Russia and the Coming of the First World War* (Manchester: Manchester University Press, 1984), 15–16 and esp. chaps. 9–11. Both Airapetov and Fuller think more highly of Obruchev's strategic understanding than does Kennan.
23. D. A. Miliutin, *Vospominaniia 1868–nachalo 1873* [Memoirs 1868–beginning of 1873] (Moscow: Rosspen, 2006), 281.
24. "Soobrazheniia ob oborone Rossii" [Considerations on the defense of Russia], 1873, quoted in Persson, *Learning from Foreign Wars*, 123–34.
25. A. M. Zaionchkovskii, *Podgotovka Rossii k imperialisticheskoi voine* [Russia's preparations for the imperialistic war] (Leningrad: Gosvoenizdat, 1926), 31, 340.
26. Fuller, *Strategy and Power*, 341; David Rich, *The Tsar's Colonels: Professionalism, Strategy, and Subversion in Late Imperial Russia* (Cambridge, MA: Harvard University Press, 1998), 88–114.
27. "Soobrazheniia ob oborone Rossii," quoted in Persson, *Learning from Foreign Wars*, 123.
28. Fuller, *Strategy and Power*, 347.
29. For introductions to Leer's thought, see Beskrovnyi, *Ocherki voennoi istoriografii Rossii*, 176–80, 206–97; Zhilin, *Russkaia voennaia mysl*, 81–83; Von Wahlde, "Military Thought," 133–42; and Bruce Menning, *Bayonets before Bullets: The Imperial Russian Army 1861–1914* (Bloomington: Indiana University Press, 1992), 125–29.
30. Azar Gat, *The Development of Military Thought: The Nineteenth Century* (Oxford: Clarendon Press, 1992), 14.
31. For a good introduction, see Heuser, *Evolution of Strategy*, chap. 4.
32. G. A. Leer, *Publichnye lektsii o voine 1870 mezhdu Frantsiei i Germaniei do Sedana vkliuchitelno* [Public lectures on the war of 1870 between France and Germany including Sedan] (Saint Petersburg: Obshchestvennaia polza, 1871), 13.
33. Leer, 22 (italics in the original).
34. G. A. Leer, *Opyt kritiko-istoricheskogo issledovaniia zakonov iskusstva vedeniia voiny (polozhitelnaia strategiia)* [The experience of historical-critical research into the laws of military art (positive strategy)] (Saint Petersburg: V. Golovin, 1869), 469–70.
35. Leer, 469.
36. Leer, 471–72. He illustrated this with the example of Napoleon I, who in 1805 had secured Prussia's neutrality during the campaign in Moravia.
37. Menning, *Bayonets before Bullets*, 36.
38. M. I. Dragomirov, "Obzor Italianskoi kampanii 1859" [Survey of the Italian campaign in 1859], *Inzhenernyi zhurnal*, no. 6 (1861), 503–6.
39. M. I. Dragomirov, *Ocherki Avstro-Prusskoi voiny v 1866 godu* [Essays on the Austro-Prussian War in 1866] (Saint Petersburg: Tipografiia Departamenta Udelov, 1867), 70.
40. Ofer Fridman has translated the introduction of the book in his edited volume *Strategiya: The Foundations of the Russian Art of Strategy* (London: Hurst, 2021), 23–73. I have used his translations when appropriate.

41. G. A. Leer, "Generalnyi shtab i ego komplektovanie v Prussii i vo Frantsii" [General Staff and its recruitment in Prussia and France] *Voennyi sbornik*, no. 11 (1868): 49–74.
42. Leer, *Entsiklopediia*, vol. 3, 193–97 (Zhomini); vol. 4, 268–70 (Klauzevits); 589–90 (Lloid).
43. Rose, *Carl von Clausewitz*, 55–56.
44. Leer, *Opyt*, 2 (italics in the original).
45. Leer, 23–24.
46. Leer, 24.
47. A. E. Snesarev, *Zhizn i trudy Klauzevitsa* [The life and work of Clausewitz] (Moscow: Kuchkovo pole, 2007), 18.
48. M. I. Dragomirov, "Uchenie o voine Klauzevitsa: Osnovnye polozheniia" [Studies of war by Clausewitz: Basic provisions], *Voennyi sbornik*, no. 10 (1888): 245–71; no. 11 (1888): 5–22. This is a translation from a French edition, corrected toward the original by M. A. Gazenkampf, professor of military administration at the General Staff Academy. The first more substantial Russian edition of *On War* appeared in 1902, translated by K. Voide: *Klauzevits: Voina (Teoriia strategii)* [Clausewitz: War (theory of strategy), 2 vols. (Saint Petersburg: Tip. Glavnogo Upraleniia Udelov, 1902).
49. L. G. Beskrovnyi, ed., *M. I. Dragomirov: Izbrannye trudy; Voprosy vospitaniia i obucheniia voisk* [M. I. Dragomirov: Selected works; Questions on the education and training of the troops] (Moscow: Voenizdat, 1956), 48, 103.
50. Beskrovnyi, 114.
51. M. I. Dragomirov, *Ocherki* [Essays] (Kiev: Tipografiia S.V. Kulzhenko, 1898), 48.
52. Beskrovnyi, *M. I. Dragomirov*: 16.
53. Beskrovnyi, 112.
54. Beskrovnyi, 110–11.
55. Dragomirov, *Ocherki* (1898), 3–136.
56. He ascribed it to Leibnitz, whereas it was Immanuel Kant who wrote it.
57. Dragomirov, *Ocherki* (1898), 61–62.
58. Beskrovnyi, *M. I. Dragomirov*, 161. On Dragomirov, see also Stanislav Yudin, "General M. I. Dragomirov (1830–1905), Voennyi myslitel i praktik" [General M. I. Dragomirov (1830–1905: Military theorist and practitioner] (PhD diss., Moscow State University, 2020).
59. L. Baikov, "Vliianie srazheniia pod Keniggretsom na taktiku" [The effect of the Battle of Königgrets on tactics], *Voennyi sbornik*, no. 6 (1872): 303–52.
60. L. L. Zeddeler, "Pekhota, artilleriia i kavaleriia v boiu i vne boia, v Germano-Frantsuzskoi voine 1870–1871 godov" [Infantry, artillery, and cavalry in battle and outside of battle], *Voennyi sbornik*, no. 7 (1872): 33–114.
61. M. I. Dragomirov, "Po povodu nekotorykh statei vyzvannykh poslednimi dvumia kampaniiami" [Regarding a few articles on the two latest campaigns], *Voennyi sbornik*, no. 12 (1872): 253–74, and no. 1 (1873): 89–106.
62. Quoted in Oleg Airapetov, *Na puti k krakhu: Russko-Iaponskaia voina 1904–05 gg* [On the road to collapse: The Russo-Japanese War 1904–5] (Moscow: Algoritm, 2014), 70–71.
63. Dominic Lieven, *The End of Tsarist Russia* (New York: Viking, 2015), 183.
64. D. A. Miliutin, "Starcheskie razmyshleniia o sovremennom polozhenii voennogo dela v Rossii" [Elderly reflections on the current situation in Russian military affairs], *Izvestiia Imperatorskoi Nikolaevskoi Voennoi Akademii*, no. 30 (1912): 833–58.

65. N. E. Makarov, *Na sluzhbe Rossii* [In the service of Russia] (Moscow: Kuchkovo pole, 2017), 415.
66. Miliutin, "Starcheskie razmyshleniia," 831.
67. John Steinberg, *All the Tsar's Men: Russia's General Staff and the Fate of the Empire* (Baltimore: Johns Hopkins University Press, 2010), 208–12.
68. Quoted in Kokoshin, *Soviet Strategic Thought*, 27. Aleksandr Neznamov (1872–1928) was a professor in the academy at the time.
69. N. P. Mikhnevich, *Osnovy strategii* [The foundations of strategy] (Saint Petersburg: Tipografiia Trenke i Fiusno, 1913), 2. Excerpts of this book are translated in Fridman, *Strategiya*, 107–36 (italics in the original).
70. Mikhnevich, *Osnovy*, 6.
71. Mikhnevich, 2.
72. Mikhnevich, 22.
73. Mikhnevich, 3–4.
74. Mikhnevich, 8, 11.
75. Mikhnevich, 4–5.
76. Mikhnevich, 17.
77. John Keep, *Power and the People: Essays on Russian History* (Boulder, CO: East European Monographs, 1995), 189.
78. Dominic Lieven, *Russia and the Origins of the First World War* (London: Macmillan, 1983), 25.
79. Lieven, 112.

# 3

# FORMING A SOVIET STRATEGY FROM THE ASHES OF WORLD WAR I

*You are millions. We are hordes and hordes and hordes.*
*Try and take us on!*
*Yes, we are Scythians! Yes, we are Asians—*
*With slanted and greedy eyes!*
. . . . . . . . . . . . . . . . . . . . . . .
*Russia is a Sphinx. Rejoicing, grieving,*
*And drenched in black blood,*
*It gazes, gazes, gazes at you,*
*With hatred and with love!*

Aleksandr Blok

Why then, if Russia's military thinking was so full of insights as the previous chapters indicate, did it fare so badly on the battlefield in the beginning of the twentieth century? The role of the czar as the supreme decision-maker was obviously paramount. Russia's engagement against Japan in 1904, although the war was started by Japan, was decided against the advice of the General Staff and was a choice driven by the desire for international prestige. Decades later the General Staff was again overruled by the political leadership when, in 1979, the Politburo decided to invade Afghanistan. The circumstances were very different, but the consequence was equally devastating. The paradox is obvious: the reasons for military involvement were to secure prestige, yet it led to the precise opposite.

In addition, the role of the home front, the economy, and the overall support for the war effort became increasingly important. As is clear from the previous chapter, some of the military strategists had fully realized this, but the economic, political, and social policies of the empire lay far beyond their abilities to influence.

This chapter examines the development of strategic thought after the collapse of the empire, the defeat in World War I, and the Civil War. The young Bolshevik state was trying to work out a strategy and doctrine for the future, with a keen eye on the latest wars. The focus here lies on works by Andrei Snesarev and Aleksandr Svechin. In addition, the roles of Mikhail Nikolaevich Tukhachevskii and Boris Mikhailovich Shaposhnikov are taken into account.

## BETWEEN TWO WORLD WARS

Three European empires collapsed in the wake of World War I: the German, the Austro-Hungarian, and the Russian. The world war had ended in defeat for the Russian army, and, even worse, the Russian Empire under the Romanovs had fallen. After the February Revolution, in 1917, the Bolsheviks seized power in October of the same year, resulting in a civil war before the Soviet Union was formally established in 1922. At the same time, Russia fought a war against Poland.

In contrast to the Napoleonic Wars and, later, World War II, during World War I no battles were fought in the Russian heartland, and it was therefore harder for the authorities to appeal to patriotic feelings.[1] In other words, Russia lost the war on the home front. It was the February Revolution, when the czar abdicated, that led to the complete erosion of discipline within the army. Compared to the average monthly figure for the entire war, the number of desertions rose fivefold every month from February to May that year.[2] The situation was exacerbated by growing food shortages. The Imperial Army disintegrated, and on January 28, 1918, the Bolsheviks ordered the creation of the Red Army. It was led by Leon Trotsky from March 1918 until November 1924.[3]

Furthermore, the Red Army, based on the Red Guards, became one of the most important tools for the young Soviet power and not only on the battlefield. It was equally important for agitation, propaganda, and literacy campaigns. All the titles and ranks from the czarist army were eradicated. The lowest rank in 1918 was "Red Army man" (*krasnoarmeets*) instead of soldier and Red Fleet man (*krasnoflotets*) for sailors. Titles for officers were abandoned, and instead simply "Red commander" (*krasnyi komandir*) was employed. By 1935, though, several of the old ranks—for example, marshal (for the army) and admiral (navy)—had already been reintroduced. In the same year, the political commissars who were appointed to secure the party line within the armed forces received a new title, *politruk* (political instructor).

During these turbulent times, the Bolsheviks decided to draft officers from the Imperial Army, the so-called military specialists. A total of about seventy-five thousand former officers served in the Red Army during the Civil War (1918–21).[4] They played an important role in the early years of the Red Army, and almost all front commanders in the war except Mikhail Vasilevich Frunze were former officers of the Imperial Army. Nearly all the leading military strategists analyzed in this chapter were military specialists.

The separate peace treaty with Germany was signed at Brest-Litovsk on March 3, 1918; it forced Russia to surrender Finland, the Baltic states, Poland, and Ukraine. This was a crushing defeat for the Bolsheviks, who moved the capital from Petrograd, which had almost become a border town, to Moscow.

The Allies started to move troops to Russian ports to prevent war matériel from falling into German hands. They were eager to keep a potential second front open against Germany in the hope that the Bolsheviks would be replaced by a government willing to continue the war. In Russia's north, British troops landed in Murmansk and then Archangel. Japanese and British troops moved into Vladivostok in April; shortly thereafter, the US government decided to add troops to the mix in the north and Russia's east. This foreign intervention quickly became a formidable propaganda tool for portraying Soviet Russia, later the Soviet Union, as a besieged country.

To the Bolshevik leadership, the enemy seemed to be everywhere. The enemy within seemed as formidable as the one without. After the Civil War, the struggle against real and imaginary enemies of the Bolshevik state continued. The quelling of the mutiny at the garrison of the Kronstadt naval base and the use of poison gas against peasants in Tambov (both events led by Tukhachevskii) were followed by a temporary retreat, in the form of the New Economic Policy. During the forced collectivization of 1928–32, which led to the disastrous famine in Ukraine, Southern Russia, and Kazakhstan, the Red Army did not play a central role. However, since the famine affected the rural population, the morale among the conscript recruits, most of whom came from the countryside, suffered.

In the early years of the Soviet Union, the Bolsheviks expected that a world revolution would follow, so they took steps to make it happen in Germany. Workers in the capitalist states would rise against their rulers and build socialism, with no regard to national boundaries. This view would deeply influence military thought; the debate that ensued among the military strategists evolved around class wars or national wars. The lessons from the Civil War were considered more important than those from World War I, mainly for ideological reasons.[5] The Red Army's commanders who had risen to power during the Civil War generally saw that conflagration as having been a war of the classes and a model for future war, whereas many of the old commanders from the Imperial Army were riveted by the lessons from World War I.

Under these circumstances, several crucial issues needed to be resolved. What would the army's relationship with the political leadership look like? Was a unified military doctrine needed, and what should it entail? In view of new technological possibilities, what would decide a future war—offensive or defensive operations?

In spite of the turmoil, Russian military thinkers continued to ponder these issues so crucial for the survival of the Soviet Union. The works by the military intellectuals we have met so far are filled with references to other, mostly Western, military thinkers, which shows that they were well connected with the main lines of military and scientific thought. In fact, Andrei Afanasevich Kokoshin, an influential military thinker in today's Russia, called the 1920s to the early 1930s "the golden age" of Russian military and military-political thought.[6] Still, as we shall see below, the repression of these theorists had severe implications on the development of Soviet strategic thought.

One of the main journals where these debates took place was the successor to *Voennyi sbornik*, initially called *Voennoe delo* (Military matters). The first issue was published on June 1, 1918. Partly reflecting the fundamental changes at the time, the journal then repeatedly changed its name: *Voennaia nauka i revoliutsiia* (Military science and revolution), 1921–22; *Voennaia mysl i revoliutsiia* (Military thought and revolution), 1922–24; and *Voina i revoliutsiia* (War and revolution), 1925–36. Finally, in 1937, it received the name that it still has today, *Voennaia mysl* (Military thought). Work on a military encyclopedia started in the 1930s under the editorship of Robert Petrovich Eideman (1895–1937). Only two volumes appeared in print before the project was abandoned, as several of the editors fell victim to the repressions of the 1930s. The first complete Soviet military encyclopedia, in eight-volumes, only came out in 1976–80.

## UNIFIED MILITARY DOCTRINE

The question of creating a military doctrine was a controversial subject intensely discussed in the early 1920s. As we have seen, this question had been discussed for years in imperial Russia, not least after the Russo-Japanese War. The importance of these discussions cannot be overstated; they played a central role in managing the relationship between politics and military strategy and even provided a direction for change.[7] They not only touched on preparing the armed forces but also the nation, the state, and the people for a future war.[8] The debates do not explain how the armed forces would operate on the battlefield in the next war, but they reveal how Russia managed the connection between policy and strategy, the organization of the armed forces, education, and how strategy and doctrine were used as a tool of change. In Høiback's words, doctrine "says *what* we do, and *why*, and *who* we are for the time being."[9]

Svechin had initiated the debate in 1920. He argued in favor of a unified doctrine, even quoting both Heinrich Heine (1797–1856) and Johann Wolfgang Goethe (1749–1832) to strengthen his argument. He accused the army of having forgotten the legacy of Suvorov and Dragomirov. Only by turning to history ("Doctrine is the daughter of history") and continuing in Dragomirov's footsteps, Svechin wrote, could a "Russian doctrine" be developed.[10]

Andrei Snesarev made an important contribution to the issue of a unified military doctrine. He joined the debate with an article in the journal *Voennoe delo*, analyzing the issue from his perspective.[11] He made the case that a unified military doctrine was needed and even ascribed the defeat in the Russo-Japanese

War to the fact that Russia did not have such a doctrine, whereas the Japanese did. He examined several definitions proposed by other military thinkers, such as V. Borisov and V. Apushkin, but found their approaches too narrow. Snesarev suggested that a unified military doctrine should consist of (1) the state's current missions or achievements, (2) an area of deep military understanding and a high level of development (here, he included the theoretical aspects of military science, military history, current military technology, etc.), (3) distribution of the result of the above to the spheres of military technology and material (e.g., instructions, statutes, and textbooks), and (4) age-old features and skills of the people in service (here, he referred to the national traits and habits of the people).

Snesarev reached a definition of a unified military doctrine: "It is a set of military-state achievements and military foundations, practical techniques, and skills of the people, which the country considers to be the best for a given historical moment and with which the military system of the state is permeated from top to bottom." He drew a line between military science and a doctrine. Military science, he wrote, is a set of generalizations within the military sphere that stand above time, place, people, and technology. "Military science can only be international," he claimed. "Doctrine—on the other hand—is national, depending on the history, the culture of the people, and technology. It is no stranger to changes."

This suggests a broad, holistic view, where the strategic objectives of the state, military science, and technology, including the morale of the people, should be systematically combined with the framework of the military doctrine. This means that the military doctrine had a political side and a technical one. The officers in favor, including not least Mikhail Frunze, argued that a unified military doctrine was needed because of its political and technical dimension.[12] The antidoctrinal camp, on the other hand, led by Trotsky, argued that no such doctrine was needed since "our state orientation has long been formed by Marxist methodology and there is no need to form it again in the bosom of the military administration."[13]

Eventually, Frunze finally won the debate, and doctrine became a central concept in Soviet military thinking. The idea and use of a doctrine was established in the Soviet Union and has endured to today, although the actual discussions ended in the mid-1930s because of the Stalinist repressions. The Russian approach to doctrine is and remains focused on the superstructure of war and conflict.

## SNESAREV AND HIS INFLUENCE ON STRATEGIC THOUGHT

Snesarev's military-political views continue to be highly valued in twenty-first-century Russia, not least his scientific and methodological approach to strategic thought.[14] His works are less known in the West but deserve attention because of the impact he had on Soviet strategic thought. He not only played an instrumental role in shaping the first Soviet military doctrine, as we have seen—he also wrote major works on Clausewitz, military geography, and the philosophy of war. Although he was repressed by Stalin, his legacy remained alive in the Soviet/Russian General Staff. For example, the former head of the General Staff, Iurii Nikolaevich Baluevskii (1947–), wrote the foreword to Snesarev's book on Clausewitz and has highlighted Snesarev's importance in laying out the foundation for a military doctrine.[15] Andrei Kokoshin mentions the importance of Snesarev in several books.[16] Also, in 2017 the current chief of the General Staff, Valerii Gerasimov, underlined Snesarev's contribution to Russian military thought, not least regarding Clausewitz.[17] In the early 1990s, his works were discussed at the highest military levels, and Gen. Mikhail Petrovich Kolesnikov (1939–2007), chief of the General Staff from 1992 to 1996, allegedly preferred Snesarev's thinking to that of Svechin.[18] His thoughts on total war, as seen below, formed an intellectual, philosophical background among Russian military thinkers in the decade before Russia's full-scale invasion of Ukraine, indicating offensive warfare involving the entire state's resources. This is yet another demonstration of the importance of studying Russian strategic thought.

Starting in 1999, the General Staff Academy hosted a center for the study of domestic military strategy, in Snesarev's name. Since 2013, a Snesarev Prize has been awarded to contributors in geostrategic studies. The corresponding member of the Academy of Military Sciences, Aleksandr Bartosh, argues that Snesarev's thoughts on war are particularly useful today in a time of nonlinear and hybrid war.[19] He highlights Snesarev's holistic view that war involves so much more than only weapons and the organization of the armed forces. It is about the relationship between economy, politics, society, and the morale of the people.

## SNESAREV'S RISE AND FALL

Both Carl von Clausewitz and Marc Bloch had the experience of fighting in wars in which their armies were defeated and the states for which they fought collapsed.[20] Snesarev had a similar experience. He was born in 1865, son of a priest, and his family moved several times when he was growing up.[21]

He spent his youth in Cossack territory, graduating from the secondary school in Novocherkassk, which long served as the capital of the Don Cossacks. At Moscow University, he studied in the physics/mathematics department, and it was only after completing these studies that he turned to a military career. Incidentally, he was also a talented singer (allegedly with a beautiful baritone) and had at one point replaced a singer at the Bolshoi Theater. He graduated from the General Staff Academy in 1899. The head of the academy during his first two years was the influential Genrikh Leer.

Initially, Snesarev was stationed in Central Asia. As an intelligence officer, he traveled widely (this being the time of the Great Game). He mapped out India and Afghanistan and served in the Turkistan Military District. He knew several of the region's languages and eventually wrote a number of fundamental works on Afghanistan, India, and military geography. His wife, Evgeniia Vasilevna Zaitseva, had supposedly at one point been courted by the Swedish explorer Sven Hedin.[22]

Snesarev was an experienced military officer, having served in both World War I and the Civil War. He decided to stay in Russia and eventually joined the ranks of the Bolsheviks. In May 1918 he was appointed to oversee the creation of the Northern Caucasus Military District, where he clashed with Stalin and Kliment Efremovich Voroshilov (1881–1969), in Tsaritsyn. Snesarev was appointed to Smolensk as the chief of parts of the Western Curtain, a defense system established after the Treaty of Brest-Litovsk to guard the demarcation line and to protect Russia from a possible invasion.

In 1919 Snesarev was appointed head of the General Staff Academy, where he initiated courses on the philosophy of war and military strategy. This was a time of "hunger and cold," as he later characterized it.[23] Being the head of the academy, he found himself at the very center of a heated debate between the "military specialists" and the Red commanders, whose training had come from practical experience in the Civil War and the Russo-Polish War (1919–20). He was at loggerheads with the Reds, who wanted to abolish theoretical studies and force the academy to rely solely on applied teachings. At the same time, wanting to renew the curriculum, he found himself at odds with some of the old professors. In effect, he fought a two-front war. Under his leadership, old subjects, such as geodesy and astronomy, were abolished, while newer topics, such as psychological warfare, fire tactics, and modern strategy, were introduced.[24]

In 1921, when Tukhachevskii was appointed head of the academy, Snesarev became director of its newly created Eastern Department. Snesarev also wrote a book about Clausewitz and translated his *On War* into Russian, both unpublished at the time.

He was arrested in 1930 when he was almost sixty and sentenced to death, a punishment that Stalin changed to ten years' imprisonment. After four years in the Solovki prison camp, he suffered a stroke, from which he never fully recovered, in spite of being released. He died in Moscow in 1937. He was rehabilitated in 1958, during the Khrushchev Thaw.

## ON WAR AND THE STATE

Snesarev's *Filosofiia voiny* (The philosophy of war) is one of his major works. Its manuscript, based on his lectures at the General Staff Academy, was finalized just before his arrest in 1930 and was first published in Russia in 2013.[25] These days, Snesarev is sometimes called "the Russian Sun Tzu."

Snesarev's book is a deep-delving and detailed work in which he explores his topic in six chapters covering the role of philosophy in the study of war, human judgments on war, war from a historical perspective, war in a scientific perspective, a moral appraisal of war, and finally war and the state. He sets out to lay the foundation for a "philosophy of war" and focuses on the questions of "why and what for" wars are fought.

His approach to war was encompassing and holistic; he examined wars not only from historical and economic perspectives but also, importantly, the moral perspective and the role of the state. Wars in the future, according to Snesarev, would become increasingly large-scale and ever more complex, requiring the entire effort of the state. This conclusion is not surprising since the text was written based on the experiences of World War I (with the introduction of airplanes and tanks) and the Civil War. He underlined how the state would already need to prepare for war in peacetime, involving not only the army and soldiers but also the entire population. In his review of Svechin's *Strategiia*, he wrote, "Strategy uses not only the sword but needs other means as well, even foreign ones such as agitation, undermining of the enemy's economy, and outdoing him in replenishing one's forces."[26]

Snesarev's outlook was mainly geopolitical, with the state having a fundamental role. He could be described as an Etatist. "The state is benevolent and not evil," he wrote, "therefore, only the state can determine questions of war and peace."[27] Consequently, he argued that a military organization "or any coercive organization is not evil but a consequence and sign of evil." It was particularly important to understand this in Russia because it was a "backward country whose people, fenced off by a deep precipice from a numerically weak intelligentsia, always felt antistate and hence [harbored] antipatriotic masses." It is no coincidence that he is very critical of Leo Tolstoy's views on war. He acknowledged Tolstoy's work as a writer but did not appreciate him as a military thinker. "He put all his resources—from that perspective not very great—on defaming, ridiculing, and humiliating the war and all the military."

Snesarev also criticized the position of the banker and pacifist Ivan Stanislavovich Bloch (1836–1901). Bloch's famous work on future war was published and translated into several languages. The original work consists of five volumes, but a condensed summary was printed in connection with the international conference on peace and disarmament in The Hague in 1899.[28] Bloch argued that war among industrial states would lead to total economic and social collapse. Therefore, war was becoming irrational and would be redundant in the future. Snesarev, with the advantage of hindsight, noted dryly, "All of the hundreds of motives [that would make war redundant], which he diligently extorted from his banker's head, were brilliantly, by actual mockery, shattered in the last Great War, 1914–1918."

In studying war, Snesarev preferred the geopolitical method since the state is the product and basic subject of geopolitical processes.[29] This may sound familiar. Some might associate this line of thinking with the Swedish political scientist and conservative politician Rudolf Kjellén (1864–1922). A German scholar finds Snesarev to be a forerunner of Carl Schmitt (1888–1985).[30] This illustrates that Soviet military thinking was totalitarian and conformed with German military thinking at that time, not least the thoughts in Erich Ludendorff's *Der totale Krieg* (Total war), published in 1935.

Throughout history, in Snesarev's view, the relationship between war and the state was always tight and inseparable. A state could be founded on five radically different points of view: religious, physical, judicial, ethical, and psychological. He examined all these aspects from the earliest times and showed how the question of the justification of a state is closely tied to that of law (*pravo*). He was slightly skeptical of the socialists' appreciation of the state but seemed confident that the state, albeit constructed in a new way, would persist.[31]

However, regardless of what constituted the foundation of a state, war was always a part of a state's evolution. Influenced by the German public lawyer Georg Jellinek (1851–1911),[32] Snesarev wrote, "What provides protection, and especially the strengthening of a state's international importance, if not wars—and mainly *offensive* ones?"[33] Wars and the weapons of the state were necessary not only for defending its territory but also its people, riches, and ideals, in order to secure its might (*mogushchestvo*) and self-sufficiency, which corresponds to its spirit and the historical vocation of its people.[34] Therefore, the state should always prepare its population for war. This, again, might sound familiar, resembling the thoughts popularized by Ludendorff in his *Der totale Krieg*. Ludendorff, incidentally, was not only born the same year as Snesarev but also died in 1937.

So, if the state is necessary and war is a part of its existence, what are the nature and size of its influence on war? Snesarev applied an "inverse function: if the state is a function of the variable called war, then war, in turn, is a function from a variable called the state."[35] He emphasized the importance of determining the goals of the state since it is "impossible to think of a state without a goal or goals, which it embodies in its activities and achievements." He analyzed various schools of thought on this topic, from Friedrich Julius Stahl, Baruch Spinoza, and John Locke to Immanuel Kant, Thomas Hobbes, and Jean-Jacques Rousseau. Stahl (1802–61) was a German political philosopher whose three-volume *Die Philosophie des Rechts nach geschichtlicher Ansicht* (The philosophy of law from a historical perspective) Snesarev had read.

The goal of the state, according to Snesarev's interpretation of these philosophical schools, is either security, freedom, or law.[36] In addition, he added that every state needs to take care of its international security, which is not always identical to "the protection of citizens and therefore cannot be summed up under the concept of protection of law."[37] Referring to Jellinek, Snesarev concluded "that without the state no society is possible and no universal human goal is achievable, that in the depths of the essence of the state there are principles, on the one hand, determining its existence, on the other, giving it a goal and direction for its work, and these principles are moral—that is, eternal, imperative, and universal."[38]

Consequently, Snesarev emphasized that "all the efforts, the works, or deprivations of an individual, a group, or all the people aimed at protecting the state and ensuring its peace, even toward its legitimate growth and expansion, are correct, appropriate, and moral acts."[39] Hence, war was the highest form of a state's justification.[40] In other words, he linked war and the armed forces to the very existence of the state, which may seem perfectly logical in view of the experiences from World War I and the Civil War. It is also a thought that still prevails in the Russian Federation of the twenty-first century.

This line of thinking, the geopolitical outlook and focus on the interests of the national state, and not necessarily on the interests of the Bolshevik Party, may have contributed to the fact that his manuscript on the philosophy of war remained unpublished for over eighty years.

## STRATEGY AND POLITICS

Lenin's fascination with Clausewitz is well documented, although it was Trotsky who made sure that part of *On War* was introduced at the General Staff Academy in the original language.[41]

Aleksandr Svechin worked closely with Snesarev, and although their biographies partly overlap, Svechin was quite different in his nontotalitarian outlook. They remained friends even if they did not always agree on everything. They were both representatives of what could be called the "German school" within the General Staff.

Svechin graduated from the General Staff Academy in 1903 and fought in both the Russo-Japanese War and World War I. For a few years, he worked in military intelligence in Warsaw. Following the Bolshevik Revolution, he joined the Red Army, and after a brief period as chief of the All-Russian Main Staff, he became a professor at the General Staff Academy, where he stayed for the rest of his life. Like Snesarev, he was imprisoned in connection with Operation Vesna, the 1930–31 repression of former officers of the Imperial Army, not least since Tukhachevskii turned against him. That time Svechin was pardoned, but in 1937 he was arrested again. A year later he was executed. He was rehabilitated in 1956, but it was not until the 1980s and 1990s that his thoughts on the strategy of attrition received recognition, not only in the Soviet Union and Russia but also in the West.

Although this book analyzes strategy and doctrine, it deserves to be noted that Svechin made a fundamental contribution to theoretical development in his introduction of the concept of "operational art," between strategy and tactics. He criticized Leer and Jomini for having too narrow an understanding of military operations. "Leer's operational lines covered the entire meaning of military operations, the head and tail of the phenomenon, since the operation almost merged, in his view, with the war."[42] At the highest level, Svechin pointed out that "strategy decides issues related to the use of armed forces, as well as to the use of all the country's resources to achieve the final military goals."[43]

Among Svechin's most famous works are *Evoliutsiia voennogo iskusstva* (The evolution of the art of war), *Klauzevits*, and his main work, *Strategiia*, which was published in 1926. Much has been written about Svechin, not least by Kokoshin, so the focus here is on Svechin's contribution to strategy and doctrine. *Strategiia* was until 1962 the only comprehensive work on strategy published in the Soviet Union, albeit forbidden for a period immediately after Svechin's execution in 1938.

His analysis did not comply with the laws of Marxism or its dialectical and historical materialism, which later became the very foundation of Soviet military thought, as we will see in the next chapter. Svechin simply noted that his knowledge of Marxism was so little that it was meaningless to try.[44] The influence of German thinkers, not least by writers such as Dietrich Heinrich von Bülow (1757–1807) and military historian Hans Delbrück (1848–1929), is clear, and he frequently quoted them from the original. Incidentally, Svechin was criticized for being, in his two-volume work, too much under the influence of Delbrück.[45]

Importantly, Svechin argued in favor of broad, inclusive strategic studies and warned against researching strategy only in the General Staff. This would lead to the creation of a "strategic caste" and ultimately a rift between strategists and tacticians.[46] He also refers to Dragomirov to underline the importance of not letting theory get the better of practice.[47]

This was a time, according to Svechin, when a new strategic landscape was being shaped, which required new methods and ways of waging war.[48] Emphasizing the primacy of politics over strategy and tactics, he claimed that strategy cannot exist outside politics. Echoing Mikhnevich, Svechin notes that it was the politician who had to set the political goal of the war. In order to set the proper goals, the politician must be well informed about his own and his enemy's resources. At the same time, he should discuss the goals with the military strategists: "The formulation of the goal should help strategy, not hinder it."[49]

In this, he was in complete agreement with Snesarev, who had noted in his manuscript on Clausewitz that "theory is good for clever people, a brother to geniuses, but she is a mute, boarded-up door to average leaders; this is her weakness. And military thought in its lofty quest will for a long time bounce between the dogmatic formulas of Bülow, Jomini, Leer, and the diffuse leadership of Clausewitz; neither they nor the other means will give a final answer; it will be somewhere in the middle."[50]

Furthermore, Svechin agreed with Nikolai Mikhnevich in arguing in favor of a strategy of attrition, rather than one of destruction. In doing so, he clashed with several colleagues, including Tukhachevskii. According to Svechin, the strategy of attrition "can strive to achieve the most decisive ultimate goals, including the complete physical extermination of the enemy." The strategy of attrition was not at all a war of "limited goals" since, he argued, the ultimate goal of the war may be far from modest.[51] This does not mean that he was against destruction of the enemy, as is sometimes claimed. The essential point is that Svechin, Snesarev, Mikhnevich, Leer, and Dragomirov had holistic views of war and conflict and that all the means of the state should be used to achieve the state's political goals. This is a premise that endures regardless of the political system in Russia and one of the lessons the West has yet to learn.

A politically defensive goal would be the most prudent for Russia, Svechin argued. He criticized those who meant that an offensive goal would put an end to internal strife, including the possibility to fight not only an enemy state but also separate political parties. "War is not a cure for the internal diseases of the state but the most serious exam on the health of internal politics."[52] The next war would be protracted and complex, Svechin predicted, as Snesarev had also done.

Tukhachevskii was one of the most talented and influential young officers in the Red Army. He took a different approach to the relationship between strategy and politics than Snesarev and Svechin. Having gained a reputation from the Russo-Polish War and the Civil War, he quickly rose in the ranks. He constantly argued for the motorization of the army, established the paratroops, and initiated the development of rocket weaponry. By coincidence, Tukhachevskii and France's later president Charles de Gaulle were imprisoned together in Ingolstadt during World War I. Both were eager to reform their respective armies and equip them with tanks.

However, in his younger years, he had an approach to the relationship between strategy and politics that was somewhat different from those of Snesarev and Svechin. He noted that "the intrusion of politics into strategy is an extreme evil," for instance, and labeled the military revolutionary councils "a thorn in the eye of our strategy. Their existence contradicts the very essence of the matter."[53] He became a proponent of class wars and world revolution of the proletariat, which was in line with the current communist ideology. This would lead to a confrontation between him and Svechin.

Another influential military theorist—then and now—was Boris Shaposhnikov. His fate was different from that of his colleagues on the General Staff in that he survived the repressions, and therefore his major work was studied from its publication in the 1920s up until today. He had graduated from the General Staff Academy in 1910, participated in World War I, and then joined the Red Army in 1918. He was head of the General Staff in 1928–31, again in 1937–40, and from July 1941 to May 1942. He was appointed marshal in 1940. Shaposhnikov was known by his contemporaries to be a very cautious man,[54] which may have helped him to be one of the few of the General Staff officers of the 1920s and 1930s to survive Stalin's repressions. Shaposhnikov also served on the court that sentenced Tukhachevskii, Iona Emmanuilovich Yakir (1896–1937), and Ieronim Petrovich Uborevich (1896–1937) to death.

Shaposhnikov's seminal work *Mozg armii* (The brain of the army) was published from 1927 to 1929 in three volumes and is still being used today at the General Staff Academy.[55] Its first two volumes start with quotes from Clausewitz, and throughout the entire work the author is engaged in a dialogue with the Prussian strategist. In fact, he ended his magnum opus by urging his readers to study Clausewitz: "We think that creating something new out of 'human weakness,' so unique to our time, would be a big mistake. America is already discovered."[56]

Shaposhnikov devoted volume 1 to examining the Austrian General Staff during World War I, the second volume to the Balkan Wars, and the third to the outbreak of World War I and the coalition wars. Being "cautious," he examined primarily the Austrian General Staff rather than the Russian or German. It is a much more detailed account than Svechin's *Strategiia* and not as succinct. Important here is the fact that Shaposhnikov, being inspired by Clausewitz, took Soviet doctrine even further. The fully accepted statement "war is a continuation of politics by other means" was extended to another level. Shaposhnikov concluded, "If war is a continuation of politics, only by other means, so is also peace a continuation of struggle, only by other means."[57] In this sense, and this is basic to Soviet doctrine and strategy, the distinction between peace and war was obliterated, except for the difference in the degree of armed force used in the perpetual conflict. This, in turn, dovetails well with the policy of "peaceful coexistence" introduced by Lenin, a topic examined in the next chapter.

Shaposhnikov's relationship to Svechin was one of mutual respect, and they shared many views, including the relationship between politics and strategy. Interestingly, in 1934 Svechin compiled a secret memorandum on future war to Voroshilov, with a reply from Shaposhnikov, who by then was serving as head of the General Staff Academy—that is, the Frunze Military Academy.[58] Svechin thought that the main enemies in a future war would be a coalition of France and Britain, supported financially and materially by the United States.

He argued that this coalition would exploit the "nationality question" in Ukraine and the Caucasus, not least since these regions were rich in wheat, oil, coal, and minerals. He recommended that the Red Army should prepare to strike against the "weakest link," namely Romania. Germany, according to Svechin, would be forced to conclude a military convention on the passage of military supplies and troops to Poland via their railways and subsequently demand access to the Polish Corridor and the adjacent quasi-state of Danzig, a large port.

Shaposhnikov did not agree with everything in Svechin's memorandum but acknowledged that it was useful for testing the Red Army's training and preparation for war. He pointed out that Britain's role in a future war would largely depend on whether Labour or the Conservatives were in power. According to Shaposhnikov, the likely enemy coalition against the Soviet Union would be other countries within the sphere of influence of the great European powers. He specified that these countries were Poland, Romania, the Baltic states, Finland, and Sweden. These countries, he claimed, were economically and politically dependent on the strong European states, geographically close to the Soviet Union and scared of the "Red danger," and "therefore interested in not only securing their borders but also extending them to the east."[59]

Neither Svechin nor Shaposhnikov proved entirely right about the enemy in a future war, but Shaposhnikov's memorandum is described today as being "a reference point for our country for many years to come."[60]

## THE ROLE OF GEOGRAPHY AND STRATEGIC INTELLIGENCE

Svechin took into account issues of military politics and strategy and, similarly, paid attention to economic and geographic problems. Not least, the exposed position of Leningrad was of great concern.[61] He compared it to both Sevastopol during the Crimean War and the French city of Nancy before World War I—in other words, as cities with unfavorable strategic positions and exposed to possible enemy attacks. The concentration of industries in the Leningrad area was of particular concern, and he warned against their further establishment there. He emphasized that the loss of economic independence would inevitably lead to the loss of strategic independence.

Geography—the hard winters, the enormous spaces—would not save Russia in a future war, Svechin warned in an article. "We must understand that 200 square kilometers is not an ocean of land," he wrote.[62] The telegraph, radio, airplanes, motor vehicles, railways—indeed all modern technology—had rendered distances less significant. He cautioned against believing too much in peace and relying on geography for protection in those dire times. "History did not handicap us strategically," he observed. Now it was imperative to organize a large military force: "Our space makes us scatter our energy and the ability to organize, which makes it difficult to gather forces to strike back. . . . It includes within its limits the most important political and strategic positions requiring serious military force, if only in order to maintain neutrality and not drift into war."[63]

He concluded with an appeal that reflects some of the views found in today's contemporary Russia: "The first step to victory is to lie in the consciousness that we are not wearing any geographic armor, that our chests are open to blows, that the enemy is not asleep, that tomorrow is made today."[64]

His article was published with an editorial comment, which noted that Svechin in general was right but one-sided in his emphasis on geography. It is worth citing the final sentence of the comment, since it reveals the official Soviet view of war: "Any war with the SSSR is a struggle against the proletarian revolution: it is a civil war; the fate of the war will be determined by the real balance of international class forces in comparison with which territorial successes alone cannot be decisive."[65]

Snesarev was also preoccupied with military geography, above all strategic intelligence. In his *Introduction to Military Geography*, from 1924, he pointed out that Russia generally had a better position than Europe since its centers of military industry were not as heavily concentrated in the capital.

Snesarev emphasized that three factors were essential to any military geographic outline: (1) the geographic location, (2) land power or island power, and (3) the relation to neighboring states.[66] Regarding the last factor, he elaborated:

> This factor has always influenced and affected the fate of the state; on the general side: the degree of its development, its security, the pace of life itself, the very possibility of life; on the military side: the need to fight, the number of troops, the defense system, the number of likely theaters of military action, the system of deployment, military spending, on the state of military science.[67]

He noted that the Soviet Union at that time had direct borders with eleven states, which made the defense of the Soviet Union complex. It led to "a large number of likely theaters of military operations, their diversity, a complex system of army deployments, high expenditures, and so on."[68]

Furthermore, he saw the links between military geography, military history, and strategy, which were "overwhelming."[69] Without military history, he argued, the military geographic data would always be too narrow, since patterns (*shablony*) will always stay too long, and new factors would be caught too late. The link to strategy was fundamental because "modern strategy with its enormous scope, especially the strategy of attrition, brings to the stage a military geography of immense content with a huge economic importance." In relation to military science, military geography touched on all the sciences related to the armed forces and war simply because, as Snesarev put it, "a person fights in the thick of geographic factors and cannot fight outside of them."[70] Here, Snesarev made a substantial contribution to "strategic geography," a topic that will be discussed further in chapter 6.

## ON STRATEGIC OFFENSIVE AND DEFENSIVE

Regarding future war, Tukhachevskii was adamant in arguing for the strategy of destruction. This developed into a major clash between him and Svechin, who, as Mikhnevich had done, argued in favor of a strategy of attrition. Svechin underlined the benefit of an active strategic defense and emphasized that "an offensive at any cost, as an a priori chosen method, leads to our troops dissolving where the enemy wants and activity degenerates into impotence."[71]

The clash of minds between Tukhachevskii and Svechin had several causes. They were of different generations, and Svechin had been educated at the prestigious General Staff Academy and had years of war experience. Tukhachevskii, in contrast, had received only a much shorter military education before World War I broke out and spent time as a prisoner of war. Apart from other explanations such as professional envy, the causes of the clash lay deeper. Already in 1927 the rift was apparent, and Tukhachevskii repeatedly attacked the "military specialists" in general, and Svechin in particular, for being "bourgeois agents" within the Red Army.

In 1931 when Svechin was arrested, Tukhachevskii, at a meeting on April 25, 1931, held in the Leningrad section of the Communist Academy of the Central Committee, publicly accused him of being "a traitor of the country."[72] He criticized Svechin for being an enemy of Soviet power, for expressing bourgeois views, and for working against the political commissars in the Red Army. He particularly criticized Svechin's views on defensive wars: "The essence of [his] *Strategiia* is defeatist when applied to the USSR. . . . It is a defense of the capitalist world from the offensive Red Army."[73]

In 1937, in Svechin's unpublished autobiography, written just before the arrest that would end with his being shot, he admitted that he was very critical of those (e.g., Tukhachevskii) who had argued that new technologies would render defense impossible. He thought that Tukhachevskii and his supporters did not sufficiently appreciate the "strategic understanding of Ludendorff and the German school."[74] He also criticized Tukhachevskii's and Vladimir Kiriakovich Triandafillov's overenthusiasm for new technologies as being the decisive factor for the Red Army in a future war.[75]

In short, revolutionary enthusiasm stood against experience and education, and the ideological "scientific law" of Marxism-Leninism stood against military science based on history and sociology. The clash would have repercussions for decades. When Tukhachevskii was rehabilitated, most of his works were republished almost immediately and recognized as outstanding. After Svechin's rehabilitation, his works were initially only published with severe cuts, and his legacy was treated with suspicion due to his service in the czarist army. As noted, it was only in the 1980s and 1990 that his reputation was rehabilitated.[76]

Furthermore, before World War II, the cult of the offensive still prevailed in Soviet military thought, as it did elsewhere. The Field Regulations from 1936 (PU-36) stated that every attack on the Soviet Union would be "repelled with all the power of the armed forces of the Soviet Union and shift the military actions to enemy territory." This concept was very strong, not least since Stalin subscribed to it. In addition, all the discussions about a strategic defense had been banned, which had disastrous consequences in June 1941.

## THE SOVIET-GERMAN MILITARY COOPERATION

German influence is evident in many of the works of Russian strategic thinkers both before and after World War I. This is hardly surprising. Germany was considered the main enemy, and the efficiency of German armed forces had been painfully obvious in World War I. Before that, German military might was, as discussed above, well established, not least through the Wars of German Unification. There had also always been a long tradition of military, political, and cultural relations between Russia and Germany, stemming from the days of Ivan IV in the mid-sixteenth century, when many Germans were in Russian service.[77] Furthermore, in the 1920s and 1930s the Soviet Union and Germany engaged in a close relationship regarding military cooperation.

That cooperation had started well before the Treaty of Rapallo in 1922. Apart from military-industrial cooperation and the setting-up of military schools (for armored, aerial, and chemical warfare) in the Soviet Union, the Soviet-German relationship also entailed exchanges of intelligence and of officers from the highest military academies for periods ranging from a few months up to a year.[78] Thus, from 1925 to 1931, a total of 156 officers studied in Germany.[79] German figures state that from 1926 to 1933, a total of 143 staff officers spent longer periods in Germany. Among the officers sent to Germany were Vladimir Triandafillov, Ieronim Uborevich, and Robert Eideman. Particularly interesting subjects of study included joint operations (*vzaimodeistvie rodov voisk*) and how the army and the navy operated together.[80]

In 1928 a commission was created to take care of the lessons learned from the cooperation.[81] A list of the most important things to evaluate was compiled: (1) organization of and methods for conducting exercises, (2) new technical means for struggle (*borba*), and (3) the most important tactical and operative views that differed from the regulations of the Red Army. This part of the

Soviet-German cooperation lasted until July 1933, when the last group of Soviet officers returned home. Earlier, on April 10, all the Soviet officers in Germany, including the military attaché, wrote a report to Voroshilov that is worth highlighting here, since it touches on the discussion of the need to train on the issue of personal initiative within the armed forces. First, they noted that in terms of artillery and means of communication, the German side was much better "than they showed to us."[82] More importantly here, the Soviet officers pointed out that whereas "our higher educational institutions were a forge of mass production," Germany's educational system was done more by hand, strictly out of need. "In our schools, there is a tendency to turn self-training into collective, brigade training." But a commander needed skills for independent work, and in Germany they put much emphasis on this, which resulted in "truly independent commanders."[83]

How significant was the Soviet-German exchange for Russian military thought? It seems reasonable to assume that the Soviet side thought it was important, but more research is needed to evaluate the effect on the thinking on strategy and doctrine. The exchanges provided the Red Army with insights into the development of the German armed forces. On the other hand, tragically, many of the highest military leaders with experience from the exchanges fell victim to Stalin's repressions.[84]

The repressions effectively stopped the debates on strategy and doctrine. Stalin's "permanently operating factors" of war were announced on February 23, 1942. Order No. 55 declared that the outcome of war is determined by permanently operating factors—not transitory ones, such as surprise. The five principles were (1) stability of the rear, (2) morale of the troops, (3) quantity and quality of divisions, (4) the army's weapons, and (5) organizational ability of the military command personnel.[85]

## THE CONSEQUENCES OF THE REPRESSIONS

Toward the end of the 1920s, in connection with the First Five-Year Plan and collectivization, the ideological pressure on the strategic military thinkers had started to increase. Operation Vesna initiated the "cleansing" of the Red Army. Over three thousand officers of the Red Army were arrested. A few years later, from 1935 to 1936, another cleansing cleared twelve thousand officers from the Red Army's ranks. However, it would get far worse. The highest leadership of the Red Army was annihilated, and from 1937 to 1938 over 35,100 of the Red Army's officers were sentenced, of whom 9,100 were either killed or sent to the gulag camps.[86]

Apart from the dreadfulness of the purges and the fear they created within the armed forces and society, it is significant to point out that not only the names of the victims were removed from the official sources—all the writings of the leading military thinkers were removed from Soviet libraries and destroyed. Marshal Georgii Konstantinovich Zhukov (1896–1974) later called those years "a veritable epidemic of slander."[87] Gen. Aleksandr Vasilevich Gorbatov (1891–1973), who was arrested in 1938 and miraculously released and reinstated in the Red Army in 1940, admitted that it was difficult to comprehend what was happening when arrest after arrest was announced.[88]

In addition, although this book primarily analyzes strategic thought, the fate of the operational concept of deep operations needs to be noted. The concept was included in the Field Regulations in 1936, but the repressions made it toxic. After Tukhachevskii was shot, in 1937, the theory of deep operations was branded as "sabotage."[89]

As for the fate of Snesarev, his observations about Afghanistan were prescient, but since his works were banned, they were not widely spread apart from being read by a few officers on the General Staff. He clearly advised against trying to invade the country. "The proud and freedom-loving character of the people and the huge mountainous area are in complete harmony with the lack of roads, making the country very difficult to conquer and especially hold on to and keep in power"[90]—words that were seemingly forgotten decades later.

Almost the entire military intelligentsia was obliterated, and the consequences on the development of military-political and military-scientific thought were severe. Strategy was removed as a subject of further study as the political leadership (i.e., Stalin) proclaimed it their monopoly.[91] Not only was there loss of self-confidence among the remaining military commanders, which hampered the initiative, according to Sergei Nikolaevich Mikhalev (1923–2005) "throughout the war," but the effects were also particularly devastating for the military scientists researching strategy and doctrine. With the loss of the institutional memory, the capacity to think about war and conflict was almost eradicated, which had serious ramifications for decades to come. The contributors to the volume *Istoriia voennoi strategii* (History of military strategy), from 2000, noted that due to the pursuit of "enemies of the people" in 1937 and 1938, "the central military apparatus was paralyzed."[92] Importantly, in spite of the rehabilitation of the repressed military thinkers in the 1950s and 1960s, the topic remained sensitive. So, for instance, Korotkov's otherwise fine work from 1980 does not discuss the consequences of the repression at all, and Marshal Konstantin Konstantinovich Rokossovsky (1896–1968), who was convicted in 1937 and pardoned in 1940, did not mention the repressions in his memoirs. According to a leading Russian military theorist, the repressions still had an impact into the 2010s.[93]

Despite this horrific and tragic period, the ability of the Red Army to fight through the war, after the initial disasters, remained unwavering.

## NOTES

*Epigraph:* Aleksandr Blok, "Scythians," January 30, 1918, translated by A. Wachtel, I. Kutik, and M. Denner, https://ruverses.com/alexander-blok/scythians/332/.
1. Lieven, *End of Tsarist Russia*, 356.
2. Oleg Airapetov, *Uchastie Rossiiskoi Imperii v Pervoi Mirovoi Voine 1914–1917* [The participation by the Russian Empire in the First World War], vol. 4, *1917: Raspad* [1917: The breakup] (Moscow Kuchkovo pole, 2015), 109, 172–73.
3. For a general overview in English, see Albert Seaton and Joan Seaton, *The Soviet Army: 1918 to the Present* (New York: Meridian, 1988).
4. A. G. Kavtaradze, *Voennye spetsialisty na sluzhbe Respubliki Sovetov 1917–1920* [The military specialists in the service of the Soviet republics 1917–20] (Moscow: Nauka, 1988), 218, 222.
5. S. N. Mikhalev, *Voennaia strategiia: Podgotovka i vedenie voin Novogo i Noveishego vremen*i [Military strategy: Preparing for and waging wars in modern and contemporary history] (Moscow: Kuchkovo pole, 2003), 492.
6. A. A. Kokoshin, *Strategicheskoe upravlenie* [Strategic control] (Moscow: Rosspen, 2003), 358.
7. Harald Høiback, "The Anatomy of Doctrine and Ways to Keep It Fit," *Journal of Strategic Studies*, no. 2 (2016): 185–97. For parts of the debate, see also his *Understanding Military Doctrine*, 43–45.
8. Kokoshin, *Soviet Strategic Thought*, 26–27.
9. Høiback, "Anatomy," 190.
10. A. Svechin, "Shto takoe voennaia doktrina?" [What is a military doctrine?], *Voennoe delo*, no. 2 (1920): 29–41. See also Mikhalev, *Voennaia strategiia*, 722–25.
11. Snesarev, "Edinaia voennaia doktrina," 225–33.
12. M. V. Frunze, "Edinaia voennaia doktrina i Krasnaia armiia" [A unified military doctrine and the Red Army], *Voennaia nauka i revoliutsiia*, no. 1 (1921): 30–46. The article was reprinted several times, notably in 1941 and in *Voennaia mysl*, no. 5 (2008): 13–24.
13. L. Trotskii, "Voennaia doktrina ili mimo-voennoe doktrinerstvo" [A military doctrine or a pseudo-military doctrinaire attitude], *Voennoe delo*, no. 2 (1921): 204–34.
14. Yuri Mikhalev, "Voenno-politicheskie vzgliady A. E. Snesareva i sovremennost, avtoreferat dissertatsii" [The military-political views of A. E. Snesarev and contemporary times] (diss. abstract, Military University, Moscow, 2008).
15. Iurii Baluevskii, "Teoreticheskie i metodologicheskie osnovy formirovaniia voennoi doktriny Rossiiskoi Federatsii" [Theoretical and methodological foundations for creating a military doctrine in the Russian Federation], *Voennaia mysl*, no. 3 (2007): 14–21.
16. Kokoshin, *Svechin*, 77–80.
17. Gerasimov, "Sovremennye voiny i aktualnye voprosy oborony strany" [Modern wars and current questions in regard to the country's defence]. *Vestnik Akademii Voennykh Nauk*, no. 2 (2017): 9.
18. Kokoshin, *Svechin*, 27–29.
19. A. A. Bartosh, *Tuman gibridnoi voiny* [The fog of hybrid war] (Moscow: Goriachaia liniia–Telekom, 2019), 14, 62.
20. Peter Paret, "Two Historians on Defeat in War and Its Causes," in his *Clausewitz in His Time: Essays in the Cultural and Intellectual History of Thinking about War* (New York: Berghahn, 2014), 113–26.

21. I. Danilenko, "Geroi Voiny i Geroi Truda" [A hero of war and a hero of labor], in A. E. Snesarev, *Pisma s fronta 1914–17* [Letters from the front 1914–17] (Moscow: Kuchkovo pole, 2012), 8–31, and V. V. Balabushevich and G. G. Kotovskii, eds., *Andrei Evgenevich Snesarev: Zhizn i nauchnaia deiatelnost* [Andrei Evgenevich Snesarev: Life and scientific work] (Moscow: Nauka, 1973).
22. A. A. Guber, "Vospominaniia o professore A. E. Snesareve" [Memories about Professor A. E. Snesarev], in Balabushevich and Kotovskii, *Andrei Evgenevich Snesarev*, 17–18.
23. V. M. Dudnik, "Voennaia deiatelnost A. E. Snesareva," in Balabushevich and Kotovskii, *Andrei Evgenevich Snesarev*, 41. See also the memoir of Kirill Meretskov, *Na sluzhbe narodu* [In the service of the people] (Moscow: Politizdat, 1968).
24. Dudnik, "Voennaia deiatelnost," 38–42.
25. Andrei Snesarev, *Filosofiia voiny* [The philosophy of war] (Moscow: Lomonosov, 2013).
26. A. Snesarev, "Retsenziia na knigu A. Svechina *Strategiia*'" [Review of A. Svechin's book *Strategy*], *Voina i revoliutsiia*, no. 4 (1927): 144–47.
27. Snesarev, *Filosofiia voiny*, 189–90, 235–36, 244–45.
28. On the discussions, see Lieven, *End of Tsarist Russia*, 152–54.
29. I. S. Danilenko, "Vydaiushchiisia voennyi teoretik i filosof XX veka" [An outstanding military theorist and philosopher of the twentieth century], in Snesarev, *Filosofiia voiny*, 27.
30. Hans-Ulrich Seidt, "Lehrjahre am Hindukusch: Kontinuität und Zäsuren russischer Geostrategie," *Zeitschrift für Außen- und Sicherheitspolitik*, no. 12 (2019): 283–99.
31. Snesarev, *Filosofiia voiny*, 216–36.
32. Jellinek wrote his main work, *Das Recht des modernen Staates: Allgemeine Staatslehre* (The law of the modern state: General theory of the state), in 1900. It was published in Russian in 1903.
33. Snesarev, *Filosofiia voiny*, 211 (italics in the original).
34. Snesarev, 211.
35. Snesarev, 212.
36. Snesarev, 242.
37. Snesarev, 243.
38. Snesarev, 244.
39. Snesarev, 245.
40. Snesarev, 245.
41. Rose, *Carl von Clausewitz*, 138–64; Jacob Kipp, "Lenin and Clausewitz: The Militarization of Marxism 1914–1921," *Military Affairs* (October 1985): 184–91.
42. Svechin, *Strategiia*, 172–73.
43. Svechin, 15.
44. Svechin, 9.
45. "Po povodu polemika t.t. Svechina i Khvesina" [Regarding the controversy between Comrades Svechin and Khvesin], *Voennyi vestnik*, no. 2 (1929): 61–62.
46. Svechin, *Strategiia*, 22.
47. Svechin, 19.
48. Svechin, 22.
49. Svechin, 37.
50. Snesarev, *Zhizn i trudy Klauzevitsa*, 124.
51. Svechin, *Strategiia*, 41, 178–79.

52. Svechin, 38.
53. M. Tukhachevskii, *Voina klassov* [War of the classes] (Moscow: Gosizdat, 1921), 36. The Military Revolutionary Council was created during the Civil War to coordinate the war. The coordination included, for instance, universal conscription and the nationalization of commercial enterprises. During this period called "war communism," the Red Army was used to forcibly extract grain from the Russian peasantry.
54. Kokoshin, *Svechin*, 76.
55. Boris Shaposhnikov, *Mozg armii* [The brain of the army], 3 vols. (Moscow: Voennyi vestnik, 1927–29).
56. Shaposhnikov, vol. 3, 376.
57. Shaposhnikov, vol. 3, 239.
58. Kokoshin, *Svechin*, 256–61.
59. Kokoshin, 261.
60. Kokoshin, 261.
61. Svechin, *Strategiia*, 35, 98; Kokoshin, *Soviet Strategic Thought*, 72.
62. A. Svechin, "Opasnye illiuzii" [Dangerous illusions], *Voennaia mysl i revoliutsiia*, no. 2 (1924), 44–55.
63. Svechin, 54–55.
64. Svechin, 55.
65. Svechin, 44.
66. A. Snesarev, *Vvedenie v voennuiu geografiiu* [Introduction to military geography] (Moscow: Tip. Voennaia akademiia R. K. K. A, 1924), 475.
67. Snesarev, 479.
68. Snesarev, 479.
69. Snesarev, 446–47.
70. Snesvarev, 447.
71. Svechin, *Strategiia*, 248.
72. Kokoshin, *Svechin*, 90–91.
73. Kokoshin, 91.
74. Kokoshin, 95; V. A. Zolotarev, ed., *Istoriia voennoi strategii* [History of military strategy] (Moscow: Kuchkovo pole, 2000), 197.
75. Kokoshin, *Svechin*, 258. Vladimir Triandafillov (1894–1931) developed the theoretical thinking behind deep operations.
76. Kokoshin, 24–27.
77. Kokoshin, *Soviet Strategic Thought*, 22; Stevens, *Russia's Wars of Emergence*, 303.
78. S. A. Gorlov, *Sovershenno sekretno: Moskva–Berlin 1920–1933* [Top secret: Moscow–Berlin 1920–33] (Moscow: IVI RAN, 1999), 146–52, 230–32.
79. Gorlov, 246.
80. Gorlov, 230.
81. Gorlov, 246.
82. Gorlov, 234.
83. Gorlov, 234.
84. Kokoshin, *Soviet Strategic Thought*, 27–28.
85. Joseph Stalin, "Prikaz Narodnogo Komissara Oborony 23 fevralia 1942 goda No 55 gorod Moskva" [Decree, People's Commissar of Defense, February 23, 1942, No. 55, Moscow City] (Gorkii: Gorkovskoe oblastnoe izdatelstvo, 1942), 8.
86. Gorlov, *Sovershenno sekretno*, 315–16; Mikhalev, *Voennaia strategiia*, 545.

87. G. K. Zhukov, *Vospominaniia i razmyshleniia* [Memoirs and thoughts], vol. 1 (Moscow: Novosti, 1990), 220.
88. A. V. Gorbatov, A. V. *Years off My Life: The Memoirs of General of the Soviet Army A.V. Gorbatov* (London: Constable, 1964), 103–4.
89. A. E. Savinkin, A. G. Kavtaradze, Iu. T. Belov, and I. V. Domnin, eds., *Postizhenie voennogo iskusstva: Ideinoe nasledie A. Svechina* [Understanding military art: The ideological heritage of A. Svechin], in *Rossiiskii voennyi sbornik* [Russian military collection], ed. A. E. Savinkin, vol. 15 (Moscow: Russkii put, 2000), 20–21.
90. Andrei Snesarev, *Afganskie uroki* [Afghan lessons] (Moscow: Russkii Put, 2003), 30–31.
91. Mikhalev, *Voennaia strategiia*, 546.
92. Zolotarev, *Istoriia voennoi strategii*, 208.
93. Kokoshin, *Svechin*, 114–15.

# 4

## THE LEGACY OF WORLD WAR II

> *We know what lies in balance at this moment,*
> *And what is happening right now.*
> *The hour for courage strikes upon our clocks,*
> *And courage will not desert us.*
> *We're not frightened by a hail of lead,*
> *We're not bitter without a roof overhead—*
> *And we will preserve you, Russian speech,*
> *Mighty Russian word!*
> *We will transmit you to our grandchildren*
> *Free and pure and rescued from captivity*
> *Forever!*
>
> ANNA AKHMATOVA, FEBRUARY 23, 1942, TASHKENT

What lessons did the Soviet military theorists draw from the cataclysmic consequences of World War II? What impact did nuclear weapons have on Soviet strategic thought? This chapter focuses on two writers: Marshal Vasily Danilovich Sokolovsky, who edited the second Soviet teaching manual on military strategy in history, and Adm. Sergei Georgievich Gorshkov, who played a crucial role in establishing an oceangoing navy.

In the immediate years following the Soviet victory, the debate on strategy and doctrine was completely dictated by Stalin. The main enemy was considered to be "American-British imperialism," which was described as having similarities to German fascism. Stalin's concept of "permanently operating factors" of war was the official military theory and could not be discussed.[1] The introduction of nuclear weapons did not immediately change the Soviet view of whom the likely enemy in a future war would be. It was not until the 1960s, following the thaw under Nikita Sergeevich Khrushchev (1894–1971), that a comprehensive text on military strategy was published, Sokolovsky's *Soviet Military Strategy*.

According to Marxism-Leninism, two fundamentally different systems stood against each other. The confrontation between the communist and the capitalist systems was inevitably going to result in a war, one that the communist system was destined to win. The capitalist West was depicted as being reactionary and on the road to its inevitable defeat.[2] At the same time, the West, and above all the United States, was seen as an imperialistic entity preparing for an attack on the Soviet Union. Therefore, the "peace-loving" Soviet Union was *forced* to take action in order to defend itself.

This thought, that Russia must simply react to what others (e.g., the West) are doing, can be traced back over the centuries; now, however, strengthened by the ideological aspect, it became much more explicit, not to say engraved, in Russian military thought. As we see below, it persists even now, although the Marxist-Leninist ideology is no longer in place.

Furthermore, Soviet military policy both before and long after World War II stressed the importance of an offensive strategy. It was not until the mid- to late 1980s that Russian strategists drew on the lessons of World War II and seriously challenged the offensive strategy.[3]

## THE COLD WAR BEGINS

The end of World War II was followed by the Cold War, the confrontation between the communist Soviet Union and the West. On a few occasions, the confrontation almost became hot.

Externally, the Soviet Union established a whole range of buffer states in Eastern Europe.[4] Stalin tried to take full control over Berlin in 1948 but did not succeed. Furthermore, the Soviet Union quelled the uprisings in Prague in both 1948 and 1968 as well as the protests in Berlin in 1953 and in Hungary in 1956. In 1968 Leonid Ilich Brezhnev (1906–82) announced his doctrine, in which the Soviet Union reserved the right to intervene militarily in other socialist countries to maintain and protect socialism. Furthermore, the Brezhnev Doctrine also contained a more active Soviet stance globally, with its pledge to support "progressive governments" and increase Soviet influence.[5]

The 1962 Cuban Missile Crisis was perhaps the closest occasion of a direct confrontation between the United States and the Soviet Union during this period. In the East, at the end of the 1960s, the Soviet Union and China were involved in a thorny border dispute.

At home, in 1945 Stalin demobilized the armed forces from more than eleven million personnel to under three million. Later, in the 1950s, the Soviet Armed Forces grew in strength to 5.7 million personnel by 1955.[6] In 1960 Khrushchev announced unilateral reductions of the Soviet ground and naval forces, to the dismay of his generals and admirals and perhaps to the astonishment of Western observers, who tended to think that the reductions were false.[7] The totalitarian regime established under Stalin remained intact until his death in 1953. In August 1949 the Soviet Union detonated its first atomic bomb; the US was no longer the only country in the world with this weapon. Under Khrushchev, a partial de-Stalinization started, and many of the repressed victims were rehabilitated, including Aleksandr Svechin and Mikhail Tukhachevsky.

The North Atlantic Treaty was also signed in 1949, followed by the Warsaw Pact in 1955. So, despite the fact that two military coalitions were standing on opposing sides, the Soviet military theorists never recognized military coalitions. In *Soviet Military Strategy*, Sokolovsky explained the Soviet position. In his view, bourgeois alliances attempt to strengthen one alliance and weaken the other and always lead to war. Consequently, the peace-loving Soviet Union "reject[ed] the formation of military coalitions." But the creation of the North Atlantic Treaty Organization (NATO) "forced the Soviet Union to unite with socialist countries in a military alliance."[8] The thought that it is the West's fault and that the Soviet Union (Russia) was forced to respond would, as is shown below, make a comeback over fifty years later.

## STRATEGY AND POLICY

The overall effect of World War II on the Soviet Union cannot be overstated. It is estimated that around twenty-seven million people lost their lives. The Red Army, according to a recent estimate, lost around 13.7 million soldiers, including prisoners of war.[9] The latter estimate is significantly higher than the official Soviet figure of ten million, revealed by Khrushchev in 1961, not to mention the current official figure from the Russian Ministry of Defense—8,668,400 million personnel, also including prisoners of war.[10] Thus, the magnitude of the disastrous war has led to uncertainty about the number of Soviet casualties in World War II and remains so today.

The experiences that Soviet military theorists studying doctrine and strategy had during World War II, however, did not have as much significance during the years after the war as might be expected. Already by 1935 Stalin had put an end to the discussions of the early 1920s. A new department of military history had been created at the Frunze Military Academy, with Boris Shaposhnikov as its director. He believed that the course on strategy that was being prepared had been approved at the political level, but the course was never held. The argument was that strategy was Stalin's personal occupation.[11] During World War II, Stalin had established the five "permanently operating factors" that in fact became the Soviet military strategy.[12]

After the war, Stalin continued to dictate the doctrine, and it was only when he died in 1953 that issues of doctrine and strategy began to be discussed in military publications, though obviously within the ideological constraints of Marxism-Leninism. A few words of clarification are needed here in order to explain how Soviet military thought developed under these ideological restrictions.

The theory of dialectical materialism (*diamat*) provided the philosophical frame. The development of humanity throughout its existence was dictated by the premise of historical materialism (*istmat*), the economy by the political economy, and politics by scientific communism. The scientific claims of Marxism-Leninism are evident and also something that was claimed to be its great difference, and advantage, compared to the capitalist system. The scientific, universal truths about the development of society were to be equated with, for instance, the laws of physics. Since the development of society was thought to be founded in science, it followed that the policy decisions made by the Communist Party were "scientifically true." This, in turn, as Wolfgang Leonhard observed, led to "a self-assurance and conviction" among the party leadership that others would perceive as arrogance.[13] His observation at least partly explains the aggressive behavior of the Soviet Union during the post–World War II period.

One consequence of the ideological constraints was a certain degree of overtheorization. Professor Ignat Semenovich Danilenko (1932–2019) describes how two schools of Soviet military thought evolved. One school was devoted to a certain theory, that of Marxism and Leninism on war and army, whereas the other school focused on a set of applied military disciplines, united and subordinated to strategy as the general theory, and the art of practical preparations and how to conduct war.[14] Both schools monopolized "their truths," which led to an absolute class doctrine regarding the nature (*priroda*) of war on one hand and an absolute focus on the military means to conduct military struggle (*borba*) on the other. Bureaucratic power struggle, not unique to Russia, certainly exacerbated the situation.[15] This "dualism" has had consequences up to the present, reflecting methodological and organizational problems for the Russian armed forces.

The second-ever official Soviet text on military strategy was published in 1962, with two revised editions published in 1963 and 1968. It was printed thirty-six years after Svechin's *Strategiia* and written by a collective of authors but published under the name of Marshal Vasily Sokolovsky, it would henceforth be referred to with Sokolovsky as the main author.[16] It was translated into several languages and became a major source for works on military history in the Soviet Union. As such, it was a major resource for Western observers. An implicit goal was apparently to impress the West with Soviet military might. According to his contemporaries, Khrushchev had instructed the authors "to frighten them [the Westerners] to death."[17]

As for the relationship between policy and strategy, the authors of *Soviet Military Strategy* briefly quoted Lenin's writings on Clausewitz's *On War*: "Politics is the reason, and war is only the tool."[18] They continued: "The acceptance of war as a tool of politics also determines the interrelation of military strategy and politics, which is based on the principle of the full dependence of the former to the latter."[19] They made it clear that military strategy is subordinate to state policy and that this "determines not only the character of strategic aims, but also the general character of strategy."[20] The Clausewitzian dictum was emphasized: "It is well known that the essence of war as a continuation of politics does not change with changing technology and armament."[21]

Although *Soviet Military Strategy* is a comprehensive work, it is almost silent on the relationship between policy and strategy. There are no in-depth discussions on the topic as there had been in the early 1920s. The absence of these discussions is telling in itself: it shows that the earlier works by Svechin, Snesarev, and Tukhachevskii had been suppressed and hence largely forgotten. The topic had become a politically sensitive subject in the Soviet Union at that time, and, clearly, a line had been drawn: it was not for the Soviet military officers to think about politics or political aims; they should concentrate their efforts on the military execution of what they were told.

*Soviet Military Strategy* was to become the last comprehensive official Soviet publication on strategy. As shown below, this does not mean that Russian military thinkers had completely stopped thinking about and debating strategic issues, but their involvement did not result in a published comprehensive work.

According to Marxism-Leninism, war and armed conflict were considered together as a sociohistorical phenomenon and an "extremely complex social phenomenon" at that.[22] Quoting both Lenin and Friedrich Engels (1820–95) and referring to Marxist-Leninist dialectics, the authors of *Soviet Military Strategy* reach this definition: "War is armed violence, organized armed conflict between the various social classes, governments, groups of governments and nations in the name of achieving definite political goals."[23] They also underline the holistic view of war and conflict in a way that today perhaps would be described as "hybrid war": "War is not the equivalent to politics in general, but makes up only a part of it." They continued: "Politics has available, in addition to war, a large arsenal of various nonviolent means which it can use for achieving its goals, without resorting to war."[24] Importantly, the authors emphasize the vital aspect of military force in future wars since "counting on 'nonmilitary' means of conflict in the course of a future war does not correspond to the methods for conducting it or to the laws of development of the means of conflict."[25]

The Soviet military thinkers determined that three basic categories of war were theoretically possible: (1) war between the imperialist and socialist camps, a world war, (2) imperialistic wars, and (3) civil wars of national liberation. A world war would be a decisive armed conflict between two opposing societal world systems. Both world war and imperialistic war were said to be aggressive and predatory; imperialistic war, moreover, was unjust. For the socialist camp, a world war would be liberating, just, and revolutionary. In scale, a world war would be one that was between the two big coalitions. The purpose of imperialistic wars was said to be to suppress national liberation movements or to seize or retain colonies. Both imperialistic wars and civil wars of national liberation would be small, local wars.[26]

## SOVIET MILITARY DOCTRINE AFTER WORLD WAR II

Military doctrine, in the view of Sokolovsky, depended on the social structure, domestic and foreign policy, and economic, political, and cultural state of the country. In general, Sokolovsky and his colleagues emphasized that military doctrine exploits the conclusions of various sciences, particularly with regard to the character of future war and the methods for conducting it and for determining the structure and preparation of the armed forces.[27] Military doctrine was summed up as "the system of officially approved, scientifically based views on the basic fundamental problems of war."[28]

In other words, military doctrine is state doctrine, and the political leadership of the state determines the basic principles of doctrine. This thought, articulated by Clausewitz, had taken root in Russia long before 1917, as mentioned above. It is one of the constants in Russian strategic thought.

Sokolovsky et alia noted that there can be "no single military doctrine for all states, since doctrine depends on the concrete conditions in which the state finds itself."[29] Developing this thought, the authors concluded that "the content and nature of military doctrine is influenced to a certain extent by the geographical location of a country and the national characteristics of its population."[30] In saying so, they echoed Snesarev's thoughts on military doctrine but without quoting him directly.[31]

As before, they emphasized the unique contribution of Soviet military science and the development of military art: strategy, operational art, and tactics. Regarding the relationship between military doctrine and strategy, Col. Gen. Nikolai Lomov (1899–1990), then chair of the Department of Strategy at the General Staff Academy, pointed out that although policy determined military strategy, there "is an internal relationship between the content of military doctrine and strategy."[32] He also emphasized that "doctrine is not a frozen dogma."[33] Hence, "military strategy is the most important part and an integral part of military doctrine."[34] This means that several of the military strategists under Khrushchev thought that policy should also relate to the theory of military strategy.[35] Importantly, this reasoning was being forwarded in the time of the Khrushchev Thaw and de-Stalinization, which can be interpreted to mean that although the military theorists remained completely loyal to the system, they seemed to be demanding to be listened to. This was not possible during the first decades of the Soviet Union.

## THE IMPACT OF NUCLEAR WEAPONS ON THE VIEW OF FUTURE WAR

The presence of nuclear weapons had a profound impact not only in the Kremlin but also on military strategic thought. In addition, missile technology was no less influential. The introduction of the first Soviet intercontinental ballistic missiles in 1957 had great political importance, not least since the missiles could be armed with thermonuclear warheads. The nuclear dimension is clearly present in *Soviet Military Strategy*, its consequences tangible, not least when future war is discussed. (On the practical level, the Soviet Strategic Rocket Forces were created in December 1959.)

Discussing the character of modern war, the authors emphasize that the factor of military technology is of utmost importance.[36] That nuclear weapons, radio-electronic devices, computers, and missile-control systems have fundamental consequences gave war a new character.

According to the authors, any armed conflict, if the nuclear powers were drawn into it, would inevitably escalate into a general nuclear war; they added that "the supreme catastrophic threat of a nuclear-rocket world war is hovering like a spectre over mankind."[37] A future world war, in terms of armed combat, would above all be a nuclear-missile war. Such a war would lead to significant changes in the military-strategic goals of both sides and cause a fundamental break in the methods of waging war and military operations.[38]

During World War II, the military-strategic goal was to defeat the enemy's armed forces in theaters of military operations and to seize vitally important regions and the administrative-political centers of the enemy. Now, in the mid-1960s, both sides would engage in mass use of nuclear missiles, with the purpose of achieving the annihilation or capitulation of the enemy in the shortest possible time. So, from then on, the Soviet military-strategic goal was, according to *Soviet Military Strategy*, to strive, simultaneously, for (1) the annihilation of the enemy's armed forces and (2) the annihilation and destruction of objectives in, and the disorganization of, the enemy's interior.[39] "The annihilation of the enemy's armed forces, the destruction of objectives in the rear areas, and the disoganization of the interior will be a single continuous process of the war," the authors explained.[40] It had become essential, at the same time, to deprive the enemy of their military, political, and economic possibilities of waging war. The means to achieve one's goals in a future war, according to Sokolovsky, was by employing mass nuclear-missile strikes: "The infliction of these assaults will be the main, decisive method of waging war."[41]

Trench warfare was a thing of the past, the authors concluded. Now, highly mobile mechanized troops would launch offensive operations through extensive maneuvers. Since the enemy would use nuclear weapons, "ground-to-ground" and "ship-to-ground," the cardinal problem for Soviet military strategy was to create a reliable protection of the rear of the country from nuclear strikes, a reliable antimissile defense.[42]

To sum up, the authors conclude that future war would be characterized by nine points:

- It would be a world war, a decisive armed clash of two opposing social world systems.
- The war would naturally end in victory for the communist system over the capitalist one.
- A decisive factor for the outcome of the war would be the economic potential of a country, including its ability to mass-produce military equipment, especially nuclear-missile weapons.
- It would be a coalition war.
- The war would be waged by mass armed forces, and therefore the attitude of the populace toward the war would have a decisive effect on its outcome.
- It would be a nuclear-missile war.
- The war would have an unprecedented spatial scope.
- Its initial period will be of decisive importance.
- Victory in the shortest possible time would be the goal, although a protracted war is possible.[43]

One of the special traits of Soviet military thought, emphasized by the authors, was scientific foresight into the character of a future war. And the arrival of nuclear weapons had led to a "fundamentally different" assessment, compared to past wars.[44] Armed conflict was now characterized by (1) the huge masses of people involved, including the civilian population, in solving military and semimilitary problems, (2) the complexity of modern military equipment, requiring special military knowledge and skills, and, finally (3) the reality that providing the needs of modern war involves strain on the economy.[45]

The Soviet theorists discussed Basil Liddell Hart's (1895–1970) book *The Strategy of Indirect Approach* and the use of "nonmilitary means." In view of World War I and its disastrous trench warfare, Liddell Hart argued that means of war in the future should include economic pressure, diplomacy, subversion, and so forth. The Soviet theorists acknowledged that there is some truth in Liddell Hart's argument. After all, war is a social phenomenon not isolated from other phenomena of social life. However, they warned against ignoring the military aspects of war. They wrote that "it was . . . military operations, armed conflict, and the use of means of violence, and not 'non-military' and 'indirect' operations in World War I that caused 10 million people to be killed. . . . World War II took almost fifty million lives."[46]

The Soviet theorists' reminder of the military aspect of war resounded into the twenty-first century. It was echoed in 2013, for example, in the now infamous speech by Chief of the General Staff Valerii Gerasimov, who expressed a ratio for the relationship between military and nonmilitary means, describing it as one to four.[47] In the years between the illegal annexation of Crimea in 2014 and the full-scale invasion of Ukraine in 2022, many analysts and politicians in the West took this formula to imply a downgrading of the military element of a future war, with more of a focus on the "hybrid" aspect of cyber and information operations. They seemed to have forgotten the "one" in the one-to-four ratio. The Russian leadership knew that those kinds of wars are hard to win, so the use of military force was never excluded from the war plans, as some in the West seemed to believe. This is an important lesson for future analysis of Russian military thought.

Soviet military theorists were preparing for a world war against a "militarily and economically powerful coalition of imperial powers." The most probable and most dangerous scenario was "a surprise attack," where a major war could break out without the threatening period.[48] Again, we see how continuities prevail, and given the enormous political, technological, economic, social, and geographic changes, the thoughts expressed by czarist and early Soviet military thinkers nevertheless persist over time.

## STRATEGIC OFFENSE VERSUS DEFENSE

The offensive strategy laid down in the 1920s remained intact. All arguments for a defensive approach derived from Svechin's and Snesarev's writings were dead and buried. The cult of the offensive had been prevalent already before World War I and not only in Russia. But by the mid-1960s it had been cemented in place by the official ideology, Marxism-Leninism, and was therefore automatically to be considered scientifically based, reflecting "objective laws."

Discussing strategic offense versus strategic defense, the authors firmly establish that only strategic offense is possible for the Soviet Union. Their reason for this was the presence of nuclear weapons. "The imperialists by no means intend to conduct a war against the socialist countries with ground forces. They are counting on nuclear, primarily strategic weapons."[49] Although the Soviet thinkers recognized the role of defense in a future war, it was only at the operational and tactical level. However, they continued, strategic defense and defensive strategy should be rejected, as they were considered to be extremely dangerous for the country.[50]

## INITIAL PERIOD OF NUCLEAR WAR

In considering a future nuclear war, its initial phase had become of particular importance. The theory of this phase had been developed in the 1920s and 1930s, until Stalin's repressions put an end to it. When he died, the Soviet military theorists again turned to this concept.

According to Sokolovsky, the pre–World War II military theorists drew the wrong conclusions regarding the initial period of the next major war. They had thought that the period would last from fifteen to twenty days, during which mobilization, concentration, and deployment of the main forces would take place. Thus, they had estimated that only limited military operations were to take place at this stage.[51] This was an erroneous conclusion, Sokolovsky remarked, especially since nuclear war had reduced the time for a possible attack, placing the initial phase of the war at the very center of war preparations. Sokolovsky concluded that the initial period had in fact become decisive for the outcome of the entire war. In order to repel a surprise nuclear attack and frustrate the enemy's aggressive schemes by inflicting a shattering blow at the right moment, the "main problem is the development of methods." What kinds of methods to achieve this was not elaborated on, other than to note that a constant high level of combat readiness should be observed.[52] Consequently, in order to prepare for a surprise attack from the United States, the Soviet Armed Forces could be mobilized totally or partially, openly, or in a concealed way.[53] However, given the improved reconnaissance means of the day, Sokolovsky concluded that the best way was to keep the armed force constantly in a maximum state of readiness.

This view of the initial period of war in the nuclear age was, in fact, a novelty in Soviet military doctrine, and it was driven by the arrival of new military technology, specifically thermonuclear weapons. Colonel General Lomov put it succinctly: "In the initial period of a future world war the main objects of armed influence are the enemy's armed forces, above all the strategic nuclear weapons, and also the most important economic centers and state administration of the enemy."[54] The border between the front and the rear had, compared to World War II, been significantly pushed back into the far depths of the country. The rear in Soviet thinking was a broad concept and basically involved the entire country's war effort.

Clearly, by the early 1960s Russia's war planners were planning to destroy cities and bomb civilians using nuclear weapons in a future war. Previously, secret war plans obtained from the Warsaw Pact had only corroborated the Soviet offensive strategy and shown that the Soviet General Staff, in reality, adhered to the concept of "launch on warning."[55] Other previously secret documents have shown that at least from 1968, Soviet exercises were all offensive, planning to reach the English Channel within days.[56]

Later, in the 1960s and 1970s, with the change in US military doctrine from "assured destruction" to "flexible response," the Soviet theorists again shifted their focus to preparing for a conventional war.[57] This trend is explored in the next chapter.

## MORALE IN A NUCLEAR WAR

Where did the Soviet military theorists stand in the discussion on the morale of the soldiers, in view of the new weapons of mass destruction? The morale of the troops was, after all, one of Stalin's five permanently operating factors. The Soviet doctrine of morale was always closely connected to ideology and therefore tended to be more political than personal.[58]

The main instrument to strengthen morale was indoctrination through the officers of the Chief Political Administration of the army and of its counterpart in the navy. It is within this area that the ideological impact of Marxism-Leninism was greatest.

The factor of morale and its importance for strategy was emphasized in Sokolovsky's *Soviet Military Strategy*. Similarly to the thinking in the 1920s, the class aspect of war is highlighted, and the Bolshevik victory in the Civil War is seen as an example of the "strong morale" of the Red Army.[59] "A member of a socialist society will always fight to win, through inspiration, fortitude, and courage," the book quoted Engels.[60] Class unity in the rear areas is said to be of utmost importance in any war. However, it notes that high and stable morale could be achieved in an army even in the absence of such unity. In those cases, a feeling of national unity might hold the country together for some time. Ideas of national independence and sovereignty take priority over class contradictions.[61] This thinking obviously reflects the experience during World War II, when the class aspect of the war was downplayed and a traditional, Russo-centric appeal gained priority. In 1943 the Russian Orthodox patriarch was restored; Russian Christianity was mobilized for the defense of the motherland, in a compromise with Marxist-Leninist teachings.

The authors of *Soviet Military Strategy* noted that the morale factor was one of the decisive elements of any war and particularly in a future nuclear war. In a thinly veiled criticism of Western military theorists, they pointed out that "any military strategy which does not take into account this most important factor, and which is based only on the superiority of material means, runs the risk of losing a lot."[62] The political-morale indoctrination, which also included the entire population, was divided into three parts: (1) the spirit of Soviet patriotism, (2) the love of country and the Communist Party, and (3) the readiness to suffer any hardships of war in order to achieve victory.[63]

Importantly, the indoctrination also contained a degree of hatred, which was considered a legitimate means of strengthening morale, not admitted or equaled in the West. Stalin had said, "It is impossible to defeat the foe without learning to hate him with all the forces of one's soul."[64] The authors of *Soviet Military Strategy* phrase it slightly differently but with the same clarity: "Hatred of the enemy should give rise to a striving to destroy the armed forces and the military industrial potential of the aggressor and to achieve complete victory in a just war."[65]

The cultivation of hatred of the enemy as part of military training could be linked to the Bolshevik idea of creating a new kind of citizen, the "new Soviet man." Through social engineering, the new Soviet man would develop into a selfless, ideologically irreproachable citizen who would work with society's best interest in mind and be prepared to sacrifice everything for his country.[66]

The new Soviet man as portrayed in the propaganda never materialized, but hatred as a part of Soviet Armed Forces indoctrination apparently did not disappear with the demise of the Soviet Union. Only this time, the hatred had also turned inward. Arkady Babchenko remarked in his book *One Soldier's War in Chechnya*, "And we began to turn wild as the cold and wet and filth drove from us all feelings apart from hatred and we hated everything on earth, including ourselves. Squabbles flared over nothing and instantly escalated beyond control."[67]

## NAVAL DOCTRINE

The Russian navy has had a long and complex history since its foundation by Peter the Great in 1696.[68] This is not the place to analyze its successes and defeats over the centuries, but it is vital to highlight the developments in the 1960s and 1970s. This is the time when the Soviet navy became a blue-water navy and submarines armed with nuclear missiles had an impact on Russian strategy and doctrine. The young Soviet Union in the 1920s had only a small naval force in the Baltic Sea and nothing in the Black Sea, the north, or in the Pacific Ocean. During the early 1930s, the Pacific and the Northern Fleets were reconstructed, and with the annexation of the Baltic states in 1940, the Soviet Union could add several naval bases in the Baltic Sea. *Soviet Military Strategy* wryly noted that the naval operations during World War II did not have any significant impact on the outcome of the war.[69]

If any single factor influenced the growth of the Soviet navy after World War II, it was the introduction of nuclear weapons. The nuclear-powered submarines armed with these new weapons became essential in the arms race. With the arrival of nuclear-powered submarines, the Russian navy was no longer tied to ground theaters but could operate at a much wider range, unprecedented in its history. It was now at an entirely new level, not to be compared to the period after the Crimean War when, during the American Civil War, Russia supported the Union and sent a squadron to New York and another to San Francisco.

Sokolovsky and his colleagues pointed out that Soviet strategy considered submarines armed with nuclear missiles to be the main fighting weapons of the navy and vastly more effective than surface vessels.[70] Although the navy was no longer tied to ground theaters but could conduct warfare on the oceans, the overall point in *Soviet Military Strategy* was that the role of the navy (and the air force) was still mainly to assist the ground forces.[71] In brief, the authors adhered to the school that claims that "Russia is a land power."

Adm. Sergei Gorshkov openly criticized this view. It was during his tenure that the Soviet Union built an oceangoing fleet. He was appointed commander in chief of the Soviet navy and deputy minister of defense in 1956 and served in both capacities until 1985.[72] However, although he managed to transform the Soviet navy (and hence the Russian navy as seen from a historical perspective) to attain unprecedented heights, he did not believe in the development of a specific naval military strategy.

The Soviet navy started to gain in strength and eventually became a bluewater navy, a force to be reckoned with. The global exercise Okean (Ocean), held in 1970, was the first to show the world that the Soviet Union was now also a superpower at sea. All four Soviet fleets participated, and the exercise included submarines, naval aircraft, and naval infantry.[73]

The central book on naval strategy, *Morskaia moshch gosudarstva* (The sea power of the state), was published by Gorshkov in 1976.[74] He argued, and tried to demonstrate, that the Soviet Union without an oceangoing fleet could not claim to be a superpower. In essence, according to Gorshkov, the Soviet Union was a maritime state. The spectacular failure of the Russian fleet in the Russo-Japanese War in 1905, he argued, was the result of a complete lack of a naval strategy.[75] He also disapproved of the traditional rivalry between the army and the navy.

Gorshkov objected to the pre–World War theory of "small wars" as well as proponents of the view that the navy existed only for defensive purposes and therefore was largely a defensive factor. The theory of small wars had been developed during the 1920s and 1930s. The military theorists who advocated this theory based their reasoning on the fact that the young Soviet Union did not have the means to build a battleship fleet capable of engaging in battle with the powerful fleets of its potential adversaries. Therefore, the Soviet Union should focus on building smaller ships, submarines, and aircraft for naval warfare.[76] This was correct at the time, although "it was a defensive concept of a weak fleet." However, in the immediate prewar period, at a time when the Soviet fleet had built a capacity for operations outside of the coastal waters, the theory of small wars still prevailed, which had a very negative impact on the development of the Soviet navy.[77]

The Soviet doctrine, as we have seen, stipulated the offensive as the only option for the Soviet Union, so Gorshkov and his like-minded colleagues saw the emphasis on the navy's defensive purpose as particularly misguided. On the contrary, Gorshkov argued, the Soviet navy could now operate well outside of its own coastal waters, which gave it a strategically offensive capability. Add to this the arrival of nuclear weapons based on both land and sea, which had a profound impact on the scope of naval warfare. The main task of modern fleets was to strike objectives in enemy territory from the sea. They had become capable of acting directly on the course of armed conflict in practically all theaters of military operations. The naval forces, according to Gorshkov, were gradually becoming the main carrier of nuclear weapons capable of striking at the enemy in all continents and seas.[78] This task for the Soviet navy was well aligned with the view expressed in *Soviet Military Strategy*, which, as we have seen, was that the offensive strategy was the right one for the Soviet Union and the defensive strategy dangerous, which led to exercises planning to reach Western Europe in days.

Gorshkov also called for not only "serious and thorough scientific research" in order to develop the fleet more extensively, but he went further. He noted that "leaders taking crucial decisions on the development of the navy" would do well to listen to the advice of research institutions and the views of naval officers on active service, as well as pay attention to their appreciation of the possibilities of industry.[79]

Importantly, he did not advocate a special naval military strategy and continued to praise the unified military strategy. He, and many other Soviet thinkers, maintained that this strategy was a unique feature of Soviet military thought. He criticized Western military theorists who wrote specifically about naval strategy or air power strategy as something separate from the totality. Soviet strategy, on the other hand, is aimed at bringing together the entire military powers of the state.[80] Having said this, he called for the study of the strategic use of each of the branches of the armed forces, including the navy, "due to their *specific* features and scope," within the framework of a unified military doctrine.[81]

This way of reasoning resembles a military version of socialist realism, as proclaimed by Stalin in 1932. Initially it was the guiding principle for the arts and literature, "national in form, socialist in content"; later it affected many other parts of Soviet culture.[82] Gorshkov's naval principle for Soviet strategy would be "specific in form, unified in content." This demonstrates clearly that the armies, as one historian put it, are "not an independent section of the social system, but an aspect of it in its totality."[83]

The importance of sea warfare had grown considerably since World War II, not only in absolute terms but also in relative terms, Gorshkov maintained. This was demonstrated by "an analysis of the present distribution of forces in the international arena and the sharp increase in the ability of modern fleets to act decisively on all fronts of armed struggle."[84] He summarized the role of the navy in strengthening Soviet sea power: (1) the universality of modern fleets enabled them to solve multifaceted tasks, *the most important one being actions against (enemy) land*, (2) the navy plays a significant role in the local wars conducted by the imperialists, (3) the navy can be used as the state's political weapon and, in the Soviet case, act as a stabilizing factor in the world, and (4) the forces of the fleet need balancing, which calls for much material expenditure.[85]

To sum up, Gorshkov did not subscribe to the traditional view that the navy's main task was to support the ground forces and defend Russia's territory. His vision was of an oceangoing fleet with the strategic task of conducting actions against enemy territory. This has not always been understood in the West. So, to say that Gorshkov "emphasized defensive military functions within the wider strategic effort" does not fully capture the sense of Gorshkov's writings.[86]

## LESSONS LEARNED—AND NOT LEARNED— FROM WORLD WAR II

The Stalinist repressions and dictatorship had a devastating effect on Soviet military thought. Whereas the military theorists who tried to contribute to the development of a military doctrine in the early 1920s were firmly rooted in previous "bourgeois" Russian and Western military thought, the next generation of thinkers were not, or, if they were, they could not say so. There was a rupture in thinking that still has effects today. After the 1920s, the tendency of Soviet military thought to glorify domestic military thinkers and despise all foreign ones became even stronger.[87] Given the slow rehabilitation of, for instance, Snesarev and Svechin, Russian military thought also largely neglected its own prewar theorists for many years after 1945.

In November 1945, the Soviet General Staff held a conference on military theory to discuss the lessons of World War II, and for the future Marshal Zhukov pointed out the following features as being exclusive for Soviet military art:

- excellent knowledge of the enemy, a correct assessment of its plans, forces, means, all of which is obtained by continuous and thorough intelligence;
- knowledge of one's own troops, their careful preparation for battle;
- operational and tactical surprise achieved by the fact that the enemy is confused about our true intentions;

- precise calculation of the men and weapons required, depending on the task;
- logistical support of the operations.[88]

It is sometimes said that armies tend to learn more from their successes than their defeats and therefore fail to learn the right lessons. This certainly seemed true during the immediate postwar years. There was a tacit ban on discussing and revising Stalin's five operating factors, as one officer noted at the time:

> In the Frunze Academy, where I served as an instructor, we collected war studies as rapidly as possible and endeavoured to draw from them all possible lessons which might be made applicable to current training. Frequently it was difficult to perform honest work because the Party line tended to draw lessons only from the Red victories, often neglecting the wealth of important material contained in those accounts which dealt with Soviet defeats. The development of new doctrine seems to be lagging, in spite of the fact that Stalin correctly has stated that the art of war makes rapid and continuous progress, and that fixed doctrine therefore is not sound. The tendency to praise the battles of the local general discourages advancement of new ideas, in spite of the Generalissimo's statement.[89]

In addition, official Soviet statements never mentioned anything about errors or mistakes. Here, the political constraints preventing an open discussion had a substantial impact on the development, or rather nondevelopment, of strategy and doctrine. It was simply easier to repeat "old truths" than to risk one's neck with innovative thoughts. Some military theorists were acutely aware of this problem and the damage it did in the longer time perspective. For instance, Makhmut Gareev, the head of the post-Soviet Academy of Military Sciences, later described the atmosphere and the personality cult under Stalin's repressive rule: "Under these conditions the scientific sphere could easily be penetrated by a mass of mediocrities which created the blank wall on which many new ideas and discoveries crumbled in the history of science.... In such a situation true scientific knowledge and abilities were not always properly regarded and individual insufficiently principled persons lost the habit of hard work."[90] Gareev also criticized the fact that there was a tendency among the commanders who had fought in the war to be content with the successes and that they did not care much about theory.

The bridge between theory and practice in Soviet military thought had now become accentuated. Consequently, two schools had developed by the end of the 1960s: one theoretical and focused on the Marxist-Leninist view of war and conflict, while the other was dedicated to applied military disciplines and practical preparations. Gareev was critical of bureaucracy and incompetence, almost echoing Miliutin decades before. Not only had the theoretical ideas on the initial period of the war not been put into practice, but the problem was also even more complex. In fact, the military system seemed to hinder innovation since "any new undertaking can be carried out in one or another area of work only with the agreement and approval of a senior chief."[91] Although no one argued against innovation, the breaking of old ideas and habits and the introduction of new scientific achievements always occurred with some difficulty, Gareev noted.

Another writer who also realized the dangers in this line of thinking was Nikolai Vasilevich Ogarkov, whose thoughts are examined in the next chapter. The extent to which this inertia in Soviet military thought was detrimental was also picked up by Nikolai Makarov, chief of the General Staff from 2008 to 2012, whom we meet in chapter 6.

This matter is not merely an academic problem but rather one with potentially devastating consequences. An illustrative example that has recently come to light with regard to World War II touches on the issue of strategic intelligence and prediction in Soviet military thought. Both Svechin and Snesarev had made important contributions in this area, but none was being applied at the time of the German invasion in 1941. Sokolovsky and his coauthors do underline the importance of strategic intelligence in peacetime and note that it should not only focus on the enemy's armed forces but also provide political, military, economic, scientific, and technical data about the possible enemies.[92] The tasks required by military strategic intelligence were listed and included gathering information about the potential enemy's military-political plans, mobilization measures, and armed forces; studying their military art; and also, importantly, gauging the level of morale of their armed forces and population. In other words, Soviet military thought both before and after the war was well prepared, in theory. In practice, it was a different matter.

The focus of Soviet intelligence briefs in the years before the unexpected German attack in 1941 tended to be solely on the number of troops, the structure of enemy forces, and their armaments, technology, and tactics—that is, "bean counting."[93] As a consequence, a mechanistic picture was painted, and no consideration was made as to the ideas underpinning it. This mechanistic view reflected the mood and mentality of the highest political leadership—in other words, Stalin. One Russian military thinker even went so far as to say that although the Soviet military command had received warning of Operation Barbarossa almost immediately after its approval, in December 1940, this made no difference to the Soviet preparations. "The highest Soviet leadership and the military command did not have enough political-military, military-strategic knowledge, not enough understanding of the character of war that Hitler's Wehrmacht was conducting."[94] That Germany was conducting a maximalist, total war was not taken into account, which resulted in the Wehrmacht's success in achieving strategic and operational surprise on June 22, 1941.

So, given the fundamental importance of Marxism-Leninism in the Soviet Union, how did it affect the content of Soviet military strategy and doctrine?

The Soviet view of war as a social phenomenon links directly to the writings of Leer and Dragomirov. And the view that war is the continuation of politics with other means came from Clausewitz. As the Finnish historian Kimmo Rentola has shown, the Soviet decision to go to war against Finland in 1939 was not made primarily for ideological reasons. It was more founded on strategic calculations and intelligence-based predictions.[95]

So, in spite of the importance of the ideology and the dialectics of Marxism-Leninism in the Soviet Union, the Soviet view on war and conflict did not differ drastically from the previous one. Instead, continuities prevailed, with thought rooted in the czarist theorists and some Western thinkers, albeit sometimes without acknowledgment. The Soviet military thinkers emphasized that the theories in *Soviet Military Strategy* relied on the *present* political and economic conditions and warned against accepting them as final and unchanging data. The Soviet military theorists encouraged and emphasized *creativity* in interpreting the conclusions.[96] Consequently, for all the scientific claims, Soviet military thought on strategy and doctrine remained rather flexible and was influenced by factors such as the international situation, technological development, geography, and domestic policy. In essence, this means that the official ideology did not have as big an impact on Soviet strategic thought as might have been expected since its roots can be traced to czarist and foreign thinkers. However, Marxism-Leninism did have a role in how strategy and doctrine was politically framed and in focusing on the study of the Civil War rather than World War I. It did color the texts and the language, as anyone who has read these works can testify. In other words, the linguistic presentation and the focus of study was different, but the core content of strategic thought remained much the same. In the 1960s and early 1970s, the biggest impact was created by the presence of nuclear weapons and ballistic missiles rather than ideology.

## NOTES

*Epigraph:* Anna Akhmatova, "Courage," in *The Complete Poems of Anna Akhmatova*, vol. 2, ed. Roberta Reeder, trans. Judith Hemschemeyer (Sommerville, MA: Zephyr, 1990), 185.

1. Kokoshin, *Soviet Strategic Thought*, 111–13.
2. Sokolovskiy, *Soviet Military Strategy*, 208–9.
3. Gareev, *M. V. Frunze*, 207–10.
4. For a well-written overview in English, see Anne Applebaum, *Iron Curtain: The Crushing of Eastern Europe 1944–1956* (London: Penguin, 2013).

5. Stephen G. Glazer, "The Brezhnev Doctrine," *International Lawyer* 5, no. 1 (1971): 169–79.
6. William Odom, *The Collapse of the Soviet Military* (New Haven, CT: Yale University Press, 1998), 39.
7. Kokoshin, *Soviet Strategic Thought*, 46–49.
8. Sokolovskiy, *Soviet Military Strategy*, 19.
9. S. N. Mikhalev, *Liudskie poteri v Velikoi Otechestvennoi voine 1941–1945, Statisticheskoe issledovanie* [Losses of human life in the Great Patriotic War 1941–45: A statistical study], 2nd ed. (Krasnoiarsk: RIO KGPU, 2000), 21–22.
10. Russian Ministry of Defense, "K voprosu o poteriakh protivoborstvuiushchikh storon na sovetsko-germanskom fronte v gody Velikoi Otechestvennoi voiny: Pravda i vymysel" [On the issue of losses of the warring parties at the Soviet-German front in the years of the Great Patriotic War: Truth and myth], 2023, https://encyclopedia.mil.ru/encyclopedia/history/more.htm?id=11359251@cmsArticle.
11. Sokolovskiy, *Soviet Military Strategy*, 118–19.
12. Stalin, "Prikaz Narodnogo komissara oborony," 8.
13. Wolfgang Leonhard, *Was ist Kommunismus? Wandlungen einer Ideologie* [What is Communism? Transformations of an ideology] (Munich: C. Bertelsmann, 1976), 99.
14. Quoted in A. A. Kokoshin, *Politologiia i sotsiologiia voennoi strategii* [The political science and sociology of military strategy] (Moscow: Lenand, 2018), 48.
15. Pavel Baev, "The Interplay of Bureaucratic, Warfighting, and Arms-Parading Traits in Russian Military-Strategic Culture," George C. Marshall European Center for Security Studies, *Strategic Insights*, no. 28 (April 2019).
16. Here I have used the English-translated version. It marks up the changes between the two previous editions. V. D. Sokolovskiy, *Soviet Military Strategy*, 3rd ed., edited with an analysis and commentary by Harriet Fast Scott (London: Macdonald & Jane's, 1968), 208–9.
17. Kokoshin, *Soviet Strategic Thought*, 50.
18. Sokolovskiy, *Soviet Military Strategy*, 14.
19. Sokolovskiy, 14–15.
20. Sokolovskiy, 16.
21. Sokolovskiy, 15.
22. Sokolovskiy, 173.
23. Sokolovskiy, 173.
24. Sokolovskiy, 174.
25. Sokolovskiy, 176.
26. Sokolovskiy, 183.
27. Sokolovskiy, 38.
28. Sokolovskiy, 38.
29. Sokolovskiy, 38.
30. Sokolovskiy, 39.
31. See chapter 3.
32. N. A. Lomov, "Sovetskaia voennaia doktrina" [Soviet military doctrine], *Voennaia mysl*, no. 1 (1963), 14–30. For the quote, see page 16.
33. Lomov, 20.
34. Lomov, 16.
35. Kokoshin, *Soviet Strategic Thought*, 50–52.
36. Sokolovskiy, *Soviet Military Strategy*, 198.

37. Sokolovskiy, 197.
38. Sokolovskiy, 197, 201–2.
39. Sokolovskiy, 202.
40. Sokolovskiy, 202.
41. Sokolovskiy, 202.
42. Sokolovskiy, 203.
43. Sokolovskiy, 208–11.
44. Sovokovskiy, 172.
45. Sokolovskiy, 175–76.
46. Sokolovskiy, 176.
47. Valerii Gerasimov, "Osnovnye tendentsii razvitiia form i sposobov primeneniia Vooruzhennykh Sil, aktualnye zadachi voennoi nauki po ikh sovershenstvovaniiu" [Principal trends in the development of the forms and methods of employing Armed Forces and current tasks of military science regarding their improvement], *Vestnik Akademii Voennykh Nauk*, no. 1 (2013), 24–29.
48. Sokolovskiy, *Soviet Military Strategy*, 188.
49. Sokolovskiy, 282.
50. Sokolovskiy, 283–84.
51. Sokolovskiy, 133–34.
52. Sokolovskiy, 210.
53. Sokolovskiy, 308.
54. Lomov, "Sovetskaia voennaia doktrina," 23.
55. Vojtech Mastny, "Imaging War in Europe: Soviet Strategic Planning," in *War Plans and Alliances in the Cold War: Threat Perceptions in the East and West*, ed. Vojtech Mastny, Sven G. Holtsmark, and Andreas Wenger (London: Routledge, 2006), 15–45.
56. Mastny, 36. For more on exercises, see Beatrice Heuser, "Military Exercises and the Dangers of Misunderstandings: The East-West Crisis of the Early 1980s," in *Military Exercises: Political Messaging and Strategic Impact*, ed. Beatrice Heuser, Tormod Heier, and Guillaume Lasconjarias, NDC Forum Papers Series, Forum Paper 26 (Rome: NATO Defense College, 2018), 113–37.
57. Kokoshin, *Soviet Strategic Thought*, 124.
58. Raymond L. Garthoff, *How Russia Makes War: Soviet Military Doctrine* (1954; e-book repr., London: Routledge, 2021), 239.
59. Sokolovskiy, *Soviet Military Strategy*, 34.
60. Sokolovskiy, 33–34.
61. Sokolovskiy, 35–36.
62. Sokolovskiy, 33.
63. Sokolovskiy, 329.
64. Quoted in Garthoff, *How Russia Makes War*, 233.
65. Sokolovskiy, *Military Strategy*, 330.
66. Sokolovskiy, 330. The literature on Soviet man (*homo sovieticus*) is vast. For a general introduction, see Mikhail Heller, *Cogs in the Wheel: The Formation of Soviet Man* (New York: Alfred A. Knopf, 1988).
67. Arkady Babchenko, *One Soldier's War in Chechnya*, trans. Nick Allen (London: Portobello Books, 2007), 17.
68. An overview of the Russian fleet in the nineteenth and early twentieth centuries can be found in V. A. Zolotarev and I. A. Kozlov, *Tri stoletiia Rossiiskogo flota:*

*XIX–nachalo XX veka* [Three centuries of the Russian fleet: From the nineteenth century to the beginning of the twentieth century] (Moscow: AST, 2004), http://militera.lib.ru/h/zolotarev_kozlov2/index.html.
69. Sokolovskiy, *Soviet Military Strategy*, 272.
70. Sokolovskiy, 200.
71. Sokolovskiy, 282–83.
72. Kevin Rowlands, ed., *21st Century Gorshkov* (Annapolis, MD: Naval Institute Press, 2017), 1–11.
73. Kokoshin, *Soviet Strategic Thought*, 130–31; Donald C. Daniel, "Trends and Patterns in Major Soviet Naval Exercises," *Naval War College Review*, no. 4 (1978): 34–41.
74. S. G. Gorshkov, *Morskaia moshch gosudarstva* [The sea power of the state], 2nd ed. (Moscow: Voenizdat, 1979).
75. Gorshkov, 312–13.
76. Gorshkov, 195–96.
77. Gorshkov, 201–2.
78. Gorshkov, 408–14.
79. Gorshkov, 270.
80. Gorshkov, 315–18.
81. Gorshkov, 317 (italics added).
82. Thomas Lahusen and Evgeny Dobrenko, "Introduction," in *Socialist Realism without Shores*, ed. Thomas Lahusen and Evgeny Dobrenko (Durham, NC: Duke University Press, 1997), 1–4.
83. Michael Howard, *The Franco-Prussian War* (1961; repr., London: Routledge, 1991), 1.
84. Gorshkov, *Morskaia moshch*, 307.
85. Gorshkov, 406–7 (italics added).
86. Andrew Lambert, *Seapower States: Maritime Culture, Continental Empires and the Conflict That Made the Modern World* (New Haven, CT: Yale University Press, 2018), 264–65.
87. Kokoshin, *Svechin*, 15.
88. Gareev, *M. V. Frunze*, 211.
89. Garthoff, *How Russia Makes War*, 59.
90. Gareev, *M. V. Frunze*, 388.
91. Gareev, 391–94.
92. Sokolovskiy, *Soviet Military Strategy*, 318–19.
93. Kokoshin, *Svechin*, 308–11.
94. Kokoshin, 309.
95. Kimmo Rentola, *How Finland Survived Stalin: From Winter War to Cold War, 1939–1940*, trans. Richard Robinson (New Haven, CT: Yale University Press, 2023), 25–27.
96. Sokolovskiy, *Soviet Military Strategy*, 386 (italics added).

# 5

# IN SEARCH OF A STRATEGY BEYOND NUCLEAR WEAPONS

*A thermonuclear war cannot be considered a continuation of politics by other means (according to the formula of Clausewitz). It would be a means of universal suicide.*
ANDREI SAKHAROV, 1968

Here the focus is on Soviet military thought at its acme—namely, during the career of Nikolai Ogarkov, chief of the General Staff from 1977 to 1984, who stands out as the most prominent military thinker of the time. His legacy serves as a bridge to current military thought. He understood the interrelationship between political and military factors and that their management could benefit the national security of the country. His contribution to developing the thinking on the "military-technical revolution" still has its value today. As discussed below, the disconnect between theory and practice was becoming even more critical.

## A TIME OF DÉTENTE AND COLD WAR

Against the backdrop of the so-called peaceful coexistence, a period of détente ensued. The concept of peaceful coexistence had been introduced in 1956 by Nikita Khrushchev as the "general line of Soviet foreign policy." In essence, it meant a pause from the Marxist-Leninist dogma of the inevitability of a war between the socialist and capitalist camps, a war that the socialist countries, led by the Soviet Union, would win. It was originally Lenin who had introduced the notion of peaceful coexistence, and it was then revived by Khrushchev. Even though this became the general line of Soviet foreign policy, it did not mean peace. The economic, political, and ideological struggle would continue, albeit without military force. In essence, it meant "an existence without war."[1]

In the 1960s, as mentioned earlier, the term "peaceful coexistence" was replaced by the Brezhnev Doctrine. The term was later reintroduced for the second time by General Secretary Mikhail Sergeevich Gorbachev (1931–2022) and, later on, in 2020, in the revised constitution of the Russian Federation.[2]

The period of détente was largely due to the improved relationship between the United States and the Soviet Union. A number of treaties were signed, which became the foundation of strategic arms reduction agreements. The Strategic Arms Limitation Talks (SALT I) began in Helsinki in 1969 and resulted in two agreements: the Treaty on the Limitations of Anti-Ballistic Missile Systems and the so-called Interim Agreement on Offensive Weapons, both signed in 1972, which imposed a freeze on the number of launchers for intercontinental ballistic missiles (ICBMs) and submarine-launched ballistic missiles (SLBMs).[3] The Helsinki Final Act, signed by thirty-five nations in 1975, culminated the détente. These agreements were followed by the Strategic Arms Limitation Treaty (SALT II), completed in June 1979, which would have limited each nation to a total of 2,400 ICBM launchers, SLBM launchers, and heavy bombers, with this number declining to 2,250 by January 1, 1981.

Important as these treaties were, they did not prevent the arms race that was continued during Brezhnev's term in office and was not halted until Gorbachev came to power.[4] The détente ended abruptly with the Soviet invasion of Afghanistan in December 1979 and the crisis in Poland in 1980, both of which paved the way for one of the coldest periods of the Cold War. From 1968 to 1987 the Soviet Armed Forces grew from 2 million to 5.2 million personnel.[5]

The decision to invade Afghanistan was taken on December 12, 1979, against Ogarkov's advice. He had argued that the Afghan problem had to be solved by political means; the Afghans had never tolerated the presence of foreigners on their soil, and Soviet troops would probably be drawn into military operations.[6] Minister of Defense Dmitrii Fedorovich Ustinov (1908–84) and the entire Politburo nonetheless made the decision to invade.[7] As Rodric Braithwaite shows, the decision was taken "with great reluctance, strongly suspecting that it would be a mistake . . . because they could not think of a better alternative."[8]

The military theorists of the Soviet Union could meet the early days of détente with increased self-confidence. In the mid-1960s, the US nuclear arsenal amounted to more than thirty thousand warheads, and by the early 1970s the Soviet Union had reached nuclear parity.[9] This "thaw" in relations also led to the Soviet signing of the Universal Copyright Convention in 1973, which led to the publication of an entire series of books, *Soviet Military Thought*, translated into English by the United States Air Force. However, despite the easing of tensions, the Soviet military thinkers continued to emphasize the "aggressive military policy of the capitalist states."[10] The wars in Vietnam and the Middle East (1967–70) were taken as proof of this. In addition, the People's Republic of

China appeared as a potential adversary to the Soviet Union at that time. China, by now a nuclear power, was thought to be preparing for a nuclear war.[11]

## STRATEGY AND POLICY

In the late 1960s and up until the late 1970s, nothing substantial was added to the debate on the relationship between policy and strategy. In his book *The Armed Forces of the Soviet State*, Andrei Antonovich Grechko (1903–76), the minister of defense and a marshal of the Soviet Union, simply repeated Lenin's dictum that the "direction of the Armed Forces by the Communist Party is the chief principle of Soviet military development."[12]

It was not until Nikolai Ogarkov became chief of the General Staff that this eternal question could be addressed in earnest. Ogarkov had a clear understanding of the interrelationship between political and military factors in a future war and was also able to express it. Ogarkov's influence and vision for the development of Soviet military strategy cannot be overstated. After the devastating blow to the military's ability to think about war and conflict and its relations to policy that was the result of the Stalinist repressions, the arrival of Ogarkov would seem to indicate that some of the prewar intellectual capacity had come back.

Ogarkov graduated from the Kuibyshev Military Engineering Academy in 1941 and then served during World War II. From 1968 to 1974, he served as first deputy chief of the General Staff, followed by three years as deputy minister of defense, before being appointed chief of the General Staff in 1977. He was unusual in that this was the first time anyone from the engineer forces had assumed such a high office, but, at the age of sixty, he had considerable experience of war and peace. He had taken part in the planning of the invasion of Czechoslovakia in 1968 and the Soviet invasion of Afghanistan in 1979, although he had argued against the latter. He had also participated in the negotiations between the United States and the Soviet Union on strategic arms control. In the West, he became (in)famous when he justified the downing of Korean Air Lines Flight 007 in 1983. He was dismissed as chief of the General Staff in 1984. Importantly, serving with him was his deputy, Makhmut Gareev, who was responsible for the development of military science. After the dissolution of the Soviet Union, Ogarkov served as an adviser to the Ministry of Defense and, more specifically, to the first deputy minister of defense (1992–97), Andrei Kokoshin, who is one of the most prominent military theorists in today's Russia.[13]

Ogarkov defined the relationship between military strategy and policy as closely related, where "policy elaborates the goals of the war, defines the means to be used to conduct it, assigns military strategy its tasks, and creates the conditions for their accomplishment, mobilizing the material and human resources necessary to meet the needs of war."[14] Importantly, he went further than most others before him, as he stated that military strategy in turn "exerts an inverse influence on policy." He specified that in deciding the goals of the war and the means to fight it, the political leadership based its decisions on the theoretical conclusions and scientific results from the research within military strategy.

## MILITARY DOCTRINE AND THE VIEW OF WAR

Ogarkov's most important publication, *Istoriia uchit bditelnost* (History teaches vigilance), was published in 1985, just after his dismissal in 1984. He did not subscribe to the view that war was a natural phenomenon of mankind; rather, he repeated the established Soviet view that war is a social phenomenon. Ogarkov linked it, true to Marxism-Leninism, to the emergence of private property. He argued that war could and had to be stopped and that the spread of socialism in the world had created real and objective conditions to abolish war from social life.[15] However, since Western "imperialism" was the main threat to peace, it was important to realize that "to achieve peace without a fight is not possible."[16] The key, and the most vital issue at this moment, he noted, was to avoid a nuclear world war.

Ogarkov identified five major areas that military doctrine should determine. They were

> the degree of probability of future war and against which enemy; the character of that war and the way it would take the country and its armed forces; the goals and missions that could be assigned to the armed forces and what kind of armed forces are necessary to meet these goals; proceeding from the above, the military programs [*voennoe stroitelstvo*] that should be accomplished and the preparations needed by the army and the country for war; and the means with which the war should be conducted if it breaks out.[17]

The sheer scope of these areas shows that the Russian/Soviet understanding of "military doctrine" (*voennaia doktrina*) is much broader than its meaning in the English-speaking Western world. *Voennaia doktrina* often translates to "grand strategy." Sometimes, in the Western world, doctrine is used in a more specific sense—for example, "naval doctrine," "nuclear doctrine," etc.—which the Soviet military thinkers frequently criticized because they considered a unified military doctrine as superior to anything else.

According to Ogarkov, the military doctrine of a country was based on the sociopolitical and economic systems of the country, the geography of the country, and the possible enemy and ensues from the state's domestic and foreign policy. The view, from Frunze, that the military doctrine had both a sociopolitical and a technical side remained steadfast, and Ogarkov underlined the interdependence of these factors. The political goals and the character of future war belonged to the sociopolitical side and hence were determined by politics.[18] He wrote, "The political goals of the war need to be fully in line with the military potential of the state, the combat capabilities of the armed forces and the means to conduct military actions. The latter should reliably be able to secure the set goals."[19] His words echo into the future as an insightful observation and one that was not remembered by his successors thirty-seven years later.

As did his predecessors, Ogarkov realized that military doctrines changed over time. The political side tended to be more constant, whereas the military technology part was more subject to change. Importantly, the military doctrine was based on the ideology and policy of a state and on its military sciences, where the theory of military art was most important and also influenced in reverse the development of military science.[20] In other words, policy ruled over everything else.

It deserves to be noted that Ogarkov, although visionary and prominent, completely adhered to the Great Russian perspective. He repeated the official line that "we have never attacked anyone" and said that the Soviet Union did not need to expand its borders.[21] But what belonged to the "Soviet people" would be defended decisively, actively, and without compromise. In other words, what is ours is ours. Ogarkov subscribed to the Leninist principle that the Soviet Union had been forced to create an army in 1917 because of the hostile international environment.

This line of thinking, that Russia had never attacked anyone and that Russia was forced by others to react, in spite of abundant historical evidence to the contrary, could be said to be a core thought of Russian strategic culture.

## OFFENSIVE VERSUS DEFENSIVE AND STRATEGIC NUCLEAR WEAPONS

The basic stance of the Soviet Union remained offensive until 1987. Despite paying lip service externally to a defensive strategy in, for instance, the Declaration of the Warsaw Pact on May 15, 1980, in reality nothing changed. The Soviet force posture remained intact and was used to pressure Poland later that year.

The reasons for keeping the offensive strategy were basically the same as they had been from the very beginning of the Soviet state: ideological and determined by policy. This is also in line with the provisions for an offensive that had entered Russian strategy since the late nineteenth century, as shown in chapter 2.

Regarding the possible use of strategic nuclear weapons, the change came in 1982 when the Soviet Union adopted the policy of no first-use. Three years earlier, in 1979, Ogarkov had stated that the Soviet Union would not use nuclear weapons first.[22] This change was based on the view that no country, not even a socialist one, could win a nuclear war. In order to compensate for the policy of no first-use, the combat readiness of the Soviet nuclear forces and the detection systems were to be upgraded and the control and communications capabilities were to be improved, according to the defense minister, Dmitrii Ustinov.[23] But, in reality, the no-first-use principle itself was not developed, and its strategic operational aspects were not specified. Furthermore, some military theorists at the time did not take this change into account and simply continued to underline the importance of a massive strategic first strike, which could decide the outcome of war.[24]

Ogarkov understood the risks of this line of thinking. He recognized that relying too much on nuclear weapons could be dangerous in the long term. He warned of inertia in military thought and emphasized that "stagnation in the development and implementation of new issues of military art and military organizational development are fraught with grave consequences." It would be outright dangerous to ignore the fast pace of technological development.[25] This warning was directed at those who perceived that possession of nuclear weapons made it unnecessary to develop the capabilities to wage a high-technology conventional war. Within the military theory community there was clear opposition to Ogarkov's views, and at one point Kokoshin overheard a critic of Ogarkov say, "Well, what he understands about military matters and contemporary military technology is that of a divisional engineer."[26]

Some scholars argue that there was a split between the communist leadership's statements about the willingness to declare no first-use of nuclear weapons and Ogarkov's belief that a nuclear war was winnable.[27] In his extensive article on military strategy, in the *Soviet Military Encyclopedia* from 1979, Ogarkov had outlined his thoughts on a future world war.[28] He envisioned a confrontation between two systems: the socialist and the capitalist. A new world war could be fought with conventional weapons only, but it could also escalate into a nuclear war, mainly involving strategic nuclear weapons. He pledged that Soviet military strategy would abide by the policy decision not to use nuclear weapons first but emphasized that any aggression with nuclear missiles against the Soviet Union or its allies would be met with a devastating retaliatory strike. A future nuclear world war was expected to be comparably short, although a protracted nuclear world war could not be ruled out. And he concluded that such a war was winnable for the entire socialist camp, due to the "just missions of the war, the superior character of these societies, and their political systems."[29] As we saw in the previous chapter, this is a continuation of the principles outlined in Sokolovsky's *Soviet Military Strategy* and does not necessarily indicate a split between the military and the politicians. Ogarkov never repeated this claim, and, after all, he was the first to declare no first-use, two years before the minister of defense, Dmitrii Ustinov, publicly did so.

Furthermore, Ogarkov repeated in his article Sokolovsky's previous provisions for the Soviet view of local wars. While the Soviet Union supported national liberation wars, it would stand up against local wars instigated by the imperialists.[30] But it was clear that the focus of the Soviet perceptions of future war was global war.

Later, in 1985, he had clearly distanced himself from any proposition that a nuclear world war would be winnable; he adhered to the principle of no first-use and argued for renewed talks with the United States in order to end the arms race. War prevention was not only possible but also necessary, Ogarkov claimed.[31] In a couple of years, this would become the new policy of Mikhail Gorbachev.

Earlier, in 1978, Ogarkov wrote an article about the dialectics of military affairs. He noted the contradictions of armed struggle, between offense and defense. In the article he included a paragraph about the impact of nuclear weapons, later deleted from his *Istoriia uchit bditelnost* of 1985. In 1978 he wrote, "This also applies fully to nuclear-missile weapons, whose rapid development stimulated military-scientific theory and practice to actively develop means and methods of counteraction. The appearance of means of defense against weapons of mass destruction in turn prompted the improvement of nuclear missile means of attack."[32]

In *Istoriia uchit bditelnost*, Ogarkov noted that armed struggle (*borba*) was especially complex and full of contradictions: between the opposing sides, in their political and strategic goals; between the needs of the armed forces and the economic capabilities of the countries; and the eternal conflict between offense and defense. He explored military history, and instead of the paragraph on nuclear weapons from 1978, he examined the two world wars. He noted that World War I had seemed to show that defense was stronger than offense, whereas World War II had shown that offense was superior. Ogarkov reached the conclusion that the contradiction between offense and defense was the inner source of the development of military affairs. The development of new offensive means always led to the development of appropriate countermeasures. Consequently, during the war and especially in the postwar period, "means of defense were developed at an accelerated rate ... whose skillful use at a certain stage balanced the means of offense and defense to some degree."[33] In this situation, when offense and defense had reached a balance, he argued, it was imperative to "study deeply every aspect of the fast contemporary technological development and not just look at the changes within military affairs from one side only."[34] The "one side only" was clearly directed at proponents of the school of thought that favored the use of nuclear weapons in a massive preemptive strike.

In addition, his reasoning shows a broader outlook, a holistic view of military affairs that several Russian military theorists have long expressed. It was also an effort to reconcile the two schools of Soviet military thought that had evolved over the years. One part was devoted to a certain theory, that of Marxism and Leninism on war and the army, whereas the other part focused on a set of applied military disciplines, united and subordinated to strategy as the general theory, and the art of practical preparations and how to conduct war.[35] Both schools monopolized "their truths," which led to an absolute class doctrine regarding the nature of war on one hand and an absolute focus on military means to conduct armed struggle (*borba*) on the other.

## REVOLUTION IN MILITARY AFFAIRS AND FUTURE WAR: IN THEORY AND PRACTICE

The term "revolution in military affairs" or, as it was often called in the Soviet Union, the "military-technical revolution," implies radical military innovation. According to the Soviet version of the definition, it consisted of a radical change in the armed forces and the methods of conducting military operations generated by scientific-technical progress in weaponry and military technology. The revolution in the postwar period referred, for instance, to the emergence of nuclear weapons, radio electronics, and automated command-and-control systems.[36] The word "revolution" is not used to mean "rapid" but rather "profound," and the development it represents leads to a fundamental change in the art of war.[37]

Since both superpowers had reached strategic nuclear parity, Ogarkov, in *Istoriia uchit bditelnost*, explicitly questioned the rationality of a nuclear world war. He dismissed the classic Clausewitzian dictum, repeated by Lenin, that war is the continuation of politics by other means, arguing that this was madness once nuclear weapons entered the equation. "Consequently, the immutable conclusion is that it would be criminal to view a thermonuclear war as a rational phenomenon or even a 'legitimate means' of the continuation of politics."[38] In line with this thinking, he also dismissed the idea of a "limited nuclear war." According to Ogarkov, such a war would be impossible to retain at that limited level and would inevitably lead to the use of the entire nuclear arsenal. "This is the harsh logic of war," he wrote.[39]

Thus, the Soviet view of nuclear weapons in a future war had gone from a "romantic period," in the 1950s and 1960s, when nuclear weapons could solve any political and military goals, through the more cautious 1970s, with the realization that nuclear wars should never be fought. Nuclear weapons, ultimately, were not primarily a military weapon but a political one.

Consequently, the military doctrine's political side had become less offensive, whereas the military technology side was still very much offensive. From 1969 onward, increasingly large-scale live and command-post exercises were conducted by the Soviet Union and the Warsaw Pact. They were designed to practice the execution of a strategic offensive operation to defeat NATO and conquer Western Europe. It was during Ogarkov's term in office that these exercises became increasingly threatening.

So, what kind of war was the Soviet General Staff planning? In the absence of Soviet archival sources, we must rely on previously secret Warsaw Pact plans and exercises: the picture remains rather bleak. The Soviet military leadership became increasingly concerned about NATO exercises in the beginning of the 1980s and feared a surprise attack. Plans were made for offensive exercises aimed at reaching the Atlantic coast within days, including the use of nuclear weapons to be launched on warning.[40]

The trauma of 1941 played a key role in the Soviet threat perception. For instance, while chairing a Warsaw Pact meeting in Minsk in September 1982, Ogarkov told the participants, "The international situation is currently very serious and extremely complicated. It is only comparable with the situation in the 1930s, shortly before the outbreak of the Second World War."[41]

Another reason seems to have been mirror-imaging. Using exercises as cover for military operations was often practiced by the Soviet Union, such as prior to the invasion of Czechoslovakia in 1968 and the threat of an invasion of Poland in 1981. So, this line of thinking about the purpose of military exercises was projected onto NATO leaders' intentions.[42]

Ogarkov believed that the military-technical revolution was changing the military art. He focused on the impact of new technologies, on automated command and control, precision strikes, and electronic warfare. According to him, it was necessary to develop the "new conventional means of warfare," such as reconnaissance strike complexes and weapons based on new physical principles, such as laser and electromagnetic weapons.[43] Consequently, he argued that the nuclear arsenal could be reduced, as it would still be sufficient. The important task ahead was to develop a new high-technology conventional arsenal for a future conventional war, one without nuclear weapons.

The developments in military technology had a profound impact on several areas, such as the space domain and, importantly, the "initial period of the war." Whereas in the 1960s, as shown above, this period in a future war would consist of massive nuclear strikes that would be decisive for the outcome, the new precision conventional weapons led to a reevaluation of the initial period of the war. Ogarkov was in the forefront of this nascent discussion. Now, the long-range conventional, precision weapons would increase the scope of the initial period of the war. "Military art has no right to lag behind the combat potential of the means of armed combat, particularly at the present stage, when, on the basis of scientific-technical progress, the main weapons systems change practically every 10–12 years," he wrote.[44] Decisive actions with conventional weapons, to a depth that encompasses the territory of an entire country at once, were now possible, something unprecedented in previous wars.

Ogarkov underlined that surprise had entered as a factor of *strategic* importance and that the time required, or available, to put the entire country on a war footing had been substantially shortened. Importantly, he argued for a centralized system between the political and military leadership in order to meet the challenges of modern war. As an example of past experience of such a system, he invoked the precedent of the State Defense Committee during World War II. In a future war, a decision-making system consisting of party, state, and economic organs would be vital for defense, he argued.[45]

During this period, perhaps paradoxically, the United States was developing the actual weapons, while Soviet thinkers wrote leading theoretical works about the fundamental impact of the new technological innovations on military art.[46] In that sense, the old, ideological Soviet dictum on "the supremacy of Soviet military theory" was correct, although not in the sense it was normally used—that is, Soviet supremacy on the battlefield and the victory in World War II. The deep understanding of the changes in military technology and their impact found no ground in the practical implementation of this "revolution." The increasingly ossified Soviet Union did not have the resources or the flexibility to change. The disconnect between theory and practice in the Soviet Union had become acute.

The reasons for Ogarkov's dismissal vary. At first it was thought that it was the result of his advocacy of excessive military spending.[47] Kokoshin claimed that in the early 1990s Ogarkov had told him that it was because of his resistance to developing even more strategic nuclear weapon systems. Allegedly, he was against developing the SS-24 and Taifun ICBMs, the latter for naval warfare. Ogarkov had argued that parity with the United States could be upheld with three to four times fewer warheads for nuclear strategic weapon systems.[48] Ogarkov thus challenged the authority of Defense Minister Ustinov on an issue directly linked to strategic deterrence and eventually lost the power struggle. Kokoshin remarked that Ogarkov's losing to Ustinov, who continued the arms race, cost the Soviet Union dearly: "The arms race (including the nuclear one) was one of the most important reasons for the collapse of the Soviet economy at the end of the 1980s and the dissolution of the Soviet state."[49]

In other words, there was a split between Ustinov and Ogarkov, not only on the issue of Afghanistan but also on matters relating to strategic deterrence. In general, Ogarkov's influence in this area has been underresearched, as the American analyst Michael Kofman notes.[50]

After Ogarkov's dismissal, the winds of change accelerated. As the political changes arrived along with Gorbachev's reforms, the impact on Soviet military doctrine was fundamental.

## GORBACHEV AND THE CHANGES OF 1985–91

During Gorbachev's six years in the Soviet Union's highest office, fundamental changes took place at all levels of society. Eventually, the Soviet Union disintegrated, as did the Soviet Armed Forces. Important milestones, for the purposes of this book, are obviously the decision to withdraw from Afghanistan, the unification of Germany, and the decision not to intervene in Eastern Europe.

In December 1988 Gorbachev announced a unilateral reduction of the Soviet Armed Forces by half a million personnel. The Soviet Armed Forces were reduced from 5.3 million to approximately 3.99 million personnel in 1990. In 1989–92, about five hundred thousand troops were withdrawn from the German Democratic Republic, Czechoslovakia, Hungary, and Poland.[51]

Gorbachev's reform policies and "new thinking" paved the way for the signing of the Intermediate-Range Nuclear Forces Treaty (INF Treaty) in 1987, thus reducing the number of nuclear missiles in Europe. The pathbreaking Treaty on Conventional Armed Forces in Europe (CFE Treaty) paved the way for substantial reductions of conventional troops on the continent.[52]

By the INF Treaty's deadline of June 1, 1991, a total of 2,692 such weapons had been destroyed, 846 by the United States and 1,846 by the Soviet Union. Importantly, the INF Treaty did not significantly alter the overall Soviet force structure.[53] Nevertheless, twenty years after it was signed, Russian president Vladimir Vladimirovich Putin (1952–) openly questioned its validity.[54] The political leadership declared what the military had tacitly been thinking at the time: that the INF Treaty had been a mistake. In 2019 the treaty was suspended by both parties.

During Gorbachev's term, the Soviet military doctrine was changed from an offensive to a defensive stance. The objective to prevent war and conflict was included in the doctrine, although the traditional aim of preparing to wage war remained. In the revised article about "military strategy" in the 1986 edition of *Voennyi entsiklopedicheskii slovar* (Military encyclopedic lexicon), a critical sentence was added: "A most important task for Soviet military strategy in contemporary conditions is the solution to the problem of preventing war."[55]

The process of change that led to the dissolution of the Soviet Union was highly complex, far beyond the scope of this book, and involved a large number of factors, including technological development, the reform policy and the revision of ideology, and radical foreign policy decisions. The growing nationalistic sentiments in the different countries and regions—including Russia—that constituted the Soviet Union was a major contributing factor to its dissolution. In the end, the centrifugal forces were uncontrollable, and the pillars of the Soviet Union—the Communist Party, the ideology, the military, and the secret police—could do nothing to prevent the Warsaw Pact and the Soviet Union from crumbling.

It should be remembered that Gorbachev's initial aim was to address the ailing Soviet economy, whereas political liberalization only came after several years. There was general agreement in the Politburo that something had to be done and that a cut in military expenditures was necessary, but there was no broad consensus as to how to achieve this.[56] However, at the Twenty-Seventh Party Congress in February 1986, Gorbachev announced that the Soviet Union would limit its military potential to "reasonable sufficiency." In the new party program approved by the congress, the wording was slightly different but carried the same meaning.

The notion of reasonable sufficiency was later developed by military and civilian theorists and was again revived in the 2000s. In essence, this principle meant not only a reduction in the Soviet Armed Forces but also an effort to bridge the gap between the political and technical side of the military doctrine. Politically, the Soviet leaders had for years proclaimed a defensive strategy, whereas the military technology side of the doctrine had remained offensive. With the fundamental changes during Gorbachev's term, this became untenable. His military reforms meant change in practice, not just rhetoric.

At the center was the view of the sources of Soviet security. The traditional outlook that military means was the guarantor of security for the Soviet Union and the entire socialist camp, symbolized by the Brezhnev Doctrine, was shifting toward Gorbachev's vision that political means would be at the center of ensuring Soviet security. Therefore, when the countries in Eastern Europe started to free themselves from the Soviet grip, the Soviet Union did not intervene.

The Soviet military theorists had to make a fundamental revision of the traditional offensive Soviet view of war, and some started to develop concepts involving the new guiding principles of the Soviet military doctrine: defense, war prevention, and reasonable sufficiency. The debate also involved civilian experts on international affairs, who were encouraged to engage in discussions on strategy and policy, paving the way, as shown below, for the deepened discussion later in the 1990s.[57] The impact on Soviet strategy and operations was essential, and the debates about its implications were vivid and rich. However, the consequences and the implementation were not fully worked out. Several key articles in the journal *Voennaia mysl* from 1987 to 1990 stressed the defensive doctrine but did not develop the question of implementation in any greater detail.

One example is the discussions on the issue of counteroffensives at the strategic level. The official statement of the doctrine had specified that should the Warsaw Pact be attacked, its forces would "give the aggressor a crushing rebuff [*otpor*]." Gen. Dmitrii Timofeev Yazov (1924–2020) explained that although the

Soviet military doctrine now considered defense as the main form of military actions, "by defense alone, however, it is not possible to defeat the aggressor. Therefore after repulsing the attack, the troops and naval forces must be capable of conducting a decisive offensive. The transition to it will take the form of a counteroffensive."[58]

Later, in 1988–90, the references to the necessity of a counteroffensive became less frequent, and, tellingly, in an article by Marshal Viktor Georgievich Kulikov (1921–2013) any reference to a counteroffensive had disappeared altogether. He wrote, "It is extremely important to study how to organize and conduct active defense, providing for effective fire defeat and conducting counterattacks and counterstrikes."[59] According to Soviet military doctrine, counterattacks take place at the tactical level, and counterstrikes at the operational. Similarly, and consistently, Maj. Gen. Stepan Andreevich Tiushkevich (1917–), in his article on defense sufficiency, made no mention at all of a counteroffensive.[60] Although the political leadership and some military theorists began to question the counteroffensive, time did not allow for further development of the implications of the more defensive Soviet military doctrine.

The debates on the implementation of a defensive stance also reflect the changes in the views on victory in war. We have seen how the cult of the offensive (by no means unique to the Soviet Union) and the total annihilation of the enemy had prevailed, whereas at the very end of the 1980s this too began to be revised. The traditional notion of quickly shifting the war into the territory of another country was deeply ingrained in the Soviet leadership, although, according to Gareev, it was not supported by theory.[61] Others took the example of the Battle of Kursk as an indication that in the present situation, defense relying on conventional weapons was more beneficial for strategic stability than offense and nuclear weapons.[62]

Furthermore, the defensive position of the Soviet military doctrine affected naval strategy. The naval leadership declared a reduction in naval personnel. Naval exercises would change in character, and they would be held closer to Soviet coasts.[63] Consequently, the Soviet navy again turned to shores closer to home.

These debates reflect a time of rapid and fundamental change, where different ideas were put forward in public and with the participation of civilians in an area that was traditionally secret and overwhelmingly military-driven. The purpose, in line with Gorbachev's "new thinking," was to gather new ideas and inspiration to replace a military strategy that had become outdated. The result was often heated and bitter debates between the civilian academics and the military. The Russian scholar and specialist in international relations and security studies Alexei Georgievich Arbatov (1951–), for instance, was accused of being "tendentious, naive, and incompetent" when, in arguing for reductions within the air defense forces, he opposed the maximalist version favored by the military.[64] Only a decade earlier, such allegations in an official Soviet journal would have jeopardized the job of the accused and, earlier still, their lives.

In the end, time had run out. The development of new concepts was overtaken by events. Germany was reunited in 1990, the East European states broke free from the Soviet grip, and in 1991 the Warsaw Pact's military and political structures fell, preceding the formal dissolution of the Soviet Union, which ceased to exist as a state in December 1991. Ogarkov's warning that inertia and the inability to adapt would lead to grave consequences turned out to be true. As Kokoshin later put it, "history has given Russia only so much time to reform the military; it would be foolish to believe that Russia has all the time it needs."[65]

At the same time, it is possible to discern that a further disconnect between the political leadership and the military emerged. Gorbachev's reduction of the Armed Forces and, importantly, the withdrawal from Afghanistan, showed that the Soviet military was not invincible. Although Ogarkov had spoken out against the invasion, ten years later the military leadership argued against a complete withdrawal.[66]

The military theorists in the General Staff tried to elaborate concepts for "defense sufficiency," whereas the plans to meet the new technological challenges indicated that even more resources should be allocated to the country's defense. The military leadership was unwilling or unable to adopt Gorbachev's *perestroika* policies to their own ranks. "Perestroika" means restructuring and was a part of Gorbachev's reform policies, initially used for trying to improve the economy. In practical terms, the General Staff implemented the INF Treaty but did not seem to do very much apart from that to continue to reform.[67] Gorbachev's unilateral troop reductions, followed by further reductions within the CFE Treaty, led to resentment within the military, not so much because of the strategic implications but more as a result of "the lack of minimal respect for the dignity of soldiers and airmen," as a Russian observer has put it.[68]

## RELEVANCE TODAY

Ogarkov's legacy, with his focus on high-technology conventional weapons, remains strong in Russia today, and he is still held in high regard. One prominent Russian military theorist told me in the early 2010s, "It seems to me that we have not had a real military thinker since Ogarkov." In essence, the development of high-technology conventional weapon systems in the 2000s is a direct legacy of Ogarkov's thought. He envisioned the "contactless battlefield" that Russian military theorists later developed and that the chief of the General Staff, Valerii Gerasimov, frequently talked about.[69]

Others have walked in his footsteps. Nikolai Makarov seems to be a kindred spirit. He was chief of the General Staff from 2008 to 2012 and the brain of a substantial military reform. Makarov often expressed concern that Russian military thinking was years behind that of the leading states. In his memoir, *Na sluzhbe Rossii* (In the service of Russia), he argued for the promotion of military thought and science, not least within the General Staff.[70] He wrote at length about the relationship between military theory and practice and the need for them to approach each other. "Why, in military affairs, to which I have given my life, is there such a rift between the theoretical ideas on future wars and the practical training of the forces?" he asked.[71]

Makarov was cautious about the future of his reform and underlined the need for a continued reform process. New features are not always applied, he complained, almost echoing Ogarkov, thirty years earlier. "Stereotypes, created during decades, a sloppiness of thought, a resistance to follow with the times and to learn from best practices in peacetime, still characterize, unfortunately, some of the generals, admirals and officers of the Armed Forces," Makarov pointed out, and ended with an appeal to continue: "It is hard, often unrewarding. But there is no other way."[72]

Furthermore, in the mid-2010s, two retired colonels, Igor Mikhailovich Popov and Musa Magomedovich Khamzatov, were worried about the state of Russian military thought. In their book *Voina budushchego: Kontseptualnye osnovy i prakticheskie vyvody; Ocherki strategicheskoi mysli* (The war of the future: A conceptual framework and practical conclusions; Essays on strategic thought), they criticize the overall "conservatism of military organizations."[73] They discuss the general unwillingness of Russian military society to listen to and learn from military thinkers who are outside of the system.[74] One of their best examples from the Russian context is Ivan Bloch, whose work in six volumes, *Budushchaia voina* (The future of war), was published in 1898. Popov and Khamzatov note, for instance, that Bloch did not have a military degree yet had a profound understanding of the essence of war.[75] They point to the United States as an example to follow to remedy the situation. There, according to the authors, not only generals and admirals can discuss military strategy but also sergeants.[76] In addition, even civilian experts such as political scientists, biologists, psychologists, journalists, information technology experts, historians, and economists can have a say in discussions about future war. This has led to a situation where the US is far ahead compared to contemporary Russian military thought. Popov and Khamzatov quote one of the great Russian military thinkers, Aleksandr Svechin, already familiar to the reader of this book, to reinforce their point. In his book *Strategiia*, Svechin pointed to the importance of having a broad discussion on strategic matters to avoid the risk of creating "a strategic caste" and a cleavage between "the enlightened and the unenlightened."[77]

Popov and Khamzatov continue their critique of Russian military society and how closed it is ("the bureaucrats"), as well as the prevalent attitude toward international conferences. Conferences, due to the influence of bureaucrats, have become an empty and dreary pastime, whereas "surprisingly enough, in the West, to take part in academic conferences, roundtables, and symposiums is not considered as a punishment but as a stimulation."[78]

Both the concept of reasonable sufficiency and Ogarkov's legacy of the need to develop high-technology conventional weapon systems survived the dissolution of the Soviet Union and remained important ideas in the search of a strategy for the Russian Federation.

## NOTES

*Epigraph:* Andrei Sakharov, "Thoughts on Progress, Peaceful Coexistence and Intellectual Freedom," *New York Times,* July 22, 1968, https://www.sakharov.space/lib/thoughts-on-peace-progress-and-intellectual-freedom.

1. "Mirnoe sosushchestvovanie" [Peaceful coexistence] in *Diplomaticheskii Slovar* [Diplomatic lexicon], vol. 2, ed. A. A. Gromyko, S. A. Golunskii, and V. M. Khvostov (Moscow: Gos. izd. politicheskoi literarury, 1961), 299; Sokolovskiy, *Soviet Military Strategy,* 176–77.
2. President of Russia, Konstitutsiia Rossiiskoi Federatsii [Constitution of the Russian Federation], July 1, 2020, § 79, www.kremlin.ru.
3. Congressional Research Service, *Arms Control and Nonproliferation: A Catalog of Treaties and Agreements,* July 8, 2024, RL33865, 49.
4. Congressional Research Service, *Arms Control and Nonproliferation,* 49–50; Odom, *Collapse of the Soviet Military,* 124–25.
5. David M. Glantz, *The Military Strategy of the Soviet Union: A History* (London: Frank Cass, 1992), 205.
6. Kokoshin, *Strategicheskoe upravlenie,* 243–45.
7. According to Gareev, Yuri Andropov told Ogarkov, "We have someone to deal with policy. You will solve the given task." Quoted in A. A. Kokoshin et al., *Sovremennye voiny i voennoe iskusstvo* [Contemporary wars and military art] (Moscow: Leland, 2015), 65.
8. Rodric Braithwaite, *Afgantsy: The Russians in Afghanistan 1979–1989* (Oxford: Oxford University Press, 2011), 57.
9. Anatoly Diakov, Timur Kadyshev, and Pavel Podvig, "Nuclear Parity and National Security in New Conditions," Center for Arms Control, Energy and Environmental Studies, Moscow Institute of Physics and Technology, https://www.armscontrol.ru/start/publications/dkp0731.htm.
10. Kokoshin, *Soviet Strategic Thought,* 126–27.
11. Kokoshin, 127.
12. A. A. Grechko, *The Armed Forces of the Soviet State: A Soviet View,* 2nd ed. Moscow, trans. and published under the auspices of the United States Air Force (Washington, DC: Government Printing Office, 1975), 24.
13. "Ogarkov, Nikolai Vasilevich" in Ogarkov, *Sovetskaia voennaia entsiklopediia,* vol. 6, 7–8; Kokoshin, *Politologiia i sotsiologiia,* 84, 110–11.

14. N. V. Ogarkov, "Strategiia voennaia" [Strategy, military], in Ogarkov, *Sovetskaia voennaia entsiklopediia*, vol. 7, 556.
15. N. V. Ogarkov, *Istoriia uchit bditelnost* [History teaches vigilance] (Moscow: Voennoe izdatelstvo, 1985), 82–90.
16. Ogarkov, 90.
17. Ogarkov, 57–58.
18. Ogarkov, 58–59.
19. Ogarkov, 59.
20. "Doktrina voennaia" [Doctrine, military] in Ogarkov, *Sovetskaia voennaia entsiklopediia*, vol. 2, 225–29.
21. Ogarkov, *Istoriia*, 79–80.
22. Ogarkov, "Strategiia voennaia," 564.
23. Kokoshin, *Soviet Strategic Thought*, 180.
24. Kokoshin, 181.
25. Ogarkov, *Istoriia*, 49, 54.
26. Kokoshin, *Strategicheskoe upravlenie*, 360.
27. Kimberly Marten Zisk, *Engaging the Enemy: Organization Theory and Soviet Military Innovation* (Princeton, NJ: Princeton University Press, 1993), 109–111.
28. Ogarkov, "Strategiia voennaia," 556–65.
29. Ogarkov, 564.
30. Ogarkov, 564.
31. Ogarkov, *Istoriia*, 82, 91.
32. N. V. Ogarkov, "Voennaia nauka i zashchita sotsialisticheskogo otechestva" [Military science and the protection of the fatherland], *Kommunist*, no. 7 (1978): 117.
33. Ogarkov, *Istoriia*, 49.
34. Ogarkov, 49.
35. Quoted in Kokoshin, *Politologiia i sotsiologiia*, 48.
36. "Revoliutsiia v voennom dele" [Revolution in military affairs], in Ogarkov, *Sovetskaia voennaia entsiklopediia*, vol. 7, 82.
37. Adamsky, *Culture of Military Innovation*, 1.
38. Ogarkov, *Istoriia*, 88–89.
39. Ogarkov, 89.
40. "Launch on warning" was a concept of nuclear weapon retaliation between the Soviet Union and the United States. With the introduction of ICBMs, it became a part of the mutually assured destruction theory (MAD). Vojtech Mastny, "Imaging War in Europe," in *War Plans and Alliances in the Cold War: Threat Perceptions in the East and West*, ed. Vojtech Mastny, Sven G. Holtsmark, and Andreas Wenger (London: Routledge, 2006), 15–45. See also Beatrice Heuser, "Military Exercises and the Dangers of Misunderstandings: The East-West Crisis of the Early 1980s," in Heuser, Heier, and Lasconjarias, *Military Exercises*, 113–37.
41. Heuser, "Military Exercises," 125–26.
42. Heuser, 127.
43. Ogarkov, *Istoriia*, 40–54; Mary C. FitzGerald, "The Impact of New Technologies on Soviet Military Thought," in *Radical Reform in Soviet Defence Policy*, ed. Roy Allison (Palgrave Macmillan: New York, 1992), 98–131.
44. N. V. Ogarkov, "Na strazhe mirnogo truda" [On guard for peaceful labor], *Kommunist*, no. 10 (1981): 80–91.
45. Ogarkov, "Na strazhe," 89–90.

46. Adamsky, *Culture of Military Innovation*, 24.
47. Dale R. Herspring, *The Soviet High Command 1967–1989: Personalities and Politics* (Princeton, NJ: Princeton University Press, 1990), 218–23; Pavel Baev, *The Russian Army in a Time of Troubles* (Oslo: International Peace Research Institute, 1996), 19.
48. Kokoshin, *Politologiia i sotsiologiia*, 302–4.
49. Kokoshin is agreeing with and quoting Dr. Aleksandr Savelev at the Primakov Institute. Kokoshin, 304, 389.
50. Michael Kofman, "The Ogarkov Reforms: The Soviet Inheritance behind Russia's Military Transformation," Russian Military Analysis, July 11, 2019, https://russianmilitaryanalysis.wordpress.com/2019/07/11/the-ogarkov-reforms-the-soviet-inheritance-behind-russias-military-transformation/. For more on Ogarkov, see also Dmitry (Dima) Adamsky, "The Two Marshals: Nikolai Ogarkov, Andrew Marshall and the Revolution in Military Affairs," in *The New Makers of Modern Strategy*, ed. Hal Brands (Princeton, NJ: Princeton University Press, 2023), 895–917.
51. Odom, *Collapse*, 272; Sergei Rogov, "Russian Defense Policy: Challenges and Developments," Occasional Paper, Institute of USA and Canada Studies and Center for Naval Analyses, February 1993, 18.
52. Roy Allison, "Soviet Policy on Conventional Force Reductions," in Allison, *Radical Reform*, 161–97.
53. Odom, *Collapse*, 147.
54. President of Russia, "Speech and the Following Discussion at the Munich Conference on Security Policy," February 10, 2007, http://en.kremlin.ru/events/president/transcripts/24034.
55. S. F. Akhromeev, ed., *Voennyi entsiklopedicheskii slovar* [Military encyclopedic lexicon], 2nd ed. (Moscow: Voennoe izdatelstvo, 1986), 712.
56. See for instance Odom, *Collapse*, 87–117.
57. Zisk, *Engaging the Enemy*, 20–22.
58. Raymond L. Garthoff, *Deterrence and the Revolution in Soviet Military Doctrine* (Washington, DC: Brookings Institution, 1990), 162.
59. V. G. Kulikov, "O voenno-strategicheskom paritete i dostatochnosti dlia oborony" [On military-strategic parity and sufficiency for defense], *Voennaia mysl*, no. 5 (1988): 3–11.
60. S. A. Tiushkevich, "Razumnaia dostatochnost dlia oborony: Parametry i kriterii" [Reasonable sufficiency for defense: Parameters and criteria], *Voennaia mysl*, no. 5 (1989): 53–61.
61. Gareev, *M. V. Frunze*, 208.
62. A. A. Kokoshin and V. Larionov, "Kurskaia bitva v svete sovremennoi oboronitelnoi doktriny" [The Battle of Kursk in light of the contemporary defensive doctrine], *Mirovaia ekonomika i mezhdunarodnye otnosheniia*, no. 8 (1987): 32–40.
63. Kokoshin, *Soviet Strategic Thought*, 191.
64. A. P. Vasilev and V. K. Rudiuk. "Dostatochna li protivovozdushnaia oborona?" [Is the air defense sufficient?], *Voennaia mysl*, no. 9 (1989): 59–68; A. G. Arbatov, "K voprosu o dostatochnosti protivovozdushnoi oborony" [To the question of air defense sufficiency], *Voennaia mysl*, no. 12 (1989): 41–45.
65. Kokoshin, *Soviet Strategic Thought*, 208.
66. Odom, *Collapse*, 460–62.

67. Odom, 136, 147.
68. Dmitri Trenin, *Post-Imperium: A Eurasian Story* (Washington, DC: Carnegie Endowment for International Peace, 2011), 4.
69. See the bibliography for references to Gerasimov's works. The Russian military literature on this topic is enormous. For a good introduction in English, see Timothy L. Thomas, *Russian Military Thought: Concepts and Elements*, MP190451V1 (McLean, VA: Mitre Corp., 2019), chap. 9.
70. Makarov, *Na sluzhbe Rossii*.
71. Makarov, 352.
72. Makarov, 421.
73. Igor Popov and Musa Khamzatov, *Voina budushchego: Kontseptualnye osnovy i prakticheskie vyvody; Ocherki strategicheskoi mysli* [The war of the future: A conceptual framework and practical conclusions; Essays on strategic thought] (Moscow: Kuchkovo pole, 2016), 13–14, 635–36.
74. Popov and Khamzatov, 102–6.
75. Popov and Khamzatov, 633.
76. Popov and Khamzatov, 96–97.
77. Svechin, *Strategiia*, 22.
78. Popov and Khamzatov, *Voina budushchego*, 106.

# 6

# IN SEARCH OF A STRATEGY FROM THE BREAKUP OF THE SOVIET UNION TO THE FULL-SCALE INVASION OF UKRAINE

> *I know that you have the power*
> *I've faith in wisdom of yours,*
> *Believing as does a dead soldier*
> *That right in the Heaven he dwells.*
> *As truly believes every being:*
> *That all that you say is true,*
> *As we go on believing,*
> *Not knowing what we do.*
>
> Bulat Okudzhava

This chapter explores the search for a new strategy, conducted against the backdrop of the dissolution of the Soviet Union and the experiences of Afghanistan and Chechnya. The war in Georgia in 2008 gave impetus to a major, and well-financed, military reform. What impact did it have on military thought about strategy and doctrine? Special attention is paid here to the topics of threat assessment, nuclear and nonnuclear deterrence, and the use of history as an instrument of security policy. The thinking of prominent theorists, such as Nikolai Makarov, Makhmut Gareev, Andrei Kokoshin, and Valerii Gerasimov, is examined. These considerations serve to clarify the context of the current Russo-Ukrainian War.

## THE END OF THE COLD WAR AND THE RUSSIAN ARMED FORCES

In the end, nothing could stop the dissolution of the Soviet Union—not the Soviet Armed Forces, not the security services. The Armed Forces did play a role in this process: first, through nonaction, and then, with the failed coup attempt in August 1991, belated action.

The fall of the Soviet Union was not the result of a revolution or a coup d'état or a military coup, nor was it the result of a defeat in a world war. It was not, in other words, as it had been when the empires of Europe fell in 1917–18. Many and complex factors, mainly domestic, contributed to its fall, and it happened quickly, especially when considered against the long centuries of Russia's history.

In speed, it was almost a reminder of the fall of czarist Russia in March 1917, when, after three hundred years on the throne, the Romanovs abdicated. Commenting on the fate of the empire, Russian author and philosopher Vasilii Rozanov (1856–1919) had remarked, "Russia wilted in two days. At the very most, three. . . . It is amazing how she suddenly fell apart, all of her, down to particles, to pieces. . . . There was no empire, no church, no army, no working class. And what remained? Strange to say, literally nothing."[1]

The Soviet Armed Forces had been one of the pillars of the Soviet Union's great-power status. In terms of nuclear weapons, the United States and the Soviet Union had reached parity. In December 1991, 61 of 101 Soviet army divisions, 7 of 10 air force armies, and 9 of 15 air defense armies were stationed outside of Russia proper. Furthermore, 44 percent of the entire manpower of the Soviet Armed Forces was outside Russia, 43 percent of the tanks, 50 percent of the strategic air force, and, importantly, 28 percent of the intercontinental ballistic missiles.[2]

Initially, there were some attempts, albeit feeble, to create unified armed forces within the newly formed Commonwealth of Independent States (CIS). Article 6 of its founding document, the Belavezha Accords of December 8, 1991, stipulated that the members of the CIS should "keep and support under a unified command a common military strategic space."[3]

In February 1992, in line with this concept of creating unified CIS armed forces, a supreme commander, Air Marshal Evgenii Ivanovich Shaposhnikov (1942–2020), was appointed. Furthermore, a draft of the CIS military doctrine was formulated in early 1992. It proposed the creation of the unified, combined armed forces, which would serve all CIS states.[4] When Shaposhnikov left his position, in November 1992, the control of a set of nuclear weapon codes, which had been Shaposhnikov's responsibility, was then handed over to the Russian defense minister, Pavel Sergeevich Grachev (1948–2012). In 1993 a number of important moves were carried out: the General Headquarters of the Joint Armed Forces was formally disbanded on June 15, 1993,[5] the position that Shaposhnikov's successor received was downgraded, and Col. Gen. Viktor Nikolaevich Samsonov (1941–2024) was appointed chief of the United Staff for the Coordination of Military Cooperation.

It had become clear that the CIS member states did not support the plans to keep the unified military structure. Instead, they began the process of creating national armed forces. Not even Russia, the de jure successor state of the Soviet Union and the dominant military power, wanted to preserve the CIS military structure. A substantial blow to the idea of joint CIS forces, therefore, came in May 1992, when the Russian Armed Forces were created. By that time, all CIS countries save Tajikistan (due to its civil war) had started to build their national armed forces. The causes of this development lie outside the scope of this book, but they illustrate the argument that the armed forces of a country do not exist in a vacuum but are rather a reflection of the society as a whole.

The most pressing issue in the 1990s was the nuclear weapons that remained in Ukraine, Belarus, and Kazakhstan. In addition, the remaining Soviet troops and military facilities in the Baltic states and East Germany were also high on the agenda.[6] Regarding the issue of nuclear weapons, the initial idea that the CIS would control Soviet nuclear weapons failed, and Russia eventually took over the remaining nuclear weapons in Belarus, Kazakhstan, and Ukraine. For some time, Ukraine had been ambivalent about relinquishing the nuclear weapons on its territory, but the issue was resolved with the provision of some financial aid from the United States and reassurance derived from the security guarantees in the Budapest Memorandum, signed in 1994. The last remaining ex-Soviet nuclear warheads were withdrawn from Kazakhstan by May 1995, Ukraine by May 1996, and Belarus by November 1996.

Agreements were reached on the withdrawal of Soviet troops from the Baltic states and Eastern Europe. This process was largely completed by 1994, although it took until 1998 before radar station Skrunda, in Latvia, was closed. According to the former chief of the Russian General Staff, Nikolai Makarov, the withdrawal, as troops and equipment returned to Russia, was messy. Much of the military equipment was left out in the open and rusted. He wrote, "When it was decided to begin cutting the numbers of the returning troops, there was no one left to take care of the military equipment. Where the disbanded military units had been located, cemeteries of military equipment piled up."[7]

Another key development during the early 1990s was the signing, on May 15, 1992, of the Collective Security Treaty (CST), formerly known as the Tashkent Treaty, the embryo of the later Collective Security Treaty Organization, or CSTO. The CST came into force in 1994 and stipulated that a Collective Security Council should be created, consisting of the "heads of participating states and the commander in chief of the CIS Joint Armed Forces."[8] As this ambition failed, the treaty was revised, and the words about joint CIS Armed Forces disappeared. It deserves to be noted that by 1995 all CIS member states, except for Tajikistan, had joined NATO's Partnership for Peace program. Russia and NATO signed the program's founding act in 1997, both sides pledging to cooperate more closely, given the changing security climate in Europe. NATO member states also reiterated their statement of December 10, 1996, that they had no intention, no plan, and no reason to deploy nuclear weapons on the territory of new members.[9] The Russia-NATO Permanent Joint Council was also set up.

Nevertheless, the Russian General Staff never stopped analyzing and planning for future war. Neither did the intelligence and security services. Importantly, the civilian and military leadership maintained a continued consensus on relying on military power as the basis for Russia's status in the international arena.[10]

## STRATEGIC GEOGRAPHY

The geostrategic position of Russia had changed fundamentally following the breakup of the Soviet Union. The western border of the Russian Federation was approximately at the same longitude as during the mid-sixteenth century under Ivan IV. Around 25 percent of the Soviet Union's territory now belonged to other states. As Makhmut Gareev remarked, "geopolitically Russia found itself pushed away from the center of Europe deep into the Eurasian continent, cut off from the most important ports of the Baltic and Black Seas."[11] The overall geopolitical situation reminded some Russian military theorists of Russia's situation in the mid-seventeenth century.[12]

Furthermore, despite the disintegration of the Soviet Armed Forces, Russia continued to use military force outside its territory. The Russian scholar Pavel Kimovich Baev (1957–) estimated that by the end of 1992, around 27,500 Russian troops were engaged in various trouble spots in the region, increasing to around 36,000 by the end of 1993. His estimate for 1994 was as high as 42,000 troops, which also included those soldiers engaged in the United Nations Protection Force in Bosnia.[13]

The defensive posture of the late 1980s never took hold, and by the 2010s the offensive force posture had returned, although under very different geopolitical and force structures.[14] The importance of territory in Russian military thought is one of the continuities over time. The preoccupation with safeguarding the long borders, primarily against an enemy coming from the west, had concerned the Russian military throughout the centuries. It did not disappear with the breakup of the Soviet Union; on the contrary, the concern with territory seemed to become even more pressing in the decades after 1991. As Baev pointed out in 1996, "the strong historical tradition of military expansion and 'winning back' territories lost in previous misfortunes also gives cause for concern." He determined that an option remained "that the Army could march under the banner of reunification of all 'eternal' Russian lands, particularly those now populated by ethnic Russians."[15] The vague identity and uncertain borders added plausibility to such a scenario.

Baev was right. Vladimir Putin framed the illegal annexation of Crimea with the argument that Russia was simply "correcting historical injustices." By 2014 he had already outlined more territorial conquests in Ukraine. In defending Russia's actions, he mentioned on March 18 that the areas involved were Russia's "historical territories." He specified Kiev, Donetsk, and Kharkov. Later, he designated the areas as "Novorossiia" and included in it "Odessa, Nikolaev, Kherson, Donetsk,

Lugansk, and Kharkov."[16] These regions had been conquered in the reign of Catherine II, at the end of the eighteenth century. In 2022 Putin compared himself with Peter I and claimed that the latter had not expanded Russian territories during the Great Northern War but simply "returned" them to Russia.[17]

This is not to say that geographic setting determines policy and strategy and that Russia is doomed to constant expansion. It is merely to point out that while geographic factors are pervasive in Russian strategic thought, geography, as Colin Gray put it, does not require political behavior of any particular kind:

> Nonetheless, it: defines the location of the national (or multinational) territory; describes the physical character of that territory in all respects; distinguishes the (national) territory of the state from the territories of other states (in one important sense geography selects neighbors and, more arguably, friends and foes); defines a polity's cultural zone or civilization (e.g., in the American case, was the region colonized by the Spanish and Portuguese, or by the French and British?); and conditions, shapes, and influences the course of a polity's historical choices.[18]

This line of thinking aligns very well with that of the Russian military thinkers of the 1920s and also of the late nineteenth century. It is worth underlining that the Russian theorists on strategic geography examined in this book link it to military history, intelligence, strategy, economy, etc. Snesarev observed, as we saw in chapter 3, that military geography touched on all the sciences related to the armed forces and war.[19]

How did Russia deal with these dramatic developments? What was the threat perception in the publicly available doctrines?

## NATIONAL SECURITY AND THREAT ASSESSMENT

Initially, it is important to remember that the explicit use of the concepts of "security policy" and "national security" is fairly new in Russia. It was only at the very end of the existence of the Soviet Union that national security began to be used as a term at the political level. During the Soviet period, the national element of security was subordinate to that of social class and the international component.[20] Since then, it has become entirely accepted. The home page of Russia's Security Council lists over thirty different documents dealing with the country's national security. The Law on Strategic Planning, adopted in 2014, also encompasses national security.[21] The main document that formulates security policy is the National Security Strategy (NSS), even though the only doctrine mentioned in the Constitution of the Russian Federation is the Military Doctrine.

The legal basis for national security comprises the constitution, the federal laws On Security and On Defense, the Military Doctrine, and other doctrinal documents.[22] The president formulates the main direction of national security in the annual presidential addresses. The notion of national security has been defined broadly. From 1997 and 2015, the NSS (initially called the National Security Concept) encompassed nine different areas: (1) defense, (2) security of the state and society, (3) higher living standards, (4) economic growth, (5) science, technology, and education, (6) health care, (7) culture, (8) ecology, and (9) strategic stability and strategic partnership. In the 2021 NSS, analyzed below, information security had its own section, and the section on culture was expanded to include Russian spiritual and moral values.[23]

The law On Security defines security policy as being a part of both domestic and foreign policy. It involves a whole range of measures: political, organizational, social and economic, military, judicial, informational, special, and other measures. All the published Military Doctrines from 1993, 2000, 2010, and 2014 show a remarkable consistency regarding the threat perception, with some significant adjustments. Importantly, as shown below, the view of the West in general and NATO in particular as potential enemies never left the General Staff. Since the doctrines are signed by the president, the political leadership was comfortable with this position, despite its public rhetoric about better relations. The official turning point was in 1999, when NATO intervened in Kosovo and Prime Minister Evgenii Maksimovich Primakov (1929–2015), on his way to Washington for an official visit, famously ordered his plane to turn back to Moscow. Incidentally, I was attending a conference in England at that time, and the Russian participants suddenly walked out of the conference.

A close reading of the NSS, the Military Doctrine, the Foreign Policy Concept, and a number of key speeches, not least the president's annual address to the Federal Assembly, reveals the following perceived external threat assessment. Russia developed its main doctrines and strategies throughout the 1990s. The Russian threat assessment in the Military Doctrines has been consistent since the first draft of the 1993 Military Doctrine.[24] In 1997 a Concept of National Security was published, as well as an updated Foreign Policy Concept.[25] Although the Military Doctrine in the initial year took a more hard-line approach to Russian national security, focusing on external military threats more than the other documents did, by the year 2000 the anti-Western view had become persistent in the political debate.[26] Throughout the 2010s, the anti-Western attitude in the doctrinal documents hardened considerably, to the point of pronounced hostility.

In the terminology of the Military Doctrine, a distinction is made between "military dangers" (*voennye opasnosti*) and "military threats" (*voennye ugrozy*), where the first can develop into the latter. In the NSS, the word "threat" (*ugroza*) is used.

One, if not the main, persistent threat is "NATO eastward expansion," which the National Security Concept had already deemed "unacceptable" in 1997.[27] In 2000 the Military Doctrine talks about the threat from "the expansion of military blocks and allies at the expense of Russia's military security."[28] Although NATO is not mentioned explicitly, it is obviously NATO that is meant. The 2010 Military Doctrine mentioned NATO explicitly and described its security plans as extending "military infrastructure at the borders of Russia."[29]

Another persistent threat discussed in Russian policy documents is the "unipolar world," based on domination by developed Western countries under the leadership of the United States. A military threat referred to in the National Security Concept 2000—that is, after NATO's intervention in Kosovo and in President Putin's first security framework document—is described as "NATO's transition to the practice of using military force outside its zone of responsibility and without UN Security Council sanction."[30] Russia has since emphasized the need to work toward a multipolar world. The multipolar world, first promoted by the then foreign minister Evgenii Primakov in the mid-1990s, is a world dominated by the interaction between different poles, where no single power should be allowed to threaten the status quo and act unilaterally without risking reciprocal action. However, after Kosovo, Russia took advantage of the "Kosovo precedent" to intervene both in Georgia in 2008 and in Crimea in 2014.[31] The military elites saw Kosovo as a template for NATO's future operations.[32]

The lessons from Chechnya and Kosovo were learned early on, as Arbatov noted:

> The main lesson learned is that the goal justifies the means. The use of force is the most efficient problem-solver, if applied decisively and massively. Negotiations are of dubious value and are to be used as a cover for military action. Legality of state actions, observation of laws and legal procedures, and humanitarian suffering are of secondary significance relative to achieving the goal. Limiting one's own troop casualties is worth imposing massive devastation and collateral fatalities on civilian populations. Foreign public opinion and the position of Western governments are to be discounted if Russian interests are at stake. A concentrated and controlled mass media campaign is the key to success.[33]

This was written in 2000 and, in the view of the current war in Ukraine, seems uncannily prescient. The "unipolar world of the United States" has been frequently criticized by Russia since then, including by the chief of the

General Staff, Valerii Gerasimov, at a meeting with the Academy of Military Sciences in 2018.[34]

In addition, the documents convey a sense of grievance at being ignored in international affairs. The 2000 National Security Concept states that "efforts to ignore the interests of Russia in solving major international problems could break international security and stability."[35] The Military Doctrine of 2000 noted that one military threat is "the effort to ignore (infringe) Russian national interests in solving international security problems."[36]

The threats in the documents published in 2000 were formulated against a background of fundamental disagreements between the United States and Russia on several issues, such as missile defense, the policies toward the Balkans and Iraq, and the unipolar world. But, as shown above, traces of these threats were consistent throughout the 1990s. It is worth noticing that Andrei Kokoshin, one of Russia's most prominent strategic thinkers and not famous for holding a hawkish standpoint, had already pointed, in 1997, to the view that NATO expansion was seen as a threat to Russian civilization.[37] Furthermore, the inability to prevent NATO's military intervention in Yugoslavia in March 1999 raised serious concerns in Moscow over Russia's international status and ability to avert potential intrusions in neighboring countries.[38]

The information sphere had grown in importance throughout the 1990s.[39] In addition to the impact of the Chechen and Balkan Wars, the Russian military theorists were starting to rediscover the writings of Snesarev and Svechin, especially their views on total war. The Military Doctrine of 2000 put a distinct emphasis on the informational aspect, listing it for the first time as one of the main threats to Russian military security.[40] The document's phrase to describe this was that the threat was "hostile information (information-technical, information-psychological) operations that damage the military security of the Russian Federation and its allies."

This threat perception also includes an awareness of a technological gap, where Russia is lagging behind the West. To rectify this, two major armament programs have been launched since 2011.[41] However, the current threat perception not only reflects concern for potential threats posed by a technologically superior enemy but also sees a direct threat to the protection of the mainland areas of Russia and the second-strike capability of the nuclear forces. In other words, these constitute an existential threat.

The current Military Doctrine describes the US Prompt Global Strike concept as a military danger. This concept was launched in 2003 when the US Department of Defense specifically identified a new mission that seeks to provide the US with the ability to strike targets anywhere on Earth with conventional weapons in as little as an hour, without relying on forward-based forces.[42]

The potential militarization of space is seen as a direct threat to the protection of the mainland areas of Russia.[43]

The internal threat assessment in both the NSS and the Military Doctrine (2014) can be summarized as consisting of these main focus points: violations of the unity and territorial integrity of the Russian Federation, attempts to change the constitutional structure of the Russian Federation by force, economic instability as a result of the financial crisis and the changing energy market, foreign intelligence services, foreign organizations, terrorism, extremism, and finally color revolutions, the latter orchestrated by the West, which also makes them threats of an external nature.

Consequently, it is important to remember that the view of the West as a threat to Russia was formulated long before the current talk about the threat of color revolutions became prominent in Russia's threat assessment. In fact, the more assertive security policy, with its great-power ambitions, was declared in the mid-1990s.[44]

## MILITARY THINKING ON CURRENT AND FUTURE WAR

The development of the threat perception is closely intertwined with the military thinking on current and future war.[45] This debate and the development of doctrines do not occur in a vacuum. Therefore, it is important to analyze the Russian view of current and future war at the strategic level, in the doctrines, and in the debate on military theory.

Regarding much of the debate in the West, there has been some confusion regarding Russian military thinking after 2014. The Western reaction has to a large degree been characterized by a lack of insight into the developments in Russian military thinking in recent years. In the West, the label "hybrid war" quickly came to be used for Russia's behavior in Ukraine, as if its actions were a new kind of warfare.[46] There have been endless writings about a "Gerasimov Doctrine," even though there is no such thing.[47] In fact, a closer study of Russian military doctrinal thinking shows that at this point (2014), there was no developed doctrinal thinking on "hybrid war."[48] When Russian military theorists write about hybrid war, it is mentioned as a Western capability.[49]

What seemed to surprise many Western observers was Russia's ability to combine military and nonmilitary means—for example, special troops, information operations, and deception as well as diplomatic, economic, and political means. The Russian terms for this are *nelineinaia voina* (nonlinear warfare) and *asimmetrichnaia voina* (asymmetrical warfare). The fixation on "hybrid" elements tended to obscure the fact that the annexation of Crimea and the military aggression in Donbas included substantial elements of conventional warfare.[50]

For the past thirty years, Russian military thinking has been influenced largely by (1) technological development and (2) the political, economic, and social changes in Russia and the outside world. The debate on military theory has reflected a number of fundamental changes: the dissolution of the Soviet Union, the reduction in Russia's territory (particularly in the western areas), and globalization. The search for a national identity, in later years becoming a policy of patriotism, has its equivalent in the debate on and search for a new Russian military strategy. International developments have also affected Russian military thinking, which is expressed in a constant discussion on the impact of the West's initial operations in the Gulf War (1990–91), Serbia (1999), Afghanistan (2001), Iraq (2003), and Libya (2011). Russia's own experiences from the wars in Georgia in 2008 and Ukraine and Syria in recent years are persistently discussed. Interestingly, Gerasimov stated that the Russian intervention in Syria in 2015 was preceded by a close study of the Soviet experience in Cuba in 1962.[51]

There is a distinction to be made between "doctrine" and "military thinking." The doctrine establishes the official position, whereas the debate between thinkers on military strategy is sometimes fierce. However, some theories from this debate may find their way into the doctrines. It can be assumed that open debate does not present the entire picture, but that it at least reflects some of the most urgent current issues.

In the mid-nineteenth century, the issues in focus were (1) the appearance of conscript armies and trained reserves, (2) the growing importance of officer education and the rise of general staffs, and (3) technological development, including the military application of the steam railway, the electromagnetic telegraph, and the rifling of muskets and cannons.[52] Nowadays, the debate revolves around questions such as (1) the relations between military and nonmilitary means, (2) the importance of nonnuclear deterrence in relation to nuclear deterrence, and (3) the role of "soft power" in contemporary warfare. Russian military thinkers have turned to basic questions of military thought, such as What is war? When and how does it start?

According to Russia's 2014 Military Doctrine, the Russian Armed Forces are prepared for four kinds of military conflicts.[53] A military conflict is described as a type of solution for interstate or intrastate tensions through the use of military force. A military conflict encompasses all kinds of armed confrontation, including large-scale, regional, and local war and armed conflicts.

An armed conflict, according to the document, is an armed clash of limited scale between states (international armed conflict) or opposing sides within the territory of a single state (internal armed conflict). It lists three different kinds of war: local, regional, and large-scale (*krupnomasshtabnaia voina*). A local war is said to have limited military-political objectives and involve mainly the states that are opposing each other. A regional war involves several states in a region and is conducted with national armed forces or with a coalition of armed forces. Each party is striving for important military-political objectives. A large-scale war is one between coalitions of states or between the great powers of the world. It could be a result of an escalating armed conflict or a local or regional war. A large-scale war requires mobilization of the country's total material and moral or spiritual resources; in other words, it would mean a total war.[54]

According to the Russian view, contemporary military conflicts are unpredictable and the time to prepare for military action has diminished.[55] The reason for this development is the increased role of nonmilitary means in military conflicts. Contemporary military conflicts are characterized as the "integrated use of military force, and by political, economic, informational or other means of a nonmilitary character through a wide use of the population's protest potential or of special operations troops." The Military Doctrine points to the use of various means of weaponry, such as hypersonic weapons, electronic warfare, UAVs, etc. In addition, the document mentions the use of "irregular armed forces and private military companies" in military operations, as well as "indirect and asymmetrical methods." As these methods are part of the Military Doctrine, it hardly needs mentioning that Russia can apply them in its military operations.

In general, the Russian debate on military strategy has been and is much richer than many outside observers realized. Throughout the 1990s and 2000s, the debates, with their various standpoints, were lively. Indeed, they were so much so that Kokoshin felt he needed to warn of false prophets: "There is always a danger in implementing pseudoscientific conclusions and recommendations. [These people] as a rule have a remarkable energy, power of persuasion, and an unshakeable faith . . . in unconditional success. The military sphere (including the military industry) has no fewer of these people than other spheres of the society, which [I] repeatedly experienced during my work as first deputy minister of defense and later secretary of Russia's Security Council."[56]

Makhmut Gareev developed his thoughts on future war in his 1995 book *Esli zavtra voina?* (If war comes tomorrow?). Gareev was one of the most influential military theorists in the Russian Federation, having served in the Soviet Armed Forces since World War II. On the General Staff, he was responsible for the development of military science. He also served as an adviser in Afghanistan from 1980 to 1981 and later was president of the Russian Academy of Military Sciences. His book is of particular interest because Gareev had retired in 1992 and could write at a time when censorship had been abolished and relations with the West had not yet deteriorated.

He subscribed to the notion, already familiar to the reader, that war and conflict are a part of the human condition, thereby leaving the official Soviet view behind that war and conflict were social phenomena. Wars could be fought with various means, economic, political, and psychological and with the decisive importance of armed struggle (*borba*).[57]

In a brief historic overview of old and new sources of military threats, he noted that Russia, as a state, would hardly have survived over the centuries if it had not been for its use of military force.[58] He thereby linked Russia's existence as a state to the armed forces and the use of force.

He thought that one of the main sources of conflict in the future would be the struggle for raw materials and survival on the planet. In this struggle, Gareev identified the United States, since it was the leading world power, as Russia's competitor. He even alleged that the US had secret military plans for war with Russia that would send much of Russia's territory back to the Middle Ages and set up the rest of it for use as a raw material resource for the West.[59] It is noteworthy that Gareev wrote this during the "honeymoon period" between post-communist Russia and the West. These thoughts would be exploited later by the political leadership under Putin.

However, Gareev forcefully rebutted any talk of Russia's joining NATO. It would be totally inadvisable, he thought, not least for the reason that Russia as a member of NATO would have to put its armed forces under NATO command; in practice, he asserted, Russian troops would be subordinate to American generals.[60] Furthermore, Russia in NATO would lead to a weakening of NATO, and Russia in NATO would be seen as a provocation against China and other countries in Asia. Consequently, the prospects of Russia's joining NATO were never taken seriously by the military or the political elite, regardless of the current discussions on broken promises.[61] The negative view of NATO persisted, and enlargement was persistently seen as a threat to Russian national security.

Precise and realistic military-political war objectives needed to be established at the strategic level; enough resources had to be allocated. These issues were within the realm of policy, according to Gareev. On the other hand, decisions about the means to achieve the objectives and the organization of operative command should be the independent responsibility of the military. The democratic states were better at organizing strategic planning than the totalitarian ones.[62] He argued for a clear division of labor in strategic planning between civilians and the military and criticized the "hybrid" practice of the Soviet Union, when Kliment Voroshilov, Nikolai Aleksandrovich Bulganin (1895–1975), and Dmitrii Ustinov, all civilians, had been appointed as ministers of defense. Gareev was very critical of Stalin's and Hitler's "meddling" in the course of World War II once it had broken out. From his personal experience of Afghanistan from 1979 to 1988, he noted that all plans, "even for comparably small fighting actions," were drawn up in Moscow, thus implying that the military's hands were tied and that, had they not been, the war might have had another outcome.

The most pressing issue for future wars was to create weapon systems that were not designed to physically destroy individual weapons but to eliminate the enemy's entire information sphere.[63] It would take almost twenty years before the political leadership fully embraced the importance of information warfare, whereas the military had been aware of this aspect since Svechin's and Snesarev's times.

Regarding the study of future war and how to conduct it, a heated debate arose in the early 2010s between two veterans of World War II. Gareev, in one corner, claimed that the study of future war must always be based on historic experiences. He ran into opposition from Stepan Tiushkevich, a professor of military history who highlighted the "crisis of military thought." (Of course, this was not a debate exclusive to Russia: Martin van Creveld has also recently written on the subject.)[64] Gareev criticized Tiushkevich for wanting to create a "megatheory" for war sciences, which he argued strongly against. He claimed that war science is "the theory of the art of war including military history" and nothing more. Tiushkevich meant that the "foundations of war sciences" should be an independent scientific discipline.[65] The debate remained unresolved, as would be expected. Meanwhile, the new chief of the General Staff, Valerii Gerasimov, began to outline his views on future war.

## FUTURE WARFARE AND MILITARY HISTORY

The future battlefield might soon be characterized by robots and automated systems, according to General Gerasimov. "With what formations and means can we fight a robotized enemy?" he asked in 2013.[66]

This thinking represents the school that for decades claimed that future wars will be "contactless," waged over huge distances, with the help of superior technology. One well-known theorist in this area was Maj. Gen. Vladimir Ivanovich Slipchenko (1935–2005), who developed his thoughts on so-called sixth-generation warfare in the 1990s and early 2000s.[67] Slipchenko was, and still is, widely read in the West as providing a blueprint for Russia's way of waging war, although the Russian debate on "new-generation warfare" has been practically nonexistent since 2013. So, after the publication of a much-read article by Sergei Chekinov and Sergei Bogdanov in which they claim that the 1990–91 Gulf War was the first "new-generation war in the history of humanity," the open discussions on this topic in Russia have been largely absent.[68]

Slipchenko championed the idea that the size and role of ground forces would diminish, if not disappear altogether, on the future battlefield.[69] Precision weapons and intelligence capabilities would be decisive. He predicted that the armed forces of the future would no longer consist of ground, naval, and air forces but rather would be made up of intelligence resources for strategic warning, strategic nonnuclear precision resources and their bearers, automated command-and-control systems, air and space resources (antimissile systems and antisatellite weapons), and, finally, the forces and means for technical supplies.

This line of thinking was heavily criticized by Gareev. In a 2005 article he deemed useless the "new modern theories about the sixth-generation warfare, buzzwords like system-network wars, asymmetrical warfare, distance warfare, and one without immediate contact on a battlefield."[70] He particularly warned against Slipchenko's thoughts on the presumed reduction of the role of tanks on the future battlefield and noted that it was dangerous to focus only on one type of weapon and ignore the rest. Gareev attacked Slipchenko explicitly, as well as other experts, on their so-called generational warfare ideas since, according to him, they had never fought in a war and their theories "had nothing to say about future war." Given these circumstances, it is therefore unlikely that a book with both their names on it published in 2005 could in fact have been a joint effort.[71] Jacob Kipp also noted in the translated version that there were several curiosities surrounding the book's publication. For instance, no editor was listed for the book, and there was an incomplete (and anonymous) introduction to Gareev's lecture, which seemed to reframe his basic argument.

In Russia, Gareev was not alone in his skepticism. In the major works of the influential theorist Andrei Kokoshin, Slipchenko is not mentioned at all, indicating that his influence was not as great as is sometimes believed.[72] Clearly, there were different schools of Russian military thought. One was focusing on the significance of military technology for the development of future war, the other on the totality of the many means to be used in a future war, not least the ground forces and the role of tanks, in addition to political, economic, and diplomatic means and information.

However, as discussed above, the insight into the important role that high-technology conventional capacities would have on the future battlefield, the "contactless battlefield," was not new. It was built on Ogarkov's thought and was promoted by both Slipchenko and Kokoshin and, later, the chief of the General Staff, Gerasimov.[73] The concept was later called "new-type warfare."[74] As shown below, Gerasimov introduced the "strategy of active defense" and the "strategy of limited actions" in 2019.[75]

## MILITARY REFORM AND STRATEGIC PLANNING

In the 1990s and early 2000s, the efforts to reform the military largely failed. The reasons for this are complex, and the causes of these failures lie beyond the scope of this book. However, at the time, Russian analysts partly blamed the military establishment for dragging their feet.[76] More seriously, it seemed the political and military leadership in those years did not have a comprehensive idea of reform and hence lacked any sense of direction. In his memoirs, Nikolai Makarov, later to become chief of the General Staff, was deeply critical of the military-political leaders during the last years of the Soviet Union and the beginning of the Russian Federation. According to him, they had lost a golden opportunity to at least start a military reform that was urgently needed. When reform got underway in the 1990s, the only thing that was done was to cut the number of personnel, without a cohesive idea to guide the decision. The then chief of the General Staff proclaimed that "our task is to survive." Makarov is still baffled: "To this day I cannot understand it.... An army [*armiia*] is a military organism whose task is not to survive but to be engaged in structured combat training." Interestingly, he did not blame the West for the lack of reform. On the contrary, Makarov stated that the Russian Federation could have afforded a comprehensive military reform, and the West had provided additional funds for it, but the Russian military leadership did not understand what was needed.[77]

The real wake-up call for reform came in 2008. Russia managed to take the territories of South Ossetia and Abkhazia from Georgia, but the performance of its Armed Forces was not at all impressive. In the early days of the eventual reform, the usual wording "military reform" had become so discredited in Russia that the new minister of defense, Anatolii Eduardovich Serdiukov (1962–), emphasized that it was not actually a military reform but rather an effort to bring order to the Armed Forces.[78]

In reality, it was the most fundamental reform of the Russian Armed Forces since the creation of the Red Army. The Russo-Georgian War provided the reformers with arguments for not postponing it any longer. At the heart of the reform of what was to become the "new look" (*novyi oblik*) Armed Forces was the transformation from a conventional mobilization army to a permanently combat-ready force.[79] During Makarov's tenure, the Russian Armed Forces not only began to adapt to contemporary realities, but also the financing of the reform was secured when the State Armament Program 2011 was approved. The political support for the reform was wholehearted.

Makarov, who was clearly proceeding from a consistent, premeditated idea, provided a list of nine steps for military reform. (This was, incidentally, a list that could be used in any reorganization, not only within the defense sector and not only in Russia.) It was comprehensive and had far-reaching requirements:

- a conceptual view of the problems to be solved;
- creation of a group of like-minded colleagues;
- formulation of a clear vision of the end result;
- detailed planning, calculations, and reasoning;
- control of all the steps and their connections;

- ability to act quickly in case of disagreements and conflicts;
- strong but just demands;
- decisiveness, courage, and boldness in performance;
- information support.[80]

The main features of the military reform were substantial changes in the system of command and control, the structure of forces, the military educational system, and the launching of a significant rearmament program. The number of personnel, including the number of officers, was reduced, as was the number of military districts. Joint strategic commands were created, and a brigade structure was formed.[81] The concept of mass mobilization was abandoned.

One of the traditional problems of a vastly inflated officer corps was also addressed. It would not be impossible to think that Alexander II's war minister, Dmitrii Miliutin (see chapter 2), would have been amused by Serdiukov's solution. When Serdiukov started, in 2008, the Russian officer corps consisted of 355,000 officers in the Armed Forces of, at least on paper, 1.1 million; in other words, one officer for roughly every three servicepeople.[82] Many positions, such as medical doctors, journalists, and jurists were replaced by civilians. At the level of Ministry of Defense and the General Staff, the officer corps was to be reduced from twenty-two thousand officers to eight thousand. Divisional and brigade commanders were put to a physical test, one of the key criteria for promotion, and as a result, up to 10 percent failed.[83]

Military science, meanwhile, was not spared from criticism. Makarov was merciless. "Military science is cut off from war," and "Russian military theorists have overslept the revolution in military affairs."[84] This did not mean that everything in Russian military science was bad, but it was a wake-up call from a reformer that things could not continue as before. Of particular concern was the relationship between military theory and practice and the need for them to come closer. "I have always been worried by the question of why, in military affairs, there is such a rift between the theoretical thoughts on future wars and the practical training of the forces," he wrote.[85]

Makarov promoted the subject of military thought within the General Staff. Partly in recognition of this problem, a Military Scientific Council was created, led by Andrei Kokoshin, in 2011. Its task was to give advice on issues of military technology issues and defense policy.[86]

Substantial efforts were also made in the realm of strategic planning. Eventually a law on strategic planning was passed, in 2014. Behind much of these efforts was the thought of Andrei Kokoshin. From his point of view, Russia had suffered a heavy defeat in the Cold War and now needed a "sober and clear assessment" of Russian strategic planning.[87] His writings divulge valuable insights into Russian thinking on military strategy, and although one of his books is titled

*Strategicheskoe upravlenie* (Strategic control), it could well have been called *Voennaia strategiia* (Military strategy).

Kokoshin listed the most important types of strategic planning. First, it was necessary to prioritize and characterize the threats to national security from a military point of view: determine who is the likely or unlikely enemy and ward off these threats in collaboration with potential partners or allies, either through the use of strategic deterrence or by securing the conditions to inflict various degrees of military defeat.[88] *Strategicheskoe sderzhivanie* (Strategic deterrence) is the official Russian term for the host of coercion activities in various operational domains.[89] In addition, in the event of total or limited war, he emphasized the necessity of deciding not only who is commander in chief but also of clarifying the relationship between the commander in chief and the General Staff and whether a *stavka* should be established or not. The stavka was a wartime Supreme Command during World War I and World War II. Furthermore, he also stressed the importance of actualizing decisions: "To implement a decision is primarily based on control over its realization." Traditionally, he remarked, one of the weakest aspects of Russian (and Soviet) strategic culture was command and control.[90]

Finally, for Kokoshin, a key issue in strategic planning was that the political leadership should be in charge of the basic combat regulations and instructions relating to certain types of armed forces and troops as well as of the main strategic actions, preparations, and conduct (*provedenie*) of the operations. These issues, he concluded, are far too important to be left with the General Staff alone and are closely connected to the implementation of the decisions made at the level of high (grand) strategy and military strategy. In other words, Kokoshin was pointing to the crucial issue of Russia's finding a balance between its declared goals and its resources, between lessons from history and the need to adapt to future demands, and between domestic and foreign threats.

The most important strategic decision, Kokoshin emphasized, was the assessment of oneself and of the most likely enemy. To assess oneself, to know one's strong and weak sides at all levels, was no less difficult than assessing the enemy. Here, it was not about the number of forces and equipment or about the number of battle-ready units at one's disposal but instead about how the political leaders needed a clear-headed understanding of what their own armed forces could and could not do: "A sober assessment of one's own possibilities has to be an important restraint in setting achievable political objectives of the war."[91]

It is doubtful, to say the least, whether the Russian political leadership had such a clear assessment of the Russian military's strengths and weaknesses, let alone allowed it to be a limitation in setting the goals, when the decision was made to go forward with a full-scale war with Ukraine on February 24, 2022.

## NUCLEAR AND NONNUCLEAR DETERRENCE: DOCTRINES AND DEBATES

Strategic deterrence, with an emphasis on nuclear deterrence, is still a pillar of Russian security policy. In the beginning of the 1990s, there was already an increasing reliance, both among the military and political elites, on nuclear forces. The Military Doctrine of 1993 had dropped the "no-first-use" principle, so that deterrence, according to Defense Minister Grachev, would be based on "a measure of uncertainty about a nuclear response to an aggression."[92] Baev pointed out that the no-first-use concept was "hypocrisy" and was never taken seriously. As discussed above, some military thinkers and political leaders did subscribe to it, not least Ogarkov and Gorbachev, but it seems safe to say that it did not take hold in the entire General Staff and Politburo.

The role of nuclear weapons in Russian security policy has traditionally been defined in the Military Doctrine, the NSS, and key presidential speeches. The Military Doctrine of 2014 states in paragraph 27 that "the Russian Federation reserves the right to utilize nuclear weapons in response to the utilization of nuclear and other types of weapons of mass destruction against it and (or) its allies, and also in the event of aggression against the Russian Federation involving the use of conventional weapons when the very existence of the state is under threat. The decision to utilize nuclear weapons is made by the president of the Russian Federation." According to the NSS, "strategic deterrence and the prevention of military conflicts are achieved by upholding nuclear deterrence at a sufficiently high level."[93] Consequently, at the doctrinal level, there was no public change in the Russian nuclear position since 2000, when the provision to use nuclear weapons in response to an attack against Russia or its allies with conventional weapons was adopted.

Interestingly, a previously secret document, "Basic Principles of the State Policy of the Russian Federation in the Domain of Nuclear Deterrence," was published for the first time on June 2, 2020.[94] Although the existence of this document was known, it had always been classified. The Soviet principle, from the mid-1980s, of not being the first to use nuclear weapons had already been abandoned in 1993. Nor has the document's publication replaced either the NSS or the Military Doctrine from 2014, even if it does reveal more details about Russia's potential use of nuclear weapons.

It specifies the conditions when Russia might use nuclear weapons:

a) upon receipt of reliable data on a launch of ballistic missiles attacking the territory of the Russian Federation and/or its allies;
b) an adversary uses nuclear weapons or other types of weapons of mass destruction against the Russian Federation and/or its allies;

c) an adversary attacks critical governmental or military sites of the Russian Federation, disruption of which would undermine nuclear forces' response actions;
d) in the event of aggression against the Russian Federation with the use of conventional weapons, when the very existence of the state is in jeopardy.[95]

It should be noted that "the very existence of the state" is a very flexible expression and that its meaning could be adapted by the political leadership depending on the situation. Moreover, point "c" is a clarification of what was already known. It means, for instance, that a cyberattack against the Russian political or military leadership that affects the country's ability to respond could result in the use of nuclear weapons.

Point "a," in essence a case of launch on warning, mentions only ballistic missiles and not cruise missiles. One probable explanation is that only ballistic missiles that are intercontinental are implied. These can be detected at a distance, using satellites and radars that are part of the strategic warning system. Also, it is more important to discover the strategic missiles because their intended goals are precisely strategic. Therefore, Russia reserves the right to respond with its own nuclear weapons even before threatening intercontinental missiles are able to reach their targets. This means that Russia also reserves the right to use nuclear weapons in response to attacks by intercontinental missiles that are conventionally armed. This stipulation is directed against the American concept of Prompt Global Strike. According to that concept, the United States aims to be equipped with the ability to strike targets worldwide using conventional weapons in as little as an hour. Any dependence on forward-based strengths is not to be tolerated.[96]

Moreover, the document "Basic Principles" also clearly states that the opponent should not know or be able to calculate when and where Russia intends to use nuclear weapons. Section 15 (d) notes that one of the principles of nuclear deterrence is "the unpredictability of a potential adversary to determine the scope, time, and place of any deployment of forces and means of nuclear deterrence"; in other words, the opponent should always hover in ignorance. This is not new nor particularly Russian, but it is worth noting that it is stated so clearly.

Russia's nuclear weapons will, in the future, be a central part of the military instrument of power, both for strategic deterrence and the defense of Russia, as well as its coercive power. The unpredictability of information about scope, time, and place is confirmed in the document, thus underlining an important, yet not new, conclusion: there will be no clear warning in advance of a nuclear attack. This is something Russia's neighbors will have to take into account.

It also deserves noting that in July 2017 the Russian president signed a document, "Foundations for Russia's Naval Activity for the Period up to 2030," that serves as a form of long-term naval strategy. This document states that if an armed conflict escalates, "a demonstration of preparedness and readiness to use nonstrategic nuclear weapons would be a strong deterrent factor."[97] In the previous version of this document, from 2012, "Foundations for Russia's Naval Activity for the Period up to 2020," the "escalate to de-escalate" concept was mentioned. This earlier version envisaged "a limited use of weapons, including precision weapons, in order to de-escalate sources of tension and resolve the conflict situation on conditions favorable to Russia."[98] Nuclear weapons are not specifically mentioned in either document but both allow for the use of a preventive strike in order to de-escalate a conflict.

In addition, neither the Nuclear Deterrence Policy nor the Military Doctrine mention anything about the preventive use of nuclear weapons to de-escalate a conflict. Suffice it to say that nuclear weapons play a significant role in Russia's strategic deterrence and can be expected to continue to do so. Nonstrategic nuclear weapons will also continue to be an important part of Russia's deterrence, along with new, long-range conventional weapon systems.

The publication of the Nuclear Deterrence Policy was preceded by both an increase in official nuclear rhetoric from the Russian political leadership from 2014 onward and an intense debate among Russian military thinkers regarding the use of nuclear weapons to de-escalate a conflict. The debate had initially started in 1999, with the publication of an article in *Voennaia mysl* titled "O primenenii iadernogo oruzhiia dlia deeskalatsii voennykh deistvii" (On the use of nuclear weapons for the de-escalation of combat).[99] But it was only in the 2010s that the debate became heated.

Konstantin Valentinovich Sivkov (1954–), at the time a known hard-liner at the Academy for Geopolitical Problems, argued in March 2014 (before the revision of the Military Doctrine had been completed) that a preventive strike with nonstrategic nuclear weapons against an enemy would not only be possible but also right.[100] He and others argued for a change in the official doctrine that would explicitly regulate Russia's possible use of a preventive nuclear strike.

It would be too easy to write off this line of thought as something coming from individual self-proclaimed experts or to trivialize it by claiming that it is the task of every military staff to make plans for any conceivable event. The West should take this debate seriously, however.

The advocates of a preemptive nuclear strike are challenging another school of thought that has been emphasizing the importance of a nonnuclear strategic deterrence for Russia. The concept of "nonnuclear deterrence" has become more important in Russian military thinking. Introduced in the Military Doctrine of

2014, the term was defined as a "complex of foreign policy, military, and military-technical measures aimed at countering aggression against the Russian Federation with nonnuclear means."[101] High-precision weapons are a major priority in the modernization of the deterrence factor in the Russian military.[102]

This concept relies on much of Ogarkov's thoughts, followed up by Kokoshin and Gareev. It stems from a perceived necessity to look beyond nuclear weapons to deter a future enemy and to develop other modern, high-precision conventional weapon systems. Kokoshin, in Ogarkov's footsteps, argued for years on the need for this concept. "Excessive confidence in nuclear deterrence in national security policy is detrimental and even dangerous for Russia," he wrote.[103] Nonnuclear deterrence, according to Kokoshin, involves high-precision long-range conventional weapons, weapons based upon new physical principles, and highly advanced information and communication systems. Possessing such capabilities would be an important "means of preventing escalation dominance by an adversary during an acute political and military crisis."[104]

Gareev, in the mid-1990s, did not see any alternative to nuclear deterrence, but he underlined the growing importance of its nonnuclear alternative.[105] In 2018 Gerasimov declared that future deterrence must mainly rely on the nonnuclear sphere, exemplified by high-precision and hypersonic weapons.[106] He also emphasized the need to develop additional electronic warfare capabilities, unmanned aerial complexes, and systems for command and control.

To summarize, the concept of nonnuclear deterrence advocates using nonnuclear weapons to deter any aggression, nuclear or otherwise. In line with Ogarkov's thought in the 1970s, it is an attempt to shift the posture away from nuclear weapons. However, as can be seen below, no unity on the issue of nonnuclear deterrence has yet to be discerned among the Russian military elites.

## "THE BLITZKRIEG OF THE TWENTY-FIRST CENTURY"

Another topic worth exploring is the debate in recent years on "the blitzkrieg of the twenty-first century." Apart from its historical origins, more recently the notion of blitzkrieg is particularly tied to the studies of the Gulf War and the initial operations of the Iraq War of 2003. This war and the example of Kosovo have both had a profound impact on Russian military thought.

Just how great the impact of the Iraq War has been on Russian military thought becomes evident in an essay, "The Blitzkrieg of the Twenty-First Century," from a thorough study *Voina budushchego* (The war of the future), in which Igor Popov and Musa Khamzatov analyze the operations in Iraq.[107] Was the engagement the last of conventional wars, or was it really a new type of war?

They do not answer categorically but claim that the impact of this war is fundamental when thinking about the future. They argue that the result was chaos and the creation of the Islamic State of Iraq and Syria and conclude that after the Cold War, "the real processes of fragmenting states" might imply that "the world is entering an epoch of long and slow-moving military conflicts in the interests of a few geopolitical forces and global elites. The seizure of territories and material riches of states only becomes an effect of such a strategy."

In addition, it is worth noting that Gerasimov has also been thinking about the blitzkrieg. In a 2016 article on the lessons from the 2015 Russian intervention in Syria, he uses the term "twenty-first-century blitzkrieg."[108] His version of the new "blitzkrieg" focuses on the combination of "color revolutions" and Prompt Global Strike. This is hardly surprising. The official Russian view has been clear from the outset: Prompt Global Strike threatens strategic stability. According to Gerasimov, even if armed with conventional warheads, the weapons could threaten Russia's critical assets and its nuclear deterrent:

> As you know, the United States has already developed and implemented the concept of Prompt Global Strike. The US military is calculated to achieve the ability to, in a few hours, deploy troops and defeat enemy targets at any point of the globe. It envisages the introduction of a promising form of warfare—of global integrated operations. It proposes the establishment as soon as possible in any region of mixed groups of forces capable of joint action to defeat the enemy in a variety of operating environments. According to the developers, this should be a kind of blitzkrieg of the twenty-first century.[109]

He added, "In the era of globalization, the weakening of state borders and development of means of communication are the most important factors changing the form of resolution of interstate conflicts. In today's conflicts, the focus of the methods used to combat them is shifting toward the integrated application of political, economic, informational, and other nonmilitary measures, implemented with the support of the military force—the so-called hybrid methods."[110]

In a public statement by the Russian Military-Historical Society in January 2015, the concept of a blitzkrieg takes a metaphorical meaning. The statement was signed by Makhmut Gareev, Vladimir Medinskii, then minister of culture, and Dmitrii Rogozin, then deputy prime minister responsible for the defense industry, among others.[111] The signatories claimed that "a blitzkrieg has started against Russia." Their understanding of a modern blitzkrieg has a distinct ideological character, and they describe it as a "war of the minds."

## SOFT POWER, CONTROLLED CHAOS, AND COLOR REVOLUTIONS

All these concepts—soft power, controlled chaos, and color revolutions—are seen as tools in the hands of the West being used to attack Russia. In fact, the Russian interpretation of the former is quite different from the conventional view of an ability to increase a country's power of attraction.[112] The use of soft power is a factor of international politics, according to Russia's 2013 document Foreign Policy Concept.[113] The 2016 Foreign Policy Concept says of the term that "in addition to traditional methods of diplomacy, 'soft power' has become an integral part of efforts to achieve foreign policy objectives."[114] In the revised version of 2023, the anti-Western rhetoric is clearly formulated. The document mentions "unfriendly" actions by "USA and its satellites," who have launched a "new type of hybrid war" against Russia.[115]

On one hand, soft power can be used as a complement to classic diplomacy. On the other, there is a risk that soft power could be used as a tool to intrude into the domestic affairs of states, aiming "among other things to finance humanitarian projects and projects relating to human rights abroad."[116] Vladimir Putin defines it as "instruments and methods to achieve foreign policy objectives without the use of weapons—information and other levers of influence."[117] And in 2018 Aleksandr Fomin, vice minister of defense, stated that "it is clear that behind the term 'soft power' hide activities such as meddling in domestic affairs by organizing color revolutions, which in turn leads to a violation of the balance of power with catastrophic consequences for regions and the entire world."[118] This reflects a militarized view, where soft power is seen as an instrument of statecraft.

In the debate on military theory, soft power is seen as one weapon among others. Gareev linked the annexation of Crimea to soft power and strategic deterrence. It was, according to him, necessary to learn from Crimea in order to "perfect our soft power, political and diplomatic means, and informational tools and thus increase effectiveness in the system for strategic deterrence."[119] It is noteworthy that soft power, in this line of thinking, is put on the same level of importance as strategic deterrence, a level usually associated with nuclear weapons and high-precision, long-range conventional weapons.

Another term used in the Russian debate on military theory is controlled chaos (*upravliaemyi khaos*). Putin used the term in his preelection article on defense in 2012.[120] It means that Russia was under attack from the West, which by various methods, political as well as economic, was destabilizing and undermining Russia's neighbors and ultimately Russia itself. It is sometimes used in connection with a discussion of soft power. Gareev equates the two.[121] Since the Russian annexation of Crimea and the aggression in Donetsk and Luhansk, military theory journals have published several articles devoted to controlled chaos and color revolutions. Aleksandr Bartosh, a corresponding member of the General Staff Academy, traces the concept of controlled chaos to the United States and claims that it was this "technology" that led to the dissolution of the Soviet Union.[122]

It is worth noticing that thoughts on the threat of color revolutions were present in Russian thinking on military strategy long before any actual color revolutions occurred.[123] However, the idea of the threat became much more developed after the Orange Revolution in Ukraine in 2004–5.

The Military Doctrine of 2014 points to a development of the use of "political forces and civic movements financed and controlled from abroad" in contemporary conflicts.[124] The most important difference from the previous Military Doctrine is that a protesting population is seen as a part of contemporary conflicts. Political and other organizations are viewed as a part of the war and are not considered as independent actors but rather as instruments of the West for undermining Russian security. Some of this reflects the Russian political leadership's official rhetoric on Ukraine, where Russia is said to be exposed to this kind of warfare by the West.

The term "color revolution" was included in the NSS for the first time in 2015 and is described as a threat to Russia's state security.[125] This also indicates that the General Staff is paying close attention to them and that in recent years it has been thinking about developing a concept to counteract "hybrid" wars against Russia and her allies.[126] Furthermore, in 2017, the General Staff Academy introduced a new course, "Army and Society." One of its purposes, according to Defense Minister Sergei Kuzhugetovich Shoigu (1955–), is to study countermeasures against color revolutions.[127] Among the subjects studied are information warfare, information security, and cultural policy, not least on counteracting the "falsification of history."

In addition, according to the Russian Criminal Code, it has been a crime since 2014 to "rehabilitate Nazism"—for instance, "to disseminate in public deliberately false information about the activities of the USSR during the Second World War" and also to spread material "expressing disrespect for society and days of military glory and memorable dates of Russia related to the defense of the fatherland."[128]

According to Sergei Chvarkov, a professor of military science, and Aleksandr Likhonosov, an associate professor and member of the General Staff Academy, a concept to counter soft power and controlled chaos might include several different strategic approaches—for example, the introduction of a strategy to make the general public aware of foreign and domestic threats to Russia's security, the creation of separate Internet networks for the Russian mass media controlled by the executive power, and the development of a strategy to increase the influence of the four traditional religions in Russia, Christianity (especially the Russian Orthodox Church), Islam, Judaism, and Buddhism. They also called for a strategy to support the "social optimism of the population." This was to be achieved by the work of ministries and other power structures to create a "national idea, national values, and a national ideology."[129]

Many of the current writings clearly carry an underlying longing for an ideology. Maj. Gen. Aleksandr Ivanovich Vladimirov (1945–), for instance, notes that Russia needs to rally the country around its "nationally vital resources": the faith (the Russian Orthodox Church), the people (Russians, *russkii*), the state (Russia), the idea (Russian culture), and the language (Russian).[130] This echoes the past, albeit not as eloquently as the nineteenth-century motto formulated by Sergei Semenovich Uvarov (1786–1855), minister of education under Nicholas I: "Autocracy, Orthodoxy, Nationality."

The efforts to introduce an ideology in Russia continued, and in 2020 some significant changes were introduced in the amended constitution.[131] Article 67 states that Russia is the legal successor of the Soviet Union and continues: "The Russian Federation, united by the millennium history, preserving the memory of the ancestors who conveyed to us ideals and belief in God . . . The Russian Federation honours the memory of the defenders of the Fatherland, ensures protection of historical truth. Diminution of the heroic deed of the people defending the Fatherland is precluded." The state ensures that children are brought up in patriotism and to respect the elders. In other words, religion, history, and patriotism are now a part of the Russian constitution, directly contradicting the first, unamended chapters of the document, where it clearly states in Article 13 that "no ideology shall be proclaimed as State ideology or as obligatory."[132]

Furthermore, Article 79 stipulates that "Russia takes measures to preserve and strengthen international peace and security, to ensure peaceful coexistence of the states and peoples, to prevent intervention into internal affairs of a State." The nostalgic Soviet term "peaceful coexistence" was thus reintroduced, showing the political leadership's efforts to build a national identity with concepts from the past.

## PATRIOTISM AND THE ROLE OF HISTORY: TOWARD AN IDEOLOGY

In developing new military strategic doctrines and concepts, Russian history has a special role.[133] This goes to the very core of the search for a national identity and the country's self-image. An important part of the "patriotic" efforts touches on both history and the military.

The use of history as a political tool is not a new phenomenon in Russia, nor is it unique to it. But given the totalitarian trajectory of Russia's political system, the consequences of this policy are substantial. One of the distinct features of the period after 1991 was the reburials. Best-known is the reburial of the last czar's family, shot in 1918 and reinterred in Saint Petersburg in 1998. Later, the widow of Alexander III, Maria Feodorovna (1847–1928) was also reburied. Also known as Princess Dagmar of Denmark and the mother of Nicholas II, she was reburied next to her husband in the Peter and Paul Cathedral eighty-seven years after she left the country. Another prominent reburial was that of Gen. Nikolai Stepanovich Batiushin (1874–1957). He had served in the army as the head of military intelligence during World War I, fought on the White side during the Civil War, fled abroad, and eventually died in Belgium. In 2004 his remains were transferred to Moscow, where he was buried with military honors. In 2005 the remains of Anton Ivanovich Denikin (1872–1947) were brought to the cemetery at Donskoi Monastery in Moscow. Denikin was a lieutenant general in the Imperial Army and had also fought on the White side. His grave is close to that of the philosopher Ivan Aleksandrovich Ilyin (1883–1954), who had been forced to leave Russia in 1922.[134] His highly contradictory ideas and thought have gained some momentum in post-Soviet Russia. He was reburied in 2005, and that year Vladimir Putin quoted him in his annual address. In the 1990s Ilyin's thoughts on patriotism were picked up by the General Staff Academy.[135]

Russia is perceived as being under attack from a hostile West, and the Russian Armed Forces are tasked with defending Russia's historical and spiritual traditions. This view ties in nicely with the many government programs on military-patriotic education and patriotic education in general. These state-run efforts clearly target the younger generation in Russia.[136] The issue of what exactly the Russian spiritual and moral traditions consist of has been a subject of discussion in Russia, addressed not least by Putin himself. At the meeting of the state-run Valdai Discussion Club in 2013, he devoted his speech to elaborating on his thinking on Russian national identity.[137] The NSS of 2015 had already codified Russian spiritual and moral values: "Traditional Russian spiritual and moral values include the priority of the spiritual over the material, protection of human life and of human rights and freedoms, the family, creative labor, service to the homeland, the norms of morals and morality, humanism, charity, fairness, mutual assistance, collectivism, the historical unity of the peoples of Russia, and the continuity of our motherland's history."[138] These were repeated and elaborated on in an entire section in the NSS of 2021.[139] Furthermore, as is shown below, Putin had an article published in July 2021 that claimed that Ukraine did not have the right to exist as an independent country.[140]

The so-called Westernization of culture is seen as a threat to Russian sovereignty. Traditional Russian spiritual, moral, and cultural-historical values are, allegedly, under active attack by the United States and its allies, as well as by transnational corporations, foreign nonprofit nongovernmental organizations, and religious, extremist, and terrorist organizations.[141]

So, what are these values that are under attack? Several things are said to be characteristic, among them patriotism, service to the fatherland and responsibility for its fate, priority of the spiritual over the material, collectivism, historical memory and the continuity of generations, and the unity of the peoples of Russia.[142] This line of thinking was developed further in a presidential decree on November 9, 2022, listing "traditional Russian spiritual and moral values."[143] The most important of these traditional Russian values, according to the new decree, are life, dignity, serving the fatherland and taking responsibility for its destiny, prioritizing the spiritual before the material, collectivism, the historic memory, and the unity of the peoples in Russia.[144]

At the same time, "destructive ideology" is defined. This allegedly comprises the values of the West. It is said to promote violence, egotism, permissiveness, immorality, and nonpatriotism and therefore constitutes "an objective threat to Russia's national interests." It is described as "alien to the Russian people."[145] Consequently, combined with the changes in history textbooks, military-political and patriotic education is an effort to create an ideology, in the absence of Marxism-Leninism, that is at the same time in direct contradiction to the constitution.

The Russian Orthodox Church has a role here, especially as primus inter pares in the efforts to build an ideology in today's Russia.[146] The concept of the *Russkii mir* (Russian world), traditionally a Russian Orthodox idea, has now become state policy.[147] According to this concept, "Holy Rus" stretches far beyond the borders of the Russian Federation and includes the entire Russian Orthodox world. It stands for the traditional Russian spiritual values that Patriarch Kirill has been lobbying for.[148] The role given to the Orthodox Church in the efforts to build a patriotic ideology also contradicts the constitution, which stipulates in Article 14 that "the Russian Federation shall be a secular state. No religion may be established as the State religion or as obligatory."

Overall, the image emerges of a Russia that, again, has turned away from the West and at the same time defends the entirety of European civilization. It echoes the myth of Moscow as the "third Rome."[149] The greatness of the empire of the past is evoked as the preferred way forward. State control and repressions of political dissent are seen as necessities to secure the future of Russia, at the same time as the younger generations will take Russia into the future as a leading high-technology nation. This may seem paradoxical, an echo from Soviet days. This underlines an important conclusion: this development challenges not only Russia but also all its neighbors.

In addition, an important but often ignored part of Russia's strategy toward the West is the instrumentalization of history and memory. It is vital to understand the implications of this development in order to grasp Russian strategy.

The Military Doctrine, a document that describes the main objectives for the Russian Armed Forces, also includes defending Russia's history.[150]

A number of concrete steps have been taken in order to strengthen the military-patriotic traditions in Russia. The historical names "Preobrazhenskii" and "Semenovskii" have been added to modern military units, alluding to the two oldest guard regiments of the Imperial Army. The first official Russian monument for the "heroes" of World War I has been erected, and a special unit has been created within the Armed Forces to combat the "falsification of history."

This development is particularly evident in the way Victory Day, May 9, is being used to create a sense of unity. It has replaced the Soviet military parades celebrating the October Revolution. Not only has the military parade on Red Square in Moscow become larger and larger, but now civilians are also marching to remember their loved ones. This practice, introduced on Victory Day 2015, was a part of a concept called the "Immortal Regiment." This was initially a local initiative that was taken over by the government and turned into a national celebration.

Russia is trying to come to terms with its czarist and Soviet past. The imperial-era Cadet Corps has been reintroduced, and the Suvorov schools for military training and the Cossack movement are being supported. The legacy of the Soviet military organization DOSAAF (Volunteer Society for Cooperation with the Army, Aviation, and Fleet) is cherished. After briefly changing its name, DOSAAF reinstated its Soviet name in 2003.[151]

The number of military-patriotic organizations is constantly growing. In May 2016 the Iunarmiia (Youth Army) was created by the Ministry of Defense. Furthermore, since 2015 the Ministry of Defense has been organizing Olympics-style military competitions that include quizzes on military history. In 2017, the centenary of the February and October Revolutions, Putin inaugurated a monument to Alexander III in Yalta adorned with words alleged to be those of Alexander III: "Russia has only two allies: its army and its fleet." In April 2023, when Putin visited the illegally annexed Ukrainian city of Kherson, he donated an icon that belonged to Alexander III's minister of war, Petr Vannovskii (1822–1904). Putin described him as "one of the most successful ministers of war in Imperial Russia."[152] Compulsory military training is being introduced into the schools, in a return to Soviet practice.[153]

## GERASIMOV AND MILITARY STRATEGY

The nonmilitary means used by the West were seen as effective in achieving political and strategic objectives. Gerasimov, the longest serving chief of the General Staff since Nikolai Obruchev (who served for sixteen years), has noted that the rules of war have changed dramatically and that nonmilitary means are four times more frequent than military means.[154] In his view, the lessons from Africa and the Middle East have demonstrated that "fully functional states can be transformed in a short period of time into an area of an embittered, armed conflict, become the victim of foreign intervention, and end up as a chaotic swamp of humanitarian catastrophe and civil war." This line of thinking obviously concerns acts against an incumbent regime—for example, in Iraq and Libya. Russia did not oppose military intervention in Mali, decided by the United Nations Security Council in 2013, in support of the government versus the separatist Tuareg militias.[155] This illustrates the fact that in Russia the use of military force was never written off. Gerasimov's (in)famous 2013 ratio of the relations between military and nonmilitary means (one to four) was sometimes misinterpreted. The belief that Russia would focus purely on nonmilitary means in a future conflict tended to hide the fact that the military option was always present. Combined with the fact that Russia did not recognize the president and government in Ukraine after 2014 made the question of Russian military intervention a matter of time. Exactly when and how the military invasion would come was, as it should be, always difficult to predict.

In March 2019 Chief of the General Staff Gerasimov gave his yearly speech at the Academy of Military Sciences.[156] Before 2014 these speeches were hardly noticed at all, but since the illegal annexation of Crimea, they have been met with great interest both in Russia and the West. The speeches are primarily directed to a Russian audience, but, in view of the West's attention, a certain amount of signaling to an external audience must be taken into account.

Gerasimov's statements were in line with the main trends of Russian military thought. In fact, much of this thinking stems from that of the former chief of the General Staff, Nikolai Makarov. Makarov's writings show that the ability to learn from the past and to adapt to realities has been a part of the development of the Russian Armed Forces for a long time, contrary to what some Western observers seem to have concluded when they focused on the so-called Gerasimov Doctrine.

Gerasimov expanded on the development of a military strategy and the need for its operationalization. "Theory without practice is dead," he stated, quoting Aleksandr Suvorov.[157] And because of this, he underlined, the practical actions of military strategy have to be based in science.

He noted that the Syrian operation had been inspired by the "strategy of limited actions." According to this strategy, each branch of weapons creates temporarily composed independent units with high mobility. These units are then to be used to support Russian national interests abroad. The most important features in realizing this strategy are to secure and maintain information supremacy, adequate readiness in command-and-control systems and support functions, and covert force deployment.[158]

Gerasimov labeled Russia's response to any threat a strategy of "active defense," meaning a combination of military and nonmilitary means. This includes military force (both regular and armed groups); information operations, cyberattacks, and diversion; and diplomatic, economic, and political measures. The term itself, active defense, is historical and was used by the Red Army during World War II. Today this is in practice nothing new and seems to be a rhetorical tool to characterize Russia's long-term campaign as a response to what the Russian leadership claims to be a Western "hybrid war" against it.

Gerasimov mentioned again threats emanating from the US plans for Prompt Global Strike as well as the "Western techniques of color revolutions and soft power." In order to meet these threats, he claims, Russia is using the strategy of active defense. During his speech, he encouraged his audience to develop this strategy further.[159]

According to the chief of the Russian General Staff, the notion of nonmilitary means also encompasses science, sports, and culture. Both open and covert measures are used, not least to create doubts about the character of a conflict. Gerasimov encouraged the academy to develop plans and operations within this field, indicating that Russian military thinkers still have to do their homework within this area.[160]

Both military and nonmilitary means are to be used to prevent the enemy. Six years on, he emphasized the importance of military means and the role of the Armed Forces, indicating that military force is still very much a part of contemporary and future wars.[161] This dovetails well with the intentions of the political leadership's ambitions. Putin's 2006 annual address had already drawn up the guiding principles for this development: "Modern Russia needs an army that has every possibility for making an adequate response to all the modern threats we face. We need armed forces able to simultaneously fight in global, regional and—if necessary—also in several local conflicts. We need armed forces that guarantee Russia's security and territorial integrity no matter what the scenario."[162]

Gerasimov's 2019 speech emphasized the importance of domestic security, of preventing the opponent's attempts to destabilize and create chaos, which would ultimately lead to the creation of ungovernable states. The role of the economy is central in case of war, he said. On the other hand, he doubted that the defense industry could deliver once the war had started. Therefore, he noted, it was important that the defense industry could already deliver what the Armed Forces needed in peacetime.

It is clear that before the large-scale invasion of Ukraine, the Russian General Staff was preoccupied with domestic security, fear of popular protest, separatism, terrorism, and other threats to the political system. The Russian Armed Forces have a domestic role to combat "fifth columnists," as both Gerasimov and

Putin have phrased it.[163] This is consistent with the perception that views color revolutions as both an external and internal threat.

## THE MARITIME DOCTRINE OF 2022

The updated Maritime Doctrine was approved by the president on July 31, 2022.[164] It was a revised version of the 2015 Maritime Doctrine, which in turn was the first revision since 2001. The Maritime Doctrine codifies the naval priorities, strategy, and procurement for all maritime assets, the military fleets, the civilian fleets, and the naval infrastructure. In other words, it is not specifically a doctrine for only the Russian navy (*Voenno-Morskoi Flot*), although it contains passages relevant for it.

This edition of the Maritime Doctrine is even more ambitious than the previous one since it reflects Russia's growing great-power ambitions. In the spirit of Adm. Sergei Gorshkov, it states that "contemporary Russia cannot exist without a powerful fleet" and that Russia will defend its national interests on the world's ocean through "sufficient seapower."[165]

The document divides Russian naval policy into six regions: Arctic, Pacific Ocean, Atlantic Ocean (including the Baltic Sea, the Sea of Azov, the Black Sea, and the Mediterranean Sea), Caspian Sea, Indian Ocean, and Antarctic. The most important regions for Russia's national interests and the "strategic and regional security of the state" are four: (1) water areas adjacent to the coast of Russia, (2) the eastern part of the Mediterranean, (3) the Black Sea, the Baltic Sea, and the Kuril Strait, and (4) areas of world sea transport communications, including the coasts of Asia and Africa.[166]

The revised Maritime Doctrine has been extended, with sections on national interests and on threats and risks to Russia's presence on the ocean. The threat comes almost exclusively from the West in general and from the United States and NATO in particular. It notes that "the role of force in international relations is not diminishing."[167] At the same time, it recognizes Russia's persistent strategic dilemma in projecting great-power status at sea—namely, that it lacks enough bases outside of Russia.[168]

Importantly, an entire section on mobilization has been added to the Maritime Doctrine, allowing insight into how Russia might engage in a maritime conflict against the West. The previous doctrine noted that civilian fishing and scientific research vessels could be mobilized to support the Russian navy.[169] The 2022 Maritime Doctrine specifies the ten most prioritized areas of mobilization preparedness that need attending to in order to strengthen Russia's naval capability and to prepare for the incorporation of civilian vessels into its Armed Forces.[170]

In sum, the Maritime Doctrine reflects the current leadership's view and its ambitions against the West, along with its efforts to create a new "world order."

## CRIMEA AND THE WAR AGAINST UKRAINE 2014

Russia's strategy had successively developed from a defensive doctrine, with its focus on preventing war, to an offensive stance that allowed for so-called preventive strikes. The wars in Chechnya and Georgia were manifestations of this change or, rather, of a return to the pre-Gorbachev era.

The Russo-Ukrainian War began in February 2014 with the illegal annexation of Crimea. It was framed by Putin as necessary to "correct an historical injustice."[171] The war also proceeded to engulf parts of Donetsk and Luhansk. Russia supported what it called "republics" financially and militarily.

With regard to the tasks of defense policy, it is noteworthy that the 2014 Military Doctrine stated that one of its responsibilities was to "support the mobilization preparedness of the economy."[172] In other words, the aim was to put the economy on a war footing. Furthermore, defense policy should "increase the effectiveness within military patriotic education for the citizens of the Russian Federation and their military service." Add to this the doctrine's view of an endangered youth that had resulted from alleged Western information operations. All this showed that Russia was taking steps to revive the national mobilization system.[173]

It could be possible to interpret the military aggressions in Crimea in 2014 and Syria in 2015 as great successes. In that sense, the Russian political and military leadership were perhaps "dizzy with success."[174] During the eight years after 2014, Russia prepared for further aggression against Ukraine and the West: financially, by building an alternative to the international banking system of the Society for Worldwide Interbank Financial Telecommunications (SWIFT), and, in the information sphere, by meddling in Western elections and increasing propaganda at home. There were many signs that Russia had turned away from the West and that the political and military leadership was not satisfied with what was happening in Ukraine.[175]

More specifically, Russia's full-scale invasion of Ukraine eventually took place against the backdrop of some important preceding events in 2021. The NSS, the most important strategy document according to the Law on Strategic Planning, was revised in July 2021, updating the one from 2015.[176] It is an instructive document since it lays out the priorities regarding Russian national interests and national security. Much of what is said in the NSS has not been implemented, but it points to the direction in which the country is heading, showing, at least, the political will about where the future lies. It sets out, as before, a number of prioritized areas, including the issues of living standards and health, defense, the information space, the environment, Russian spiritual and moral values, and strategic stability.

Russia is preparing itself for a long-term conflict with the West. The importance of military force to achieve geopolitical aims is increasing.[177] There is a growing risk that armed conflicts will escalate into local and regional wars, including those involving nuclear powers. Space and the information space are being identified as "new spheres of warfare."[178] The Internet and international information-technology companies are claimed to be spreading "false information." Russia's youth, according to the NSS, are ever more threatened by "destructive influence."

All the paragraphs from the previous NSS documents regarding the need for cooperation with the United States and NATO in order to maintain strategic stability are gone, as are the formulations about cooperation with the European Union. The foreign policy section has been reduced from twenty paragraphs to seven. The anti-Western rhetoric has increased, and there are various formulations about "unfriendly states" and the West's attempt to "preserve its hegemony." At the same time, the NSS states that the Western, liberal model is in crisis and simultaneously attempting to undermine traditional values, distort world history, revise views on Russia's role and place in it, and rehabilitate fascism.[179] All references to Ukraine have been excluded, except for the paragraph that stipulates that Russia wants to strengthen its ties with the Belarusian and Ukrainian peoples. For Russia, the protests against election fraud in Belarus were organized by the West and not a result of genuine domestic dissatisfaction with President Alexander Lukashenko or stolen elections. Rather, all this was being done to damage Russia and its relations with traditional allies.

The threats against Russia are considered in the NSS to be many. The US contribution to NATO's missile defense in Europe and NATO's position at the borders of Russia are such threats, as was also stated in the previous NSS. The new document decries that the United States is planning to deploy medium-range missiles in Europe and the Pacific region, which threatens strategic stability.[180] In order to secure the country's defense, the Russian Armed Forces, other troops (*drugie voiska*), and military formations (*voinskie formirovanie i organy*) are assigned fourteen priorities.[181] Among the most important are to improve the Russian Federation's military planning in order to develop and implement interrelated political, military, military-technical, diplomatic, economic, informational, and other measures. Again, the holistic view of war and conflict is clear and is reminiscent of the writings of Snesarev and Svechin.

Second, in addition to the release of the NSS, Putin published an article in which he used history to claim Russia's right to Ukraine, dismiss Ukraine's right to exist, and tie into all the official doctrines and strategies examined above. This is not the place to examine all the falsehoods in Putin's article. Suffice it to say that at the time it was published, July 12, 2021, it demonstrated a revisionist Russia preparing to "correct an historical injustice."[182]

## THE FULL-SCALE INVASION

It was clear from the beginning of the war against Ukraine, in its high-intensity phase that started in February 2022, that several contradictions were waiting for future historians to examine. This was not the war the Russian Armed Forces had prepared for. The huge Soviet mobilization army had been dismantled, and Russia had been trying to build mobile armed forces far different from anything that resembled the Battle of Kursk. It was not the war the military theorists had been developing concepts for. It took eight months, for example, before a single field commander was appointed.[183]

Instead, the war developed as a "nineteenth-century war fought with twentieth-century tactics and twenty-first-century weaponry," as the historian Serhii Plokhy has eloquently put it.[184] Another deficiency was that not enough soldiers, around two hundred thousand, were deployed to conquer such a large country, with a population of over forty million.[185] By way of comparison, the invasion of Czechoslovakia in 1968 required up to half a million troops, for a country with approximately fourteen million.

So, what happened? It was obviously supposed to be a "blitzkrieg of the twenty-first century" relying mainly on airborne troops and special forces deployed with the purpose of removing the elected political leadership in Ukraine. According to a 2021 report by the Royal United Services Institute, Russia's Federal Security Service (FSB) was tasked with planning for the occupation of Ukraine; it proceeded to devise such a plan together with the defense minister, Shoigu, as well as Gerasimov and elements within the presidential administration.[186] Since the initial decision to wage a war in Ukraine was apparently taken within a small circle including Putin and the security services, it is perhaps useful to consider a comparison to Afghanistan in 1979. The decision to invade Afghanistan was primarily taken by three people, the troika of KGB chairman Yuri Vladimirovich Andropov (1914–84), Foreign Minister Andrei Andreevich Gromyko (1909–89), and Defense Minister Dmitrii Ustinov. The other members of the Politburo were more or less excluded, including even Leonid Brezhnev, the general secretary of the Communist Party, and Nikolai Ogarkov, the chief of the General Staff, who objected but in the end had no choice but to comply; everyone just had to go along.[187] This is important since it illustrates the fact that on both occasions the decision to go to war was made in a small circle and that the security service, the KGB, had an influential role in that decision. Furthermore, it indicates that the Soviet decision-making process in 1979 was flawed and that this is still the case in Russia today.

Ahead of the war in 2022, there were military voices of warning. For instance, Col. Gen. Leonid Grigorevich Ivashov (1943–), former aide to Defense Minister Ustinov, warned of the consequences, as did Mikhail Mikhailovich Khodarenok (1954–), a former General Staff officer, but it seemed they were talking to deaf ears.[188]

In a soul-searching article in the journal *Voennaia mysl* published a year after the invasion, Col. Oleg Tumakov pointed out several errors with regard to the military-political work within the Armed Forces—for example, the morale preparations of the forces.[189] The hasty decision to start "the special operation," he wrote, made it impossible to convey to every soldier the purpose of the operation and his place and role in it. Secondly, the information about the "social political situation" in Ukraine did not correspond with reality. "Instead of being greeted with flowers and bread in the Russian-speaking areas, our rear columns met civil resistance," he wrote. Third, the information about the morale and psychological state of the Ukrainian Armed Forces was incorrect, and the expectation of mass surrender did not materialize. His success in getting such a highly critical article published in the Ministry of Defense's own journal could indicate that there is dissatisfaction about the performance of the Armed Forces within the Russian military elite. But, given the harsh sentences against "discrediting the Armed Forces," it is perhaps more likely that it is the result of an effort to protect one's own back against criticism and avoid being the scapegoat.

Kokoshin noted, in 2003, that Russia had lost and won wars throughout its history, often at the price of enormous loss of human life. "Today, Russia cannot allow itself to suffer these kinds of losses because in the kind of society it is trying to create, the value of human life is becoming higher, and also for reasons of demography."[190] Additionally, in the military concepts envisaged for future operations, the military thinkers understood that an excessive loss of civilian lives would strengthen the political resolve of the adversary.[191]

In view of the current war in Ukraine, it seems this admonition was nothing more than wishful thinking since Russia has ruthlessly inflicted heavy civilian losses in Ukraine. The Russian Armed Forces have also suffered heavy losses in the war, again displaying a total disregard for human life. This illustrates, apart from the cruelties and war crimes committed by Russia, that the gap between theory and practice in the Russian military has been a constant feature over the centuries.

The current war is framed by Putin as being an existential war for Russia; in other words, he connects war and the armed forces to the very existence of the state. This is an echo from centuries ago and shows that the armed forces are believed to be an integral part of the Russian state. The implications, both for Russia and its surrounding countries, are far-reaching.

## NOTES

*Epigraph:* "The Prayer of Francois Villion," 1963, trans. Maya Jouravel, https://ruverses.com/bulat-okudzhava/francois-villon-s-prayer/8704/.

1. Vasilii Rozanov, "Apokalips nashego vremeni," in *Opavshie listia* (Moscow: Sovremennik, 1992), 472.
2. Rogov, "Russian Defense Policy, 17.
3. Soglashenie o sozdanii Sodruzhestvo Nezavisimykh Gosudarstv [Agreement on the creation of the Commonwealth of Independent States], December 8, 1991, http://www.cis.minsk.by/page.php?id=176. See also Gudrun Persson, "Conflicts and Contradictions: Military Relations in the Post-Soviet Space," in *What Has Remained of the USSR? Exploring the Erosion of the Post-Soviet Space*, ed. Arkady Moshes and Andras Racz, FIIA Report no. 58 (Helsinki: Finnish Institute of International Affairs, 2019), 43–60.
4. Marcel de Haas, "An Analysis of Soviet, CIS and Russian Military Doctrines 1990–2000," *Journal of Slavic Military Studies*, no. 4 (2001): 1–14.
5. Andrei Zagorski, "CIS Regional Security Policy Structures," in *Security Dilemmas in Russia and Eurasia*, ed. Roy Allison and Christoph Bluth (London: Royal Institute of International Affairs, 1998), 281–91.
6. In Russian, such military installations are *voennye obekty*, which have personnel but do not qualify as "military bases" (*voennye bazy*).
7. Makarov, *Na sluzhbe Rossii*, 346–48.
8. "Treaty on CIS Collective Security Published," Article 3, in *Russia and the Commonwealth of Independent States: Documents, Data, and Analysis*, ed. Zbigniew Brzezinski and Paige Sullivan (New York: M. E. Sharpe, 1997), 541–42.
9. Founding Act on Mutual Relations, Cooperation and Security between NATO and the Russian Federation, May 27, 1997, https://www.nato.int/cps/en/natohq/official_texts_25470.htm?selectedLocale=en. See also M. E. Sarotte, *Not One Inch: America, Russia, and the Making of the Post–Cold War Stalemate* (New Haven, CT: Yale University Press, 2021), 270–77.
10. Mary C. FitzGerald, "Russia's New Military Doctrine," *Naval War College Review*, no. 2 (Spring 1993): 25.
11. Makhmut Gareev, *Esli zavtra voina?* [If war comes tomorrow?] (Moscow: VlaDar, 1995), 94.
12. Rogov, "Russian Defense Policy," 43.
13. Bettina Renz, *Russia's Military Revival* (Cambridge, UK: Polity Press, 2018), 123.
14. Clint Reach et al., "Russia's Evolution toward a Unified Strategic Operation: The Influence of Geography and Conventional Capacity," Research Report (Santa Monica, CA: RAND Corp., 2023), 14–15.
15. Baev, *Russian Army*, 25.
16. President of Russia, "Meeting of the Valdai International Discussion Club," October 24, 2014, http://en.kremlin.ru/events/president/news/46860.
17. President of Russia, "Meeting with Young Entrepreneurs, Engineers and Scientists," June 9, 2022, http://en.kremlin.ru/events/president/news/68606.

18. Colin Gray, "A Debate on Geopolitics: The Continued Primacy of Geography," *Orbis*, no. 2 (1996): 247–59.
19. Snesvarev, *Vvedenie*, 447.
20. Kokoshin, *Soviet Strategic Thought*, 194.
21. Federal Law No. 172, O strategicheskom planirovanii v Rossiiskoi Federatsii [On the strategic planning of the Russian Federation], June 28, 2014, http://www.kremlin.ru/acts/bank/38630.
22. *Voennaia entsiklopediia v vosmi tomakh* [Military encyclopedia in eight volumes], vol. 1, ed. I. N. Rodionov (Moscow: Voennoe Izdatelstvo, 1997), 399; Federal Law No. 390, O bezopasnosti [On security], December 28, 2010, http://kremlin.ru/acts/bank/32417; Federal Law No. 61, Ob oborone [On defense], May 31, 1996, http://kremlin.ru/acts/bank/9446.
23. President of Russia, Decree No. 400, Strategiia natsionalnoi bezopasnosti Rossiiskoi Federatsii [The National Security Strategy of the Russian Federation], July 2, 2021, http://www.scrf.gov.ru/ (hereafter cited as National Security Strategy [2021]).
24. The 1993 Military Doctrine was never published in full; its main points were summarized in "Osnovnye polozheniia voennoi doktriny Rossiiskoi Federatsii" [Main provisions of the Military Doctrine of the Russian Federation], *Izvestiia*, November 18, 1993, 1, 4.
25. President of Russia, Decree No. 1300, Kontseptsiia vneshnei politiki Rossiiskoi Federatsii [The Foreign Policy Concept of the Russian Federation], December 17, 1997.
26. Margo Light, "In Search of an Identity: Russian Foreign Policy and the End of Ideology," *Journal of Communist Studies and Transition Politics* 19, no. 3 (2003): 42–59.
27. President of Russia, Decree No. 1300, Kontseptsiia natsionalnoi bezopasnosti Rossiiskoi Federatsii [The National Security Concept of the Russian Federation], December 17, 1997, § I.
28. President of Russia, Decree No. 706, Voennaia doktrina Rossiiskoi Federatsii [The Military Doctrine of the Russian Federation], April 2000 (hereafter cited as Military Doctrine [2000]), § 5.
29. President of Russia, Voennaia doktrina Rossiiskoi Federatsii [The Military Doctrine of the Russian Federation], February 5, 2010, § 8.
30. President of Russia, Decree No. 24, Kontseptsiia natsionalnoi bezopasnosti [The Concept of National Security], January 10, 2000 (hereafter cited as Concept of National Security [2000]), § III.
31. President of Russia, "Poslanie Prezidenta Rossiiskoi Federatsii" [Address by the president of Russia], March 18, 2014, http://www.kremlin.ru.
32. Stephen Blank, *Threats to Russian Security: The View from Moscow* (Carlisle, PA: Strategic Studies Institute, 2000), 4.
33. Alexei G. Arbatov, "The Transformation of Russian Military Doctrine: Lessons Learned from Kosovo and Chechnya," *Marshall Center Papers*, no. 2 (July 2000), https://www.marshallcenter.org/en/publications/marshall-center-papers/transformation-russian-military-doctrine-lessons-learned-kosovo-and-chechnya/transformation-russian-military#toc-notes.
34. Valerii Gerasimov, "Vliianie sovremennogo kharaktera vooruzhennoi borby na napravlennost stroitelstva i razvitiia Strategiia sil Rossiiskoi Federatsii: Prioritetnye zadachi voennoi nauki v obespechenii oborony strany" [The influence of the

contemporary nature of armed struggle on the focus of the construction and development of the Armed Forces of the Russian Federation: Priority tasks of military science in safeguarding the country's defense], *Vestnik Akademii Voennykh Nauk*, no. 2 (2018), 16–22.
35. Concept of National Security (2000), § I.
36. Military Doctrine (2000), § 5.
37. Andrei Kokoshin, "Reflections on Russia's Past, Present, and Future," paper, Strengthening Democratic Institutions Project, Belfer Center for Science and International Affairs, Harvard Kennedy School, June 1997.
38. Roy Allison, *Russia, the West, and Military Intervention* (Oxford: Oxford University Press, 2013), 44, 69.
39. Oscar Jonsson, *The Russian Understanding of War* (Washington, DC: Georgetown University Press, 2019), 94–123.
40. A translated version can be found at https://www.armscontrol.org/act/2000-05/russias-military-doctrine.
41. Susanne Oxenstierna, "Russian Military Expenditure," in *Russian Military Capability: 2016*, ed. Gudrun Persson, FOI-R--3474--SE (Stockholm: Swedish Defence Research Agency, 2012), 133–50. See also in the same volume, Tomas Malmlöf with contributions from Roger Roffey, "The Russian Defence Industry and Procurement," 152–77.
42. Amy F. Woolf, *Conventional Prompt Global Strike and Long-Range Ballistic Missiles: Background and Issues*, Report R41464, version 47 (Washington, DC: Congressional Research Service, 2019).
43. President of Russia, Decree No. 2976, Voennaia doktrina Rossiiskoi Federatsii [The Military Doctrine of the Russian Federation], December 2014 (hereafter cited as Military Doctrine [2014]), § 12 d, § 14 b, § 15 c, §§ 21 l–n, http://www.scrf.gov.ru/.
44. Peter Truscott, *Russia First: Breaking with the West* (London: I. B. Tauris, 1997), 270–71. For more on this development, see also Anne Clunan, *The Social Construction of Russia's Resurgence: Aspirations, Identity, and Security Interests* (Baltimore: Johns Hopkins University Press, 2009).
45. This section is an updated version from Gudrun Persson, "On War and Peace: Russian Security Policy and Military-Strategic Thinking," in *Putin's Russia: Economy, Defence and Foreign Policy*, ed. Steven Rosefielde (Singapore: World Scientific, 2020), 347–77.
46. See, e.g., András Rácz, *Russia's Hybrid War in Ukraine: Breaking the Enemy's Ability to Resist*, FIIA Report 43 (Helsinki: Finnish Institute of International Affairs, 2015).
47. Mark Galeotti, "I'm Sorry for Creating the 'Gerasimov Doctrine,'" *Foreign Policy*, March 5, 2018, http://foreignpolicy.com/2018/03/05/im-sorry-for-creating-the-gerasimov-doctrine/.
48. Gudrun Persson, "Mellan krig och fred: Militärstrategiskt tänkande i Ryssland" [Between war and peace: Military strategic thought in Russia], in Örnen, *Björnen och Draken: Militärt tänkande i tre stormakter* [The eagle, the bear, and the dragon: Military thought in three great powers], ed. Robert Dalsjö, Kaan Korkmaz, and Gudrun Persson, FOI-R--4103--SE (Stockholm: Swedish Defence Research Agency, 2015), 46–64.
49. For examples in English, see Keir Giles, "Russia's 'New' Tools for Confronting the West: Continuity and Innovation in Moscow's Exercise of Power" (research paper,

Chatham House, London, March 2016); Ofer Fridman, *Russian "Hybrid Warfare": Resurgence and Politicisation* (London: Hurst, 2018).
50. Michael Kofman et al., *Lessons from Russia's Operations in Crimea and Eastern Ukraine*, Research Report No. RR-1498-A (Santa Monica, CA: RAND Corp., 2017).
51. Viktor Baranets, "Nachalnik Genshtaba Vooruzhennykh sil Rossii general armii Valerii Gerasimov: 'My perelomili khrebet udarnym silam terrorizma'" [Chief of the General Staff of the Russian Armed Forces Valeriy Gerasimov: "We have broken the back of the shock troops of terrorism"], Komsomolskaia Pravda Online, December 26, 2017, https://www.kp.ru/daily/26775/3808693/.
52. Persson, *Learning from Foreign Wars*, 11–23.
53. Military Doctrine (2014), § 8.
54. Military Doctrine (2014), § 8.
55. Military Doctrine (2014), § 15.
56. Kokoshin, *Svechin*, 366.
57. Gareev, *Esli zavtra voina?*, 7.
58. Gareev, 13–14.
59. Gareev, 25–26.
60. Gareev, 39.
61. For a recent study of this discussion, see Sarotte, *Not One Inch*.
62. Gareev, *Esli zavtra voina?*, 174–76.
63. Gareev, 51.
64. Martin van Creveld, "The Crisis of Military Thought," in *Military Thinking in the 21st Century*, ed. Gudrun Persson, Carolina Vendil Pallin, and Tommy Jeppsson (Stockholm: Swedish Academy of War Sciences, 2015), 61–71.
65. M. Gareev, "Vyrvat eres s kornem" [Uproot the heresy], *Voenno-promyshlennyi kurer*, no. 21 (June 2013); M. Gareev "Iskusstvo reshitelnykh deistvii" [The art of decisive actions], *Voenno-promyshlennyi kurer*, no. 22 (June 12, 2013); S. Tiushkevich and V. Burenok, "Krizis voennoi mysli" [The crisis of military thought], *Voenno-promyshlennyi kurer*, no. 24 (June 26, 2013); M. Gareev, "Eshche raz o sisteme znanii o sovremennoi voine" [Once again on the system of knowledge about modern war], *Voenno-promyshlennyi kurer*, no. 29 (July 31, 2013).
66. Gerasimov, "Osnovnye tendentsii razvitiia, 24–29.
67. V. I. Slipchenko, *Voina budushchego* [Future war] (Moscow: Moskovskii Obshchestvennyi nauchnyi fond, 1999). See also Mary C. FitzGerald, "The Russian Military's Strategy for 'Sixth Generation' Warfare," *Orbis*, no. 3 (1994): 457–76.
68. S. G. Chekinov and S. A. Bogdanov, "O kharaktere i soderzhanii voiny novogo pokoleniia" [The nature and content of a new-generation war], *Voennaia mysl*, no. 10 (2013): 13–24. See also Rácz, "Russia's Hybrid War."
69. Vladimir Slipchenko, "K kakoi voine dolzhny gotovitsia vooruzhennye sily?" [What kind of war should the Armed Forces prepare for?], *Otechestennye zapiski*, no. 8 (2002), http://www.strana-oz.ru/2002/8/k-kakoy-voyne-dolzhny-gotovitsya-vooruzhennye-sily.
70. M. Gareev, "Otstaivaia natsionalnyie interesy" [Defending national interests], *Voenno-promyshlennyi kurer*, no. 47 (December 14–20, 2005).
71. Makhmut Gareev and Vladimir Slipchenko, *Future War*, with an introduction by Jacob W. Kipp (Fort Leavenworth, KS: Foreign Military Studies Office, 2007), v, xvi.
72. On Slipchenko, see Konyshev and Sergunin, *Sovremennaia voennaia strategiia*, 89–96.

73. Gerasimov, "Osnovnye tendentsii razvitiia," 24–29.
74. Timothy Thomas, "The Evolving Nature of Russia's Way of War," *Military Review*, July/August 2017, 34–42. For a recent example of Western writings about Slipchenko, see Charles Bartles, "Sixth-Generation War and Russia's Global Theatres of Military Activity," in *Russian Grand Strategy in the Era of Global Power Competition*, ed. Andrew Monaghan (Manchester: Manchester University Press, 2022), 71–97.
75. Gerasimov, "Razvitie voennoi strategii," 6–11.
76. Rogov, "Russian Defense Policy," 57.
77. Makarov, *Na sluzhbe Rossi*, 337–38.
78. Quoted in Golts, *Voennaia reforma*, 125.
79. Much has been written on this topic. See, e.g., Golts, 128–37, and Renz, *Russia's Military Revival*, 61–72.
80. Makarov, *Na sluzhbe Rossi*, 384–87.
81. Golts, *Voennaia reforma*, 112–59; Renz, *Russia's Military Revival*, 61–72.
82. Golts, *Voennaia reforma*, 124–25.
83. Golts, 140.
84. Quoted in Golts, 136.
85. Makarov, *Na sluzhbe Rossi*, 352.
86. Viktor Litovkin, "Andrei Kokoshin: My budem dumat o budushchem" [Andrei Kokoshin: We will think about the future], *Nezavisimoe voennoe obozrenie*, May 20, 2011, https://nvo.ng.ru/realty/2011-05-20/1_kokoshin.html.
87. Kokoshin, *Strategicheskoe upravlenie*, 10.
88. Kokoshin, 28–30.
89. Dmitry (Dima) Adamsky, *The Russian Way of Deterrence: Strategic Culture, Coercion, and War* (Stanford, CA: Stanford University Press, 2023), 3. Russian strategic thought tends not to differentiate between coercion, deterrence, and compellence, as is customary in the West.
90. Kokoshin, *Svechin*, 367.
91. Kokoshin, 363–65.
92. Quoted in Baev, *Russian Army*, 43.
93. National Security Strategy (2021), § 40.
94. President of Russia, Decree No. 355, Ob osnovakh gosudarstvennoi politiki Rossiiskoi Federatsii v oblasti iadernogo sderzhivaniia [Basic principles of the state policy of the Russian Federation in the domain of nuclear deterrence], June 2, 2020.
95. President of Russia, Decree No. 355, Ob osnovakh gosudarstvennoi politiki, § 19.
96. Jakob Hedenskog and Gudrun Persson, "Russian Security Policy," in *Russian Military Capability in a Ten-Year Perspective: 2019*, ed. Fredrik Westerlund and Susanne Oxenstierna, FOI-R--4758--SE Stockholm: Swedish Defence Research Agency, December (2019), 79–96.
97. President of Russia, Decree No. 327, Osnovy gosudarstvennoi politiki RF v oblasti voenno-morskoi deiatelnosti na period do 2030 g [Foundations for Russia's naval activity for the period up to 2030], July 20, 2017.
98. Quoted in Katazyna Zysk, "Nonstrategic Nuclear Weapons in Russia's Evolving Military Doctrine," *Bulletin of the Atomic Scientists*, no. 5 (2017): 322–27.
99. V. I. Levshin, A. V. Nedelin, and M. E. Sosnovskii, "O primenenii iadernogo oruzhiia dlia deeskalatsii voennykh deistvii" [On the use of nuclear weapons for the de-escalation of combat actions], *Voennaia mysl*, no. 3 (1999): 34–37.

100. Konstantin Sivkov, "Pravo na udar" [The right to strike], *Voenno-promyshlennyi kurer*, no. 8 (March 5, 2014).
101. Military Doctrine (2014), § 8.
102. Roger McDermott and Tor Bukkvoll, *Russia in the Precision-Strike Regime: Military Theory, Procurement and Operational Impact*, FFI Rapport 17/00979 (Kjeller: Norwegian Defence Research Establishment, 2017).
103. Andrei Kokoshin, "Ensuring Strategic Stability in the Past and Present: Theoretical and Applied Questions" (paper, Belfer Center for Science and International Affairs, Harvard Kennedy School, June 2011), 58; Kokoshin, *Strategicheskoe upravlenie*, 321–22.
104. Kokoshin, *O sisteme neiadernogo (prediadernogo)*, 28.
105. Gareev, *Esli zavtra voina?*, 74–78.
106. Gerasimov, "Vliianie sovremennogo kharaktera, 21."
107. Popov and Khamzatov, *Voina budushchego*, 510–36.
108. Valerii Gerasimov, "Po opytu Sirii," [The Syrian experience], *Voenno-promyshlennyi kurer*, March 7, 2016.
109. Gerasimov.
110. Gerasimov.
111. Russian Military-Historical Society, "Zaiavlenie Rossiiskogo Voenno-Istoricheskogo Obshchestva" [Statement, Russian Military-Historical Society], January 13, 2015.
112. On soft power, see Joseph Nye, *Soft Power: The Means to Success in World Politics* (New York: PublicAffairs, 2004), chap. 1.
113. President of Russia, Decree No. 251, Kontseptsiia vneshnei politiki Rossiiskoi Federatsii [Foreign Policy Concept of the Russian Federation], February 12, 2013, (hereafter cited as Foreign Policy Concept [2013]), § 20.
114. President of Russia, Decree No. 640, Kontseptsiia vneshnei politiki Rossiiskoi Federatsii [Foreign Policy Concept of the Russian Federation], November 30, 2016, § 9.
115. President of Russia, Decree No. 229, Kontseptsiia vneshnei politiki Rossiiskoi Federatsii [Foreign Policy Concept of the Russian Federation], March 31, 2023, § 13.
116. Foreign Policy Concept (2013), § 20.
117. Vladimir Putin, "Byt silnymi: Garantii natsionalnoi bezopasnosti dlia Rossii" [Be strong: National security guarantees for Russia], *Rossiiskaia gazeta*, February 20, 2012.
118. VII Moscow Conference on International Security, "Podvedenie itogov MCIS 2018 general-polkovnikom Aleksandrom Fominym" [Summary of the results of the MCIS 2018 by Col. Gen. Aleksandr Fomin], April 5, 2018, video, https://www.youtube.com/watch?v=ZLB7Zxq1pQo.
119. Makhmut Gareev, "Velikaia pobeda i sobytiia na Ukraine" [The great victory and the events in Ukraine], *Vestnik Akademii Voennykh Nauk*, no. 2 (2014): 10.
120. Putin, "Byt silnymi."
121. Makhmut Gareev, "Na 'miagkuiu silu' naidutsia zhestkie otvety" [To 'soft power' there are sharp responses], *Voenno-promyshlennyi kurer*, December 4, 2013.
122. A. A. Bartosh, "Model upravliaemogo khaosa v sfere voennoi bezopasnosti" [The model of controlled chaos in the sphere of military security], *Vestnik Akademii Voennych Nauk*, no. 1 (2014): 69–77.
123. Persson, "Mellan krig och fred," 57.
124. Military Doctrine (2014), § 15.

125. President of Russia, Decree No. 683, Strategiia natsionalnoi bezopasnosti Rossiiskoi Federatsii [National Security Strategy of the Russian Federation], December 31, 2015 (hereafter cited as National Security Strategy [2015]), § 43.
126. Valerii Gerasimov, "Sovremennye voiny i aktualnye voprosy oborony strany" [Modern wars and current questions in regard to the country's defense], *Vestnik Akademii Voennykh Nauk*, no. 2 (2017): 13.
127. "Minoborony RF nachalo kurs lektsii 'Armiia i obshchestvo'" [The Ministry of Defense of the Russian Federation started a course of lectures "Army and Society"], TASS, January 12, 2017, http://tass.ru/armiya-i-opk/3934635.
128. Federal Law No. 128, O vnesenii izmenenii v otdelnye zakonodatelnye akty RF [On the amendments of certain legislative acts], May 5, 2014, http://publication.pravo.gov.ru/document/0001201405050051.
129. S. V. Chvarkov and A. G. Likhonosov. "Novyi mnogovektornyi kharakter ugroz bezopasnosti Rossii, vozrosshii udelnyi ves 'miagkoi sily' i nevoennykh sposobov protivoborotstva na mezhdunarodnoi arene" [The new multivector nature of threats to Russia's security, the increased share of soft power, and the nonmilitary measures of countering them at the international level], *Vestnik Akademii Voennykh Nauk*, no. 2 (2017): 27–30.
130. Aleksandr I. Vladimirov, *Osnovy obshchei teorii voiny, chast I: Osnovy teorii voin* [Foundations of the general theory of war, volume 1: Foundations of the theory of war] (Moscow: Universitet Sinergiia, 2013), 486–87.
131. The Constitution of the Russian Federation, adopted by popular vote on December 12, 1993, with amendments approved by an all-Russian vote on July 1, 2020. For the direct quotes, I have used the English translation published by the Russian Foreign Ministry. It can be found here: https://mid.ru/upload/medialibrary/fa3/xwhwumdwunawy9iprvhcxdqds1lzxqdx/CONSTITUTION-Eng.pdf.
132. The Constitution of the Russian Federation, Article 13:2.
133. See also Gudrun Persson, "Russia and the Baltic Sea: A Background," in *Strategic Challenges in the Baltic Sea Region: Russia, Deterrence and Reassurance*, ed. Ann-Sofie Dahl (Washington DC, Georgetown University Press, 2018), 17–31.
134. Gudrun Persson, *Det sovjetiska arvet* [The Soviet legacy] (Stockholm: SNS Förlag, 2011), 183–84.
135. I. V. Domnin, ed., *Russkoe zarubezhe: Gosudarstvenno-patrioticheskaia i voennaia mysl* [Russian émigrés: State-patriotic and military thought], in *Rossiiskii voennyi sbornik* [Russian military collection], vol. 6, ed. A. E. Savinkin (Moscow: GA VS, 1994), 39–64.
136. Gudrun Persson, "Security Policy and Military Strategic Thinking," in *Russian Military Capability in a Ten-Year Perspective*, ed. Jakob Hedenskog and Carolina Vendil Pallin, FOI-R--3734--SE (Stockholm: Swedish Defense Research Agency, 2013), 71–88.
137. President of Russia, "Meeting of the Valdai International Discussion Club," September 19, 2013, http://en.kremlin.ru/events/president/news/19243.
138. National Security Strategy (2015), 2015, § 78.
139. National Security Strategy (2021), §§ 84–93.
140. President of Russia, "Article by Vladimir Putin 'On the Historical Unity of Russians and Ukrainians,'" July 12, 2021, http://en.kremlin.ru/events/president/news/66181.

141. National Security Strategy (2021), § 87.
142. National Security Strategy (2021), § 91
143. President of Russia, Decree No. 809, Osnovy gosudarstvennoi politiki po sokhraneniiu i ukrepleniiu traditsionnykh rossiiskikh dukhovno-nravstvennykh tsennostei [Fundamentals of state policy for the preservation and strengthening traditional Russian spiritual and moral values], November 9, 2022, www.kremlin.ru.
144. Osnovy gosudarstvennoi politiki, § 5.
145. Osnovy gosudarstvennoi politiki, § 14.
146. Gudrun Persson, "Vilka är vi? Rysk identitet och den nationella säkerheten" [Who are we? Russian identity and national security], *Nordisk Østforum*, no. 3 (2014): 199–214.
147. Dmitry Adamsky, *Russian Nuclear Orthodoxy: Religion, Politics, and Strategy* (Stanford, CA: Stanford University Press, 2019), particularly chaps. 7 and 8.
148. For Kirill's sermons and speeches on this topic, see http://www.patriarchia.ru/.
149. According to this political and theological thought, Moscow is seen as the third Rome and successor to ancient Rome and Constantinople. Filofei, an Orthodox monk, first used this concept in 1523–24. See also Gudrun Persson, Carolina Vendil Pallin, and Maria Engqvist, "Ryssland ändrar grundlagen: Innehåll och konsekvenser" [Russia changes the constitution: Content and consequences], Memo 7091, Swedish Defence Research Agency, May, 2020.
150. Military Doctrine (2014), § 13.
151. DOSAAF Rossii, "Istoriia organizatsiia" [History of the organization], http://www.dosaaf.ru/about/history/.
152. On the Iunarmiia, see the website https://yunarmy.ru/headquarters/about/. On the military competitions, see https://www.france24.com/en/europe/20220823-what-russia-s-international-army-games-tell-us-about-the-war-in-ukraine. On the monument, see President of Russia, "Unveiling of Monument to Alexander III," November 18, 2017, http://en.kremlin.ru/events/president/news/56125. On Putin's visit to Kherson, see Aleksandr Dobrovolskii, "Paskhalnyi podarok Putina: Ikona prinadlezhala generalu, kotoryi vnedril 'trekhlineiki'" [Putin's Easter gift: The icon belonged to the general who introduced the "three-ruler" system], *Moskovskii komsomolets*, April 18, 2023, https://www.mk.ru/social/2023/04/18/paskhalnyy-podarok-putina-ikona-prinadlezhala-generalu-kotoryy-vnedril-trekhlineyki.html.
153. "Basic Military Training Course to Be Added to Russian School Curricula Next Year," TASS, November 9, 2022, https://tass.com/society/1534113.
154. Gerasimov, "Osnovnye tendentsii razvitiia," 24–29.
155. Xenia Avezov and Timo Smit, "The Consensus on Mali and International Conflict Management in a Multipolar World," SIPRI Policy Brief, September 2014.
156. Gerasimov, "Razvitie voennoi strategii," 6–11.
157. Gerasimov, 8.
158. Gerasimov, 9.
159. Gerasimov, 7.
160. Gerasimov, "Vliianie sovremennogo kharaktera," 17.
161. Gerasimov, "Razvitie voennoi strategii," 6–7.
162. President of Russia "Annual Address to the Federal Assembly," May 10, 2006, http://en.kremlin.ru/events/president/transcripts/23577.

163. See, e.g., Gerasimov, "Razvitie voennoi strategii," and President of Russia, "Address by President of the Russian Federation," March 18, 2014.
164. President of Russia, Decree No. 512, Morskaia Doktrina Rossiiskoi Federatsii [Maritime Doctrine of the Russian Federation], July 31, 2022 (hereafter cited as Maritime Doctrine [2022]), www.kremlin.ru.
165. Maritime Doctrine (2022), §§ 104–5.
166. Maritime Doctrine (2022), § 15.
167. Maritime Doctrine (2022), § 20–22.
168. Maritime Doctrine (2022), § 23:6.
169. President of Russia, Decree n/a, "Morskaia Doktrina Rossiiskoi Federatsii" [The Maritime Doctrine of the Russian Federation], July 26, 2015, http://www.kremlin.ru, § 8.
170. Maritime Doctrine (2022), §§ 84–85.
171. President of Russia, "Address by the President of the Russian Federation," March 18, 2014, http://en.kremlin.ru.
172. Military Doctrine (2014), § 21.
173. Julian Cooper, *If War Comes Tomorrow: How Russia Prepares for Possible Armed Aggression*, Whitehall Report 4–16 (London: Royal United Services Institute, 2016).
174. Stalin's phrase in a speech in 1930, published in *Pravda*, in which he criticized overzealous officials in the collectivization.
175. For an overview in English, see, e.g., Owen Matthews, *Overreach: The Inside Story of Putin's War against Ukraine* (London: Mudlark, 2022), and Mark Galeotti, *Putin's Wars: From Chechnya to Ukraine* (Oxford: Osprey, 2022), esp. chap. 29.
176. National Security Strategy (2021); Federal Law No. 172. O strategicheskom, Article 11.
177. National Security Strategy (2021), § 34.
178. National Security Strategy (2021), § 17.
179. National Security Strategy (2021), § 19.
180. National Security Strategy (2021), § 36.
181. National Security Strategy (2021), § 40.
182. President of Russia, "Article by Vladimir Putin."
183. Mykhaylo Zabrodskyi et. al., *Preliminary Lessons in Conventional Warfighting from Russia's Invasion of Ukraine: February–July 2022*," RUSI Special Report (London: Royal United Services Institute, 2022), 45–47.
184. Serhii Plokhy, *The Russo-Ukrainian War* (Dublin: Allen Lane, 2023), 295.
185. Plokhy, 143.
186. Zabrodskyi et al., *Preliminary Lessons*, 7–8.
187. See Zabrodskyi et al., chap. 5.
188. Leonid Ivashov, "Obrashchenie Obshcherossiiskogo ofitserskogo sobraniia k prezidentu i grazhdanam Rossiiskoi Federatsii" [Statement by the All-Russian Officers Assembly to the president and citizens of the Russian Federation], January 28, 2022, http://www.cooc.su/news/obrashhenie_obshherossijskogo_oficerskogo_sobranija_k_prezidentu_i_grazhdanam_rossijskoj_federacii/2022-01-31-79?ysclid=lnd5i4rsee402579256; Mikhail Khodarenok, "Prognozy krovozhadnykh politologov: O vostorzhennykh iastrebakh i toroplivykh kukushkakh" [Forecasts of bloodthirsty political scientists: About enthusiastic hawks and hurried cuckoos], *Nezavisimoe voennoe obozrenie*, February 3, 2022, https://nvo.ng.ru/realty/2022-02-03/3_1175_donbass.html.

189. O. G. Tumakov, "Osnovnye napravleniia sovershenstvovaniia voenno-politicheskoi raboty pri podgotovke operatsii" [The basic directions for improving military-political work in preparing for an operation], *Voennaia mysl,* no. 2 (2023): 38–48.
190. Kokoshin, *Strategicheskoe upravlenie,* 9–10.
191. Michael Kofman et al., *Russian Military Strategy: Core Tenets and Operational Concepts* (Arlington, VA: Center for Naval Analyses, 2021), 69.

# 7

# CONCLUSIONS AND THOUGHTS ON THE ART OF WINNING

*The war ended.... Now we were going to live.... We were going to love.... But we had forgotten all that, we didn't know how to do it.*

SVETLANA ALEXIEVICH

Strategists in the Russian Federation are rediscovering the early Soviet military theorists as part of their efforts to redevelop strategy. As discussed earlier, the debate revolves around four key concerns: (1) whether or not the character of war has changed fundamentally, (2) the relationship between military and nonmilitary means, (3) the importance of nonnuclear deterrence in relation to nuclear deterrence, and (4) the role of the so-called color revolutions and controlled chaos in contemporary warfare.

The renaissance of interest in Russia's own military theorists includes those on the White side, who went into exile after 1917. The writings of Evgenii Eduardovich Messner (1891–1974) about wars of rebellion (*miatezhevoiny*) are considered important today in relation to the discussion of color revolutions. Messner was a former officer in the czarist army, joined the White side during the Civil War, and was forced to emigrate afterward. Some of his writings are freely available on the Internet.[1] Another rediscovered theorist is Anton Antonovich Kersnovskii (1907–44), who volunteered very briefly on the White side despite being only thirteen years old, emigrated in 1920, and spent most of his life in Paris. Among other things, he wrote the four-volume *Istoriia russkoi armii* (History of the Russian army).[2]

This book set out to trace how Russian strategic thought has developed through the centuries, particularly in cataclysmic times. At the beginning of this journey, I expected, perhaps naively, to find more evidence of change, given the enormous technological and political transformations that occurred. The czarist empire fell, ending three hundred years of Romanovs at the throne, and only seventy-four years later the Soviet empire fell. However, the main conclusion is that continuities are more frequent than radical change.

At times, some of the constants have been less pronounced; nonetheless, they have not disappeared. So, for instance, the age-old belief that Russia is forced to react to actions by hostile Western countries keeps coming back. The fact that wars start unannounced was a realization in Russia already at the beginning of the twentieth century.

There are several main constants. First, Russian military doctrine and strategy constitute an inclusive whole, comprising policy, diplomacy, economy, information, military force, intelligence operations, and morale of the nation (ideology). Armed force is only one of the instruments of wielding power and achieving political goals. This view of strategy is sometimes misunderstood in the West, which often treats it in a much narrower way.

Second, warfare has been treated as a science throughout the centuries in Russia. As is shown in previous chapters, the content and application of military science has been an ongoing discussion and, at times, an issue of dispute. Where is the boundary between science and art? This question revolves around yet another question: What kind of science is military science? There have been many variations on this theme, but history is a cornerstone of Russian strategic thought. Lately, Kokoshin has been pushing to introduce sociology into the equation.

This scientific approach, again, is often misunderstood in the West. Soviet strategists at times criticized their American counterparts for having a narrow, technical understanding of military affairs. In 1970 a Soviet strategist wrote, "The efforts of American strategists have yielded a whole system of concepts that may be applicable and even useful in the analysis of the purely military correlations of forces, but lead to unavoidable distortions when applied to politics and such political problems as international and national security. In this approach, the very question of war is, as it were, isolated from politics, from the analysis of whether or not war can bring about the desired political objectives."[3]

Hence, the primacy of policy over Russian strategy is yet another constant sometimes ignored by Western analysts. This is a paradox since the insight that "war should never be thought of as something autonomous, but always as an instrument of policy," comes from Clausewitz.

The offensive strategy is another constant. Attempts have been made to change to a defensive strategy, but those efforts were never allowed the time to develop before the offensive strategy returned. The view of the West as the main enemy is persistent. This is evident from Russia's war plans in the 1870s, Boris Shaposhnikov's idea that Europe intended to expand eastward (which was true in the case of Nazi Germany), and the Soviet Union's threat perception during the Cold War. The Russian leadership is implementing this idea again today—that the West is the adversary and is expanding eastward—to justify its invasion of Ukraine, but it does not make it truer.

Furthermore, another constant had entered Russian strategic thought by the early nineteenth century. Building on the experience of expansion, Suvorov's victories in Europe, and Russia's success in 1815, the strategy of protecting Russia by waging war away from Russia proper had by then become central to its strategic outlook.

The main changes to the offensive Russian strategic outlook occurred on at least three occasions. After the first Crimean War, a defensive doctrine was adopted. The major driver for this was partly the defeat in the war but more importantly the result of domestic changes and reform, including the impressions of the Wars of German Unification, in the 1860s and the technological changes in firepower.

Mikhail Gorbachev's introduction of a defensive doctrine was another major change of possible strategic implications. Again, the domestic factors provided the main impetus. Earlier, there was the change in strategic thought from Jomini (with his eternal laws of warfare) to Clausewitz. This transformation took place against the background of the fall of the Romanov Empire and the Bolshevik takeover. Although reading Clausewitz was promoted by Lenin, his thought was also championed by two of the leading military theorists in the early 1920s. In the late 1980s, the Clausewitzian and now Soviet dictum that "war is a continuation of politics" was considered obsolete in view of a nuclear war. Soviet theorists concluded that a nuclear war was impossible to win, leading to a defensive doctrine.

However, these changes in Russian strategic thought did not have time to take root—not in the mid-nineteenth century, not in the early 1920s, and not before the fall of the Soviet Union, and the offensive doctrine returned, combined with renewed attention to Clausewitz. How can this be explained?

Factors that influence thought on strategy and doctrine, as set out at the beginning of this book, were on one hand the hard factors, such as technology and geography, and on the other soft factors, such as policy (domestic and foreign), history, and foreign military thought. This book demonstrates that the soft factors generally have a stronger impact on Russian strategy than the hard ones. Incidentally, Adamsky also found that Russian strategy tended to rely heavily on the soft aspects and human mass to make up for technological-material inferiority.[4] Consequently, policy, both domestic and foreign, and history tend to explain more about Russia's strategic thought than technological and geographic factors. Geography does have an impact, but it is more of an indirect influence, creating an argument for, or feeling of, insecurity. So, for instance, the breakup of the Soviet Union did not lead Russia to continue Gorbachev's defensive doctrine. Instead, it was abandoned quickly, and the offensive doctrine was reintroduced. Technology and new weapon systems should not be ignored, obviously, and the arrival of nuclear weapons had a significant impact on Russian strategy and doctrine, but over time the soft factors dominated.

Subsequently, one of this book's important conclusions, one often misunderstood in the West, is that Russia primarily acts for its own reasons (despite Russian rhetoric to the contrary), national interests, and intelligence-based predictions, not necessarily as a reaction to Western actions. Domestic factors, as we have seen, such as fear of uprisings, and the strategic calculations of waging the war away from the Russian heartland influence Russian strategic thought to a large degree.

The "action-reaction" paradigm, which attributes the decisive role to changes in Western strategy, is inadequate to explain Soviet and Russian strategic thought.[5] The months leading up to the Russian full-scale invasion of Ukraine in 2022 are yet another case in point. The United States and United Kingdom leaked intelligence about Russian movements in an effort to dissuade Russia from going to war, yet this signaling had no effect on Russia's behavior. Ambassador Raymond L. Garthoff, one of the leading American analysts of Soviet military doctrine, once said that "we are probably more sophisticated military technical analysts; . . . they may well be the better political historians."[6] Nevertheless, Russian strategic thought on military doctrine and policy has suffered from an inability to translate it into practice. As we have seen time and again, Russian military thinkers have thought deeply, and often insightfully, on war and conflict. But the inability to implement the concepts in practice is evidently clear.

In fact, the gap between theory and practice is one of the continuities of Russian military thought that has severe implications for making and implementing strategic decisions. This is not about the inability to think, as sometimes alleged, but it illustrates that the armed forces of any country are a reflection of its society. The authoritarian and sometimes totalitarian rule in Russia is characterized by central control, yet the difficulties in implementing decisions seem inherent in the Russian armed forces. Kokoshin even identified the disconnect as "one of the weakest points in our national strategic culture."[7] The chiefs of the General Staff, Makarov and Ogarkov, also observed this gap, as did Miliutin in the nineteenth century.

Another factor with a significant impact on Russian strategic thought is the repressive political system that has restrained its development. Even if it is not possible to demonstrate a direct causal connection, there is enough evidence as well as eyewitness accounts that testify to at least a probable cause. Repeatedly, formidable Russian and Soviet thinkers have been ousted by the czars or the Politburo. Suvorov died in disgrace. Miliutin retired to his estate and was never called for again, although, in fairness, he was promoted to field marshal in 1896. His grave was destroyed by the Bolsheviks, and only in 2016, the two hundredth anniversary of his birthday, was a tombstone erected. During the Soviet era, several of the most prominent military theorists were killed in Stalin's purges. This led to an atmosphere of fear and mistrust, with effects to this day, as Kokoshin has pointed out. The repression has also led to a memory loss. The leading thinkers of the 1920s became "nonpersons," so their works could only be read in secrecy, if at all.[8]

In the current increasingly repressive political system under Vladimir Putin, the fears of the past are becoming more visible. Russia today complains about the West and then does what it perceives the West is doing, using methods of their own invention. One explanation, as is evident from this book, is mirror-imaging. Since the thought on total war, asymmetry, and nonlinear means were already well developed in Soviet Russia in the 1920s, the image is projected against the West. Another explanation for this tendency is the collective loss of memory, due to the repressive political system and the inclination of the top leader, whether Nicholas II, Stalin, or Putin, to consider himself the best and only strategist.

The military has tried, on occasion, to speak out, as described in chapters 5 and 6, but these are lonely voices that obviously were not listened to. This brings us to another observation by some of the theorists in this book—namely, the importance of having a broader debate about strategy, military science, and future war. Svechin was explicit in warning of a "strategic caste." Popov and Khamzatov point to the United States as an example to follow in this regard. There, even civilian experts such as political scientists, biologists, psychologists, journalists, information-technology experts, historians, and economists can have a say in thinking about future war.[9] Kokoshin underlines that the US publicizes important strategic documents, which helps commanders at all levels to familiarize themselves with their content, thereby increasing their realization.[10]

It is perhaps ironic that on February 9, 2023, almost a year into the war against Ukraine, the well-known hard-liner Col. Gen. Leonid Ivashov pointed to the consequences of this. He observed, "But to silence someone, this does not mean that you have become stronger. If sober-minded people are muzzled, then you only become dumber and more corrupt, but not stronger in any way. We are being defeated by intellect. And in our country, instead of intellect, people are twisting arms, intimidating, and imprisoning. In such a situation, the country always loses and does not have long to live."[11]

Furthermore, it is not possible to understand Russian strategic thought without considering the influence from abroad, mainly from Western thinkers and theorists. Suvorov's reading recommendations appear in chapter 1 and are but one case in point. Throughout the period examined here, Russian theorists took inspiration from all the leading Western military thinkers, related to their work, adapted and developed doctrines to suit Russian conditions, and then more often than not called them "Soviet" or "Russian." The influence of any Chinese theorists, or even Sun Tzu, is almost entirely absent, except for during the past two decades when Russia's relationship with China began to develop. One military theorist remarked recently that the influence of Sun Tzu in Russian strategic and military thought is still almost invisible.[12]

The long-held conviction in some Russian intellectual circles that Russia is culturally and intellectually independent of the West and that Russian/Soviet military doctrine is unique is another constant. Living in exile in Paris, Kersnovskii summarized Russia's national military doctrine from the eighteenth century and onward as "superiority of the spirit over the material, Russian uniqueness [*samobytnost*], superiority of quality before quantity, religious and national pride."[13] The strategic outlook was, he noted, "to look at the entire picture" of war and military affairs.

Fifty years after Kersnovskii, in 2000 Vladimir Antonovich Zolotarev (1946–) noted that Russian military strategy was characterized by "national uniqueness; reliance primarily on our own national forces; continentality; peripheral focus; alternate neutralization of threats from the west, east, and south; proportional development of forces, with a primary focus on ground forces; decisiveness of action; flexible combination of attack and defense; positional and maneuver forms of combat."[14] Policy directs strategy, but sometimes the military aspect also influences policy, Zolotarev repeats. Apart from economic factors, he also highlights ideology as an important factor in setting the strategic goals.

The idea of Russian uniqueness in strategic thought needs to be nuanced, as this book shows. In his detailed study of the Russian military enlightenment, Miakinkov reached the same conclusion.[15]

Throughout this book, the debate has revolved around two main schools of thought. One emphasizes the need for modern technology, while the other stresses the qualities of the soldier. Traditionalists warn against exaggerating the importance of advanced technology to win future wars and advocate a focus on soft factors, such as history, morale and ideology. Russian scholars argue that they see themselves as defenders of Clausewitz and Svechin.[16] The technologists stress the importance of new weapon systems that will shape future war and even the meaning of victory as we see below. This is something of an oversimplification, to be sure, but Danilenko's observation that during the Soviet period the two schools monopolized their dogmas is important. To some extent, bureaucratic infighting has certainly played a role, which is not unique to Russia. However, the consequences of the dualism continue to be reflected in methodological and organizational problems for the Russian Armed Forces. This dualism also influences national identity and Russian interpretations of history, with severe consequences for Russia itself as well as for neighboring countries.

Technical and organizational innovations, as shown in chapter 2, in any time or indeed any large organization always entail risk, and their consequences are not always easy to predict. Introducing an innovation, which may seem innocent enough, is a large undertaking that is not easy to correct. Therefore, one can expect large organizations, such as armies, to show a certain reluctance to jump too quickly to adjust to change. On the other hand, a general wait-and-see attitude is potentially dangerous and can lead to devastating results, as Ogarkov and Makarov observed. Much of the problem lies in finding a balance in peacetime between adapting to change and determining the actual value of innovations for war. There is a balance to be found between novelty and tradition, between leaping to conclusions and resisting change. The fact that armed force is directly linked to the security of the state does not make the situation an easy one. It is hardly surprising, therefore, that armies are often described as being marked by a curious contradiction. On one hand, they are oriented toward the present and future in their efforts to make the most rational use of their means and to be as efficient as possible. On the other, they are often perceived by both insiders and outsiders as the bearers of traditional values represented by ceremonies that should be preserved at all costs. This balancing act between future and past becomes more evident in times of radical change.

A balance needs to be found between technology and morale. The pre-1914 European armies were later accused of disregarding technology and putting too much emphasis on morale. The experience of World War I certainly seems to vindicate this criticism. Nevertheless, many wars of the twentieth and twenty-first centuries have demonstrated again and again that an army with strong morale, regardless of its technological inferiority, can win wars.

Why, then, are so few Russian military theorists known abroad and in Russia? Baev claims that the Russian army traditionally existed in a sort of "cultural vacuum" and that Russian generals and admirals left no distinguished writings that had won acclaim. On the surface, this may be true, as may be his explanation that the Russian intelligentsia was opposed to the absolutism of which the army was also part and parcel.[17] Nevertheless, the evidence in this book suggests that from the czarist era up until the present, there have been several military theorists who thought deeply and intelligently about war and conflict. In some cases, they even became members of international war academies. But they did not become world-renowned names, such as Machiavelli, Clausewitz, and Liddell Hart. One explanation is the political system in which they worked, not in the sense that it prevented thought but rather that the military strategists were left at the mercy of a single ruler. In czarist times, they could easily fall from power and be sent into oblivion; during Stalin's, they were killed. Another factor is the extreme secrecy surrounding all things military in Russia. It was only during Gorbachev's time in office that civilians were encouraged to contribute to Russian strategic thought on war, army, and conflict. The skepticism, however, against the engagement of civilians in the debate about war and conflict is still profound in the Russian military, almost one hundred years since Svechin's warning about the danger of a strategic caste.

## RUSSIA AS A GEOPOLITICAL ACTOR: WHAT NEXT?

These conclusions open the way for a few broader, personal reflections on Russian strategic behavior. Why does Russia act in the way it does? I propose four recurring conditions—four variables, if you will—that influence Russian strategic actions over time, with severe consequences for its neighbors and the world.[18]

The first variable is the army's position as a founding—that is, integral—part of Russia as a state. There is a close link between the military and political elites that connects military power and the survivability of the ruler or regime. Russia has over the centuries devoted an unusual amount of economic and human resources to war and conflict. The Russian historian Vasilii Osipovich Kliuchevskii (1841–1911) had already described the link in his writings about Peter the Great and the military reforms: "This is not just a matter of national defense request: the reform had a profound impact on the society. . . . The war was the main driving leverage of Peter's transforming activity, and military reform was its starting point. The Great Reformer built the new state as a huge garrison."[19] And when Nicholas II abdicated, he did so to the chief of staff of the armed forces. Only the army could uphold the sovereignty of Russia.[20]

Sergei Iulevich Witte (1849–1915), Nicholas II's prime minister and a staunch antimilitarist, later remarked in his memoirs, "In truth, what is it that has essentially upheld Russian statehood? Not only primarily, but exclusively, the army. Who created the Russian Empire, transforming the semi-Asiatic Muscovite czardom into the most influential, most dominant, grandest European power? Only the power of the army's bayonet. The world bowed not to our culture, not to our bureaucratized church, not to our wealth and prosperity. It bowed to our might."[21]

Petr Berngardovich Struve (1870–1944), a liberal politician, philosopher, and historian who had fled Bolshevik Russia, later reflected from his exile: "To revive Russia without the army or apart from the army is impossible. The army is not these or those generals, no matter how great their services. . . . The army is the living personification of the official existence of Russia."[22]

The army's position as a state builder might explain the almost complete absence of military coups in Russia. In more recent times, for instance, the ousting of Khrushchev in 1964 was supported by the military, but, importantly, it was not instigated by them. In a telling example from 1990, when the political leadership carried out unilateral reductions of the Soviet Armed Forces and decided to leave Eastern Europe, the military leadership did nothing. "We tried," said Ivashov, when the retired United States Army lieutenant general and academic William Odom asked him about the event in 1995, "but we had no leader. We begged Yazov to lead a coup, but he always asked, 'What will we do with the power if we take it?'"[23] Yazov later participated in the feeble coup attempt of August 1991, in a sequence of events that echoed the failed attempt by the Decembrists in 1825.

The second variable is territorial expansion, driven in part by economic reasons and in part to "protect" the heartland and preferably wage wars away from it. From 1500 to 1917, Russia expanded by an average of 130 square kilometers per day. The Soviet Union, in turn, built up an entire chain of buffer states, through annexation and coercion. The Russian Federation gradually tried to expand its territory by using armed force in Georgia in 2008 and capturing Crimea from Ukraine, which in turn was followed by the military aggression in Donbas (2014–22) and then the full-scale invasion. The uncertainty of its borders has played a critical role in the history of Russia, today especially so. From the Russian military's perspective, territories are crucial to the survival of Russia. The Soviet Union, even at the height of its global power, used to describe itself as encircled. Accordingly, Russia today claims to be fighting a defensive campaign in order to protect Russia proper.

The third variable is the demand for prestige and international great-power status on one hand and an explicit feeling of insecurity on the other. In the late nineteenth century, according to William Fuller, two errors resulted in a mismatch between Russia's strategy and its policy: one was an excessive sense of military inferiority and the other a reluctance to accept any diminution in Russia's international standing and prestige, which led to an avoidable overextension.[24] Rather than recognize this, Russia overstretched, with disastrous consequences. Much of the same overextension eventually led to the breakup of the Soviet Union a century later.

And the fourth variable is the nationality question. Russia is not and has never been a homogeneous nation-state. Although Russians dominate today, the 2021 census showed that there are almost 150 ethnic minorities in Russia.[25] Miliutin reflected on this issue in the mid-nineteenth century, as we saw in chapter 2, and maintained that the predominance of Russians did not necessarily mean the oppression of other nationalities. At the same time, he advocated a brutal intervention in Poland in 1863. The Great Russian perspective prevailed.

Deploring the dissolution of the Soviet Union, Aleksandr Nikolaevich Yakovlev (1923–2005), "the father of perestroika," noted that he and the Soviet leadership under Gorbachev had ignored the nationalities.[26] Although Russia's borders with and influence on neighboring countries have fluctuated over the centuries, it nevertheless retained its Great Russian perspective, its imperial form, including after both 1917 and 1991.

For the future, these four variables are going to be handled, and balanced, by Russia's leaders, regardless of who is in power in the Kremlin. All of this touches on the question of Russian identity, once described by Putin as a "national sport": Who are we? What kind of state will Russia be in the future, and what kind of relationship should it have with Europe and the West? In turn, its neighbors and the rest of the world need to prepare for the fact that Russia is presently demonstrating that it is neither able to deal with these factors nor break free of the vicious circle in which it appears to be floundering. In particular, the West needs to relate to the four variables mentioned above and consider its long-term relations with a future Russia.

For ten years before the full-scale invasion of Ukraine in 2022, it was often said, both in Russian and Western analyses, that Putin did not have a strategy but only acted as a brilliant tactician, thereby implying that the current political leadership was simply being opportunistic. This was obviously a superficial statement. There is no contradiction between pursuing strategic goals and the exploitation of tactical opportunities. As Richard Pipes put it, "strategy is not getting what one wants but knowing what one wants and what it takes to get it."[27] Strategy can fail, obviously. According to Richard Betts, strategy fails when some link in the planned chain of cause and effect, from low-level tactics to high-level political outcomes, is broken, when military objectives come to be pursued for their own sake without reference to their political effect, or when policy initiatives depend on military options that are infeasible.[28] Given Russia's history of successes and failures in its strategic choices, it is clear that the challenges ahead, for neighboring countries and the West, are formidable.

In the beginning of the twentieth century, Russian military thinkers worried about the technological gap between Russia and Europe. Today, the gap remains, and Russia has far to go to catch up. But, as discussed above, concepts have been developed involving other means of force—the so-called nonmilitary means. Consequently, almost every part of society is increasingly seen as a battlefield that spans everything from nuclear weapons to history, culture, and science. This has echoes of the Soviet period.

Importantly, thought and doctrine on future war need to find a balance between perceived threats and the resources available to meet them. Therefore, political support is essential in any country and in any time. At the moment, the West is seen as the main threat to Russian national security, and the response has been to launch a full-scale invasion against Ukraine and eliminate any dissent at home. The authoritarian, increasingly totalitarian political system, with a strong figurehead at the top, is described as "the right one" for Russia, feeding into the tradition of Russian great-powerness. The current political leadership often quotes words ascribed to Alexander III: "Russia has only two allies: its army and its fleet."

## THE ART OF WINNING

Finally, in light of the Russo-Ukrainian War, a few words need to be said about the Russian discussion on the meaning of victory in contemporary wars. The first phase of the Russian attack on Ukraine, in 2022, could be said to have vindicated Dragomirov—that is, if you do not know why you fight, you will not win. Obviously, technological superiority is important, but without the will to fight, victory is far away. To rely solely on advanced technical superiority has often proved inadequate. The recent Western interventions in Afghanistan and Iraq demonstrate this.[29]

Moreover, the supporters of Slipchenko's ideas on the contactless battlefield claimed that the concept of "victory" would change fundamentally. According to their line of thinking, strategically offensive weapons could early on and at a distance destroy an enemy's energy supplies, communications, and political system. Victory could thereby be proclaimed without the need for ground troops. The experience from Kosovo in 1999 clearly influenced these thoughts.

Kokoshin focuses on the lessons from the Iraq War, a war that had, and continues to have, a great impact on Russian military thought. He points out the obvious—namely, that a military victory does not always transform into a political one.[30] Although his example is the Iraq War, he also points to Afghanistan in 1979 and to the initial phase of the Crimean War in 1853, when Russian forces achieved several victories over the Turkish forces.[31]

To secure a political victory in modern wars, several issues need to be resolved. Kokoshin points to factors such as information dominance, asymmetrical strategies, and having a proper plan for the postwar management of the defeated enemy.[32] One increasingly important problem, according to Kokoshin, is securing permanent political control of a war and the military operations that are part of it. To achieve this, a reliable control system is needed. However, the lack of control to manage and implement decisions is one of the weak sides of Russian strategic culture, he adds.[33] In the end, referring to Clausewitz, he concludes that to win in contemporary wars, it is necessary to defeat the enemy's will to fight.[34]

Popov and Khamzatov discuss the question of what victory means in contemporary wars.[35] The key factors are the material, morale, informational, and cognitive factors. Factor $C$, for "chance," is included in their diagram. Each of these factors needs to be correctly assessed and predicted in order to achieve victory. They recognize that the diagram is more useful at the tactical level than the strategic, simply because the complexity increases at the higher level. But the authors underline the importance of assessing immaterial factors, such as morale, informational, and cognitive aspects, rather than focusing solely on the number of troops, tanks, and airplanes, in order to achieve victory instead of humiliating defeat in the future.

Vladimirov quotes Kersnovskii: "Wars are not waged with the purpose of killing but of winning."[36] Vladimirov draws on Clausewitz's writings and then reaches the conclusion that Russia must have an army that can win because this is a requirement for a great power such as Russia. The very foundation of such armed forces, according to Vladimirov, is an ideology that encompasses the entire nation and supports Russia's historical legacy and great-power status.

This echoes the totalitarian thoughts of Snesarev (see chapter 3), who elaborated the concept of total war. Vladimirov also expresses his high regard for Snesarev.[37] "War is the highest justification of the state," Snesarev argues. The implications are far-reaching and telling. It might be argued that this school of thought was made irrelevant by the experiences of World War II. However, the West must realize that Snesarev's thinking is being studied and greatly appreciated in twenty-first century Russia. He also emphasized the need to prepare for protracted wars, as Svechin had done. Does this mean Russia is preparing for a long war today? It is impossible to say, but it is evident that Russian strategic theorists have thought long and hard about the probability of a long war.

History shows that the home front is central in winning any war, as Russia knows very well. In a time when the Russian military leadership claims that not only are the borders between war and peace becoming blurred but also the line between offensive and defensive operations, the concept of "controlled chaos," using asymmetrical as well as symmetrical means of force, is being invoked.

Consequently, the Russian Federation does have a strategy that is continuously developing. The West must realize the all-encompassing Russian view of war and conflict and the political primacy of strategy. A failure to do so will result in serious errors of analysis and rude awakenings in the future. History has just begun—again.

## NOTES

*Epigraph:* Svetlana Alexievich, *The Unwomanly Face of War*, translated by Richard Pevear and Larissa Volokhonsky (New York: Random House, 2017), 222.

1. I. V. Domnin and V. I. Marchenkov, eds., *Khochesh mira, pobedi miatezhevoinu! Tvorcheskoe naslediia E. Messnera* [If you want peace, win the war of rebellion! The creative heritage of E. Messner], in *Rossiiskii voennyi sbornik* [Russian military collection], ed. A. E. Savinkin, vol. 21 (Moscow: Voennyi universitet, Russkii put,

2005), https://archive.org/details/MessnerMutinyWAR. See also I. V. Domnin, ed., *Voennaia mysl v izgnanii: Tvorchestvo russkoi voennoi emigratsii* [Military thought in exile: The creativity of the Russian military emigrés], in *Rossiiskii voennyi sbornik* [Russian military collection], ed. E. Savinkin, vol. 16 (Moscow: Voennyi universitet, Russkii put, 1999).
2. Anton Kersnovskii, *Istoriia russkoi armii* [History of the Russian army], 4 vols. (1933–38; repr., Moscow: Golos, 1992).
3. Quoted in Richard Pipes, *Survival Is Not Enough: Soviet Realities and America's Future* (New York: Simon & Schuster, 1984), 86.
4. Adamsky, *Russian Way of Deterrence*, 64–67.
5. For an analysis of Soviet thought during the Cold War, see Mastny, *War Plans*, 28–38.
6. Garthoff, *Journey through the Cold War*, 266.
7. Kokoshin, *Svechin*, 367.
8. Kokoshin, 24.
9. Popov and Khamzatov, *Voina budushchego*, 96–97.
10. Kokoshin, *Politologiia i sotsiologiia*, 471.
11. Evgenii Senshin, "'Esli nyneshnii konflikt okhvatit strany NATO, tseliu Aliansa stanet razgrom Rossii': General-Polkovnik Leonid Ivashov—o voine i oshibkakh Kremlia" ["If the current conflict engulfs NATO countries, the alliance's objective will be to defeat Russia": Colonel-General Leonid Ivashov—about the war and the Kremlin's mistakes], *Republic*, February 9, 2023, https://republic.ru/posts/107160.
12. Kokoshin et al., *Sovremennye voiny*, 69.
13. Kersnovskii, *Istoriia russkoi armii*, vol. 1, 164–69.
14. V. A. Zolotarev, ed., *Istoriia voennoi strategii Rossii* [A history of Russia's military strategy], (Moscow: Kuchkovo pole, 2000), 6.
15. Miakinkov, *War and Enlightenment*, 231–36.
16. Konyshev and Sergunin, *Sovremennaia voennaia strategiia*, 87–88; Igor Popov, *Voennaia mysl sovremennoi Rossii* [Military thought in contemporary Russia], 2007, http://futurewarfare.narod.ru/theoryRF.html.
17. Baev, *Russian Army*, 13–14.
18. Inspired by Odom, *Collapse*, 397–404.
19. Golts, *Voennaia reforma*, 259–60.
20. Richard Pipes, *The Russian Revolution* (New York: Vintage Books, 1991), 316.
21. Quoted in Richard Pipes, "Militarism and the Soviet State," *Daedalus*, no. 4 (1980): 1–12.
22. A. E. Savinkin, I. V. Domnin, and Iu. T. Belov, eds., *Kakaia armiia nuzhna Rossii? Vzgliad iz istorii* [What kind of army does Russia need? A view from history], in *Rossiiskii voennyi sbornik* [Russian military collection], ed. A. E. Savinkin, vol. 9 (Moscow: Voennyi universitet, 1995), 7.
23. Odom, *Collapse*, 339.
24. Fuller, *Strategy and Power*, 462–63.
25. Rosstat, Vserossiiskaia perepis naseleniia 2020 g [All-Russian population census 2020], vol. 5, table 1, https://rosstat.gov.ru/vpn/2020.
26. Public lecture, Swedish Society for the Study of Russia, Central and Eastern Europe and Central Asia, Stockholm, March 18, 2003.
27. Pipes, *Survival Is Not Enough*, 55.
28. Richard K. Betts, "Is Strategy an Illusion?," *International Security* 25, no. 2 (2000): 7.

29. John Stone, *Military Strategy: The Politics and Technique of War* (London: Bloomsbury Academic, 2018), vii.
30. Kokoshin, *Politologiia i sotsiologiia*, 452.
31. Kokoshin et al., *Sovremennye voiny*, 63–65.
32. Kokoshin, *Politologiia i sotsiologiia*, 475–80.
33. Kokoshin et al., *Sovremennye voiny*, 67.
34. Kokoshin et al., 68.
35. Popov and Khamzatov, *Voina budushchego*, 444–72.
36. Vladimirov, *Osnovy*, vol. 1, 281–82.
37. Vladimirov, vol. 1, 97–98.

# SELECTED BIBLIOGRAPHY

Adamsky, Dima. *The Culture of Military Innovation: The Impact of Cultural Factors on the Revolution in Military Affairs in Russia, the US, and Israel*. Stanford, CA: Stanford Security Studies, 2010.
Adamsky, Dmitry. *Russian Nuclear Orthodoxy: Religion, Politics, and Strategy*. Stanford, CA: Stanford University Press, 2019.
Adamsky, Dmitry (Dima). *The Russian Way of Deterrence: Strategic Culture, Coercion, and War*. Stanford, CA: Stanford University Press, 2023.
Airapetov, Oleg. *Na puti k krakhu: Russko-Iaponskaia voina 1904–05 gg* [On the road of collapse: The Russo-Japanese War 1904–5]. Moscow: Algoritm, 2014.
———. *Uchastie Rossiiskoi Imperii v Pervoi Mirovoi Voine 1914–1917* [The participation by the Russian Empire in the First World War 1914–17]. Vol. 4, *1917 Raspad* [The breakup]. Moscow: Kuchkovo pole, 2015.
———. *Zabytaia karera "russkogo Moltke" Nikolai Nikolaevich Obruchev (1830–1904)* [The forgotten career of the "Russian Moltke" Nikolai Nikolaevich Obruchev (1830–1904)]. Saint Petersburg: Aleteia, 1998.
Akhromeev, S. F., ed. *Voennyi entsiklopedicheskii slovar* [Military encyclopedic lexicon], 2nd ed. Moscow: Voennoe izdatelstvo, 1986.
Alekseeva, T. A. "Strategicheskaia kultura: Evoliutsiia kontseptsii" [Strategic culture: Evolution of the concept]. *Polis*, no. 2 (2012): 130–47.
Allison, Roy. *Russia, the West, and Military Intervention*. Oxford: Oxford University Press, 2013.
Allison, Roy, and Christoph Bluth, eds. *Security Dilemmas in Russia and Eurasia*. London: Royal Institute of International Affairs, 1998.
Applebaum, Anne. *Iron Curtain: The Crushing of Eastern Europe 1944–1956*. London: Penguin, 2013.
Arbatov, A. G. "K voprosu o dostatochnosti protivovozdushnoi oborony" [To the question of air defense sufficiency]. *Voennaia mysl*, no. 12 (1989): 41–45.
Arbatov, Alexei G. "The Transformation of Russian Military Doctrine: Lessons Learned from Kosovo and Chechnya." *Marshall Center Papers*, no. 2, July (2000). https://www.marshallcenter.org/en/publications/marshall-center-papers/transformation-russian-military-doctrine-lessons-learned-kosovo-and-chechnya/transformation-russian-military#toc-notes.

Baev, Pavel. "The Interplay of Bureaucratic, Warfighting, and Arms-Parading Traits in Russian Military-Strategic Culture." George C. Marshall European Center for Security Studies. *Strategic Insights*, no. 28, April (2019). https://www.marshallcenter.org/en/publications/security-insights/interplay-bureaucratic-warfighting-and-arms-parading-traits-russian-military-strategic-culture.

———. *The Russian Army in a Time of Troubles*. Oslo: Prio, 1996.

Balabushevich, V. V., and G. G. Kotovskii, eds. *Andrei Evgenevich Snesarev: Zhizn i nauchnaia deiatelnost* [Andrei Evgenevich Snesarev: Life and scientific work]. Moscow: Nauka, 1973.

Baluevskii, Iurii. "Teoreticheskie i metodologicheskie osnovy formirovaniia voennoi doktriny Rossiiskoi Federatsii" [Theoretical and methodological foundations for creating a military doctrine in the Russian Federation]. *Voennaia mysl*, no. 3 (2007): 14–21.

Bartosh, A. A. "Model upravliaemogo khaosa v sfere voennoi bezopasnosti" [The model of controlled chaos in the sphere of military security]. *Vestnik Akademii Voennych Nauk*, no. 1 (2014): 69–77.

———. "Strategicheskaia kultura kak instrument voenno-politicheskogo analiza" [Strategic culture as an instrument of military-political analysis]. *Voennaia mysl*, no. 7 (2020): 6–21.

———. *Tuman gibridnoi voiny* [The fog of hybrid war]. Moscow: Goriachaia liniia–Telekom, 2019.

Beskrovnyi, L. G., ed. *M. I. Dragomirov: Izbrannye trudy; Voprosy vospitaniia i obucheniia voisk* [M. I. Dragomirov: Selected works; Questions on the education and training of the troops]. Moscow: Voenizdat, 1956.

———. *Ocherki voennoi istoriografii Rossii* [Essays on the military historiography of Russia]. Moscow: Izdatelstvo Akademii nauk SSSR, 1962.

———, ed. *Russkaia voenno-teoreticheskaia mysl XIX i nachala XX vekov* [Russian military-theoretical thought in the 19th century and the beginning of the 20th century]. Moscow: Voennoe izdatelstvo Ministerstva Oborony Soiuza SSR, 1960.

Bloch, Marc. *Strange Defeat: A Statement of Evidence Written in 1940*. London: W. W. Norton, 1999.

Braithwaite, Rodric. *Afgantsy: The Russians in Afghanistan 1979–1989*. Oxford: Oxford University Press, 2011.

Brands, Hal, ed. *The New Makers of Modern Strategy*. Princeton, NJ: Princeton University Press, 2023.

Chekinov, S. G., and S. A. Bogdanov. "O kharaktere i soderzhanii voiny novogo pokoleniia" [The nature and content of a new-generation war]. *Voennaia mysl*, no. 10 (2013): 13–24.

Chvarkov, S. V., and A. G. Likhonosov. "Novyi mnogovektornyi kharakter ugroz bezopasnosti Rossii, vozrosshii udelnyi ves 'miagkoi sily' i nevoennykh sposobov protivoborotstva na mezhdunarodnoi arene" [The new multivector nature of threats to Russia's security, the increased share of soft power, and the nonmilitary measures of countering them at the international level]. *Vestnik Akademii Voennykh Nauk*, no. 2 (2017): 27–30.

Cooper, Julian. *If War Comes Tomorrow: How Russia Prepares for Possible Armed Aggression*. Whitehall Report 4–16. London: Royal United Services Institute, 2016.

Creveld, Martin van. *The Art of War: War and Military Thought*. London: Cassel, 2000.

———. "The Crisis of Military Thought." In *Military Thinking in the 21st Century*, edited by Gudrun Persson, Carolina Vendil Pallin, and Tommy Jeppsson, 61–71. Stockholm: Swedish Academy of War Sciences, 2015.

Dahl, Ann-Sofie, ed. *Strategic Challenges in the Baltic Sea Region: Russia, Deterrence and Reassurance*. Washington, DC: Georgetown University Press, 2018.

Danilenko. I. S. "Vydaiushchiisia voennyi teoretik i filosof XX veka" [An outstanding military theorist and philosopher of the twentieth century]. In Snesarev, *Filosofiia voiny*, 5–32.

Diakov, Anatoly, Timur Kadyshev, and Pavel Podvig. "Nuclear Parity and National Security in New Conditions." Center for Arms Control, Energy and Environmental Studies, Moscow Institute of Physics and Technology. https://www.armscontrol.ru/start/publications/dkp0731.htm.

Domnin, I. V., ed. *Ne chislom, a umeniem: Voennaia sistema A. V. Suvorova* [Not by numbers but by skills: The military system of A. V. Suvorov]. In *Rossiiskii voennyi sbornik* [Russian military collection], edited by A. E. Savinkin, vol. 18. Moscow: Voennyi universitet, Russkii put, 2001.

———, ed. *Russkoe zarubezhe: Gosudarstvenno-patrioticheskaia i voennaia mysl* [Russian émigrés: State-patriotic and military thought]. In *Rossiiskii voennyi sbornik* [Russian military collection], edited by A. E. Savinkin, vol. 6. Moscow: GA VS, 1994.

———, ed. *Voennaia mysl v izgnanii: Tvorchestvo russkoi voennoi emigratsii* [Military thought in exile: The creativity of the Russian military emigrés]. In *Rossiiskii voennyi sbornik* [Russian military collection], edited by A. E. Savinkin, vol. 16. Moscow: Voennyi universitet, Russkii put, 1999.

Domnin, I. V., and V. I. Marchenkov, eds. *Khochesh mira, pobedi miatezhevoinu! Tvorcheskoe naslediia E. Messnera* [If you want peace, win the war of rebellion! The creative heritage of E. Messner]. In *Rossiiskii voennyi sbornik* [Russian military collection], edited by A. E. Savinkin, vol. 21. Moscow: Voennyi universitet, Russkii put, 2005.

Dragomirov, M. I. "Obzor Italianskoi kampanii 1859" [Survey of the Italian campaign in 1859]. *Inzhenernyi zhurnal*, no. 6 (1861): 503–6.

———. *Ocherki* [Essays]. Kiev: Tipografiia S. V. Kulzhenko, 1898.

———. *Ocherki Avstro-Prusskoi voiny v 1866 godu* [Essays on the Austro-Prussian War in 1866] Saint Petersburg: Tipografiia Departamenta Udelov, 1867.

———. "Po povodu nekotorykh statei vyzvannykh poslednimi dvumia kampaniiami" [Regarding a few articles on the two latest campaigns]. *Voennyi sbornik*, no. 12 (1872): 253–74; no. 1 (1873): 89–106.

———. "Uchenie o voine Klauzevitsa: Osnovnye polozheniia" [Studies of war by Clausewitz: Basic provisions]. *Voennyi sbornik*, no. 10 (1888): 245–71; no. 11 (1888): 5–22.

Duffy, Christopher. *Russia's Military Way to the West*. 1981. Facsimile ed., Knighton, Wales: Terence Wise, 1994.

Eitelhuber, Norbert. *Russland im 21. Jahrhundert: Reif für eine multipolare Welt?* [Russia in the 21st century: Ripe for a multipolar world?]. Frankfurt am Main: Peter Lang, 2015.

Figes, Orlando. *The Story of Russia*. London: Bloomsbury, 2022.

FitzGerald, Mary C. "The Impact of New Technologies on Soviet Military Thought." In *Radical Reform in Soviet Defence Policy*, edited by Roy Allison, 98–131. New York: Palgrave Macmillan, 1992.

———. "The Russian Military's Strategy for 'Sixth Generation' Warfare." *Orbis*, no. 3 (1994): 457–76.

Fridman, Ofer. *Russian "Hybrid Warfare": Resurgence and Politicisation*. London: Hurst, 2018.

———, ed. *Strategiya: The Foundations of the Russian Art of Strategy*. London: Hurst, 2021.

## Selected Bibliography

Frunze, M. V. "Edinaia voennaia doktrina i Krasnaia armiia" [A unified military doctrine and the Red Army]. *Voennaia nauka i revoliutsiia*, no. 1 (1921): 30–46.

Fuller, William C., Jr. *Strategy and Power in Russia 1600–1914*. New York: Free Press, 1992.

Galeotti, Mark. *Putin's Wars: From Chechnya to Ukraine*. Oxford: Osprey, 2022.

Gareev, M. A. *Moia poslednaia voina* [My last war]. Moscow: Inan, 1996.

Gareev, Makhmut. *Esli zavtra voina?* [If war comes tomorrow?]. Moscow: VlaDar, 1995.

———. "Velikaia pobeda i sobytiia na Ukraine" [The great victory and the events in Ukraine]. *Vestnik Akademii Voennykh Nauk*, no. 2 (2014): 4–10.

Gareev, Makhmut, and Vladimir Slipchenko. *Future War*. Introduction by Jacob W. Kipp. Fort Leavenworth, KS: Foreign Military Studies Office, 2007.

Gareev, Makhmut Akhmetovich. *M. V. Frunze, Military Theorist*. Washington, DC: Pergamon-Brassey's, 1988.

Garthoff, Raymond L. *Deterrence and the Revolution in Soviet Military Doctrine*. Washington, DC: Brookings Institution, 1990.

———. *How Russia Makes War: Soviet Military Doctrine*. 1954. E-book reprint, London: Routledge, 2021.

———. *A Journey through the Cold War: A Memoir of Containment and Coexistence*. Washington, DC: Brookings Institution Press, 2001.

Gat, Azar. *A History of Military Thought from the Enlightenment to the Cold War*. Oxford: Oxford University Press, 2001.

Gerasimov, Valerii. "Osnovnye tendentsii razvitiia form i sposobov primeneniia Vooruzhennykh Sil, aktualnye zadachi voennoi nauki po ikh sovershenstvovaniiu" [Principal trends in the development of the forms and methods of employing armed forces and current tasks of military science regarding their improvement]. *Vestnik Akademii Voennykh Nauk*, no. 1 (2013): 24–29.

———. "Po opytu Sirii" [The Syrian experience]. *Voenno-promyshlennyi kurer*, March 7, 2016.

———. "Razvitie voennoi strategii v sovremennykh usloviiakh: Zadachi voennoi nauki" [The development of military strategy in contemporary conditions: Tasks for military science]. *Vestnik Akademii Voennykh Nauk*, no. 2 (2019): 6–11.

———. "Sovremennye voiny i aktualnye voprosy oborony strany" [Modern wars and current questions in regard to the country's defense]. *Vestnik Akademii Voennykh Nauk*, no. 2 (2017): 9–13.

———. "Vliianie sovremennogo kharaktera vooruzhennoi borby na napravlennost stroitelstva i razvitiia Vooruzhennykh Sil Rossiiskoi Federatsii: Prioritetnye zadachi voennoi nauki v obespechenii oborony strany" [The influence of the contemporary nature of armed struggle on the focus of the construction and development of the Armed Forces of the Russian Federation: Priority tasks of military science in safeguarding the country's defense]. *Vestnik Akademii Voennykh Nauk*, no. 2 (2018): 16–22.

Giles, Keir. "Russia's 'New' Tools for Confronting the West: Continuity and Innovation in Moscow's Exercise of Power." Research paper, Chatham House, London, March 2016.

Glantz, David M. *The Military Strategy of the Soviet Union: A History*. London: Frank Cass, 1992.

Golts, Aleksandr. *Voennaia reforma i rossiiskii militarizm* [Military reform and Russian militarism]. Uppsala: Acta Universitatis Upsaliensis, 2017.

Goncharov, V., ed. *Russkaia voennaia mysl XVIII vek* [Russian military thought in the 18th century]. Moscow: Terra Fantastica, 2003.

Gorbatov, A. V. *Years Off My Life: The Memoirs of General of the Soviet Army A. V. Gorbatov*. London: Constable, 1964.
Gorlov, S. A. *Sovershenno sekretno: Moskva–Berlin 1920–1933* [Top secret: Moscow–Berlin 1920–33]. Moscow: IVI RAN, 1999.
Gorshkov, S. G. *Morskaia moshch gosudarstva* [The sea power of the state]. 2nd ed. Moscow: Voenizdat, 1979.
Gray, Colin. "A Debate on Geopolitics: The Continued Primacy of Geography." *Orbis*, no. 2 (1996): 247–59.
Grechko, A. A. *The Armed Forces of the Soviet State: A Soviet View*. 2nd ed. Moscow. Translated and published under the auspices of the US Air Force. Washington, DC: Government Printing Office, 1975.
Gromyko, A. A., S. A. Golunskii, and V. M. Khvostov, eds. *Diplomaticheskii Slovar* [Diplomatic lexicon]. 3 vols. Moscow: Gos. izd. politicheskoi literarury, 1960–64.
Harrison, Richard W. *The Russian Way of War: Operational Art, 1904–1940*. Lawrence: University Press of Kansas, 2001.
Herspring, Dale R. *The Soviet High Command 1967–1989: Personalities and Politics*. Princeton, NJ: Princeton University Press, 1990.
Heuser, Beatrice. *The Evolution of Strategy: Thinking War from Antiquity to the Present*. Cambridge: Cambridge University Press, 2010.
———. *Strategy before Clausewitz: Linking Warfare and Statecraft*. Oxford: Routledge, 2018.
Heuser, Beatrice, Tormod Heier, and Guillaume Lasconjarias, eds. *Military Exercises: Political Messaging and Strategic Impact*. NDC Forum Papers, no. 26. Rome: NATO Defense College, 2018.
Higham, Robin, and Frederick W. Kagan, eds. *The Military History of the Soviet Union*. New York: Palgrave, 2002.
Howard, Michael. *The Franco-Prussian War*. 1961. Reprint, London: Routledge, 1991.
Huntington, Samuel P. *The Soldier and the State: The Theory and Politics of Civil-Military Relations*. 1957. Reprint, Cambridge, MA: Belknap Press of Harvard University Press, 1995.
Høiback, Harald. "The Anatomy of Doctrine and Ways to Keep It Fit." *Journal of Strategic Studies*, no. 2 (2016): 185–97.
———. *Understanding Military Doctrine: A Multidisciplinary Approach*. London: Routledge, 2013.
Ivashov, Leonid. "Obrashchenie Obshcherossiiskogo ofitserskogo sobraniia k prezidentu i grazhdanam Rossiiskoi Federatsii" [Statement by the All-Russian Officers Assembly to the president and citizens of the Russian Federation]. January 28, 2022. http://www.cooc.su/news/obrashhenie_obshherossijskogo_oficerskogo_sobranija_k_prezidentu_i_grazhdanam_rossijskoj_federacii/2022-01-31-79?ysclid=lnd5i4rsee402579256.
Jomini, Antoine Henri de. *The Art of War: Restored Edition*. Kingston, Ontario: Legacy Books, 2008.
Jonsson, Oscar. *The Russian Understanding of War: Blurring the Lines between War and Peace*. Washington, DC: Georgetown University Press, 2019.
Kagan, Frederick W., and Robin Higham, eds. *The Military History of Tsarist Russia*. New York: Palgrave, 2002.
Kavtaradze, A. G. *Voennye spetsialisty na sluzhbe Respubliki Sovetov 1917–1920* [The military specialists in the service of the Soviet republics 1917–20]. Moscow: Nauka, 1988.

Keep, John L. H. *Power and the People: Essays on Russian History*. Boulder, CO: East European Monographs, 1995.
——. *Soldiers of the Tsar: Army and Society in Russia 1462–1874*. Oxford: Clarendon Press, 1985.
Kennedy, Paul. *The Rise and Fall of the Great Powers: Economic Change and Military Conflict from 1550 to 2000*. London: Fontana Press, 1988.
Kersnovskii, Anton. *Istoriia russkoi armii* [History of the Russian army]. 4 vols. Moscow: Golos, 1992.
Khodarenok, Mikhail. "Prognozy krovozhadnykh politologov: O vostorzhennykh iastrebakh i toroplivykh kukushkakh" [Forecasts of bloodthirsty political scientists: About enthusiastic hawks and hurried cuckoos]. *Nezavisimoe voennoe obozrenie*, February 3, 2022. https://nvo.ng.ru/realty/2022-02-03/3_1175_donbass.html.
Kipp, Jacob. "Lenin and Clausewitz: The Militarization of Marxism 1914–1921." *Military Affairs* (October 1985): 184–91.
Kofman, Michael, Anya Fink, Dmitry Gorenburg, Mary Chesnut, Jeffrey Edmonds, and Julian Waller. With contributions by Kasey Stricklin and Samuel Bendett. *Russian Military Strategy: Core Tenets and Operational Concepts*. Arlington, VA: Center for Naval Analyses, 2021.
Kofman, Michael, Katya Migacheva, Brian Nichiporuk, Andrew Radin, Olesya Tkacheva, and Jenny Oberholtzer. *Lessons from Russia's Operations in Crimea and Eastern Ukraine*. Research Report No. RR-1498-A. Santa Monica, CA: RAND Corp., 2017.
Kokoshin, A. A. *O sisteme neiadernogo (prediadernogo) sderzhivaniia v oboronnoi politike Rossii* [About the system of nonnuclear (prenuclear) deterrence in Russia's defense policy]. Moscow: Izdatelstvo Moskovskogo universiteta, 2012.
——. *Politologiia i sotsiologiia voennoi strategii* [The political science and sociology of military strategy]. Moscow: Lenand, 2018.
——. *Soviet Strategic Thought, 1917–91*. Cambridge, MA: MIT Press, 1998.
——. *Strategicheskoe upravlenie* [Strategic control]. Moscow: Rosspen, 2003.
——. *Voporosy prikladnoi teorii voiny* [Questions of an applied theory of war]. Moscow: Izd. dom Vysshei shkoly ekonomiki, 2018.
——. *Vydaiushchiisia otechestvennyi voennyi teoretik i voenachalnik Aleksandr Andreevich Svechin* [The outstanding Russian military theorist and military commander Aleksandr Andreevich Svechin]. Moscow: Izd. Moskovoskogo universiteta, 2013.
Kokoshin, A. A., and V. Larionov. "Kurskaia bitva v svete sovremennoi oboronitelnoi doktriny" [The Battle of Kursk in light of the contemporary defensive doctrine]. *Mirovaia ekonomika i mezhdunarodnye otnosheniia*, no. 8 (1987): 32–40.
Kokoshin, A. A., V. A. Veselov, A. V. Liss, and I. S. Fisenko. *Sovremennye voiny i voennoe iskusstvo* [Contemporary wars and military art]. Moscow: Leland, 2015.
Kokoshin, Andrei. "Ensuring Strategic Stability in the Past and Present: Theoretical and Applied Questions." Paper, Belfer Center for Science and International Affairs, Harvard Kennedy School, June 2011.
——. "Reflections on Russia's Past, Present, and Future." Paper, Strengthening Democratic Institutions Project, Belfer Center for Science and International Affairs, Harvard Kennedy School, June 1997.
Konyshev, V. N., and A. A. Sergunin. *Sovremennaia voennaia strategiia* [Contemporary Military Strategy]. Moscow: Aspekt Press, 2014.
Korotkov, Ivan A. *Istoriia sovetskoi voennoi mysli: Kratkii ocherk 1917–iiun 1940* [History of Soviet military thought: A short essay 1917–June 1941]. Moscow: Nauka, 1980.

Kulikov, V. G. "O voenno-strategicheskom paritete i dostatochnosti dlia oborony" [On military-strategic parity and sufficiency for defense]. *Voennaia mysl*, no. 5 (1988): 3–11.

Lahusen, Thomas, and Evgeny Dobrenko, eds. *Socialist Realism without Shores*. Durham, NC: Duke University Press, 1997.

Lambert, Andrew. *Seapower States: Maritime Culture, Continental Empires and the Conflict That Made the Modern World*. New Haven, CT: Yale University Press, 2018.

Lantis J. S. "Strategic Culture: From Clausewitz to Constructivism." In *Strategic Culture and Weapons of Mass Destruction: Initiatives in Strategic Studies; Issues and Policies*, edited by J. L. Johnson, K. M. Kartchner, and J. A. Larsen, 33–52. New York: Palgrave Macmillan, 2009.

LeDonne, John. *The Grand Strategy of the Russian Empire, 1650–1831*. Oxford: Oxford University Press, 2004.

Leer, G. A., ed. *Entsiklopediia voennykh i morskikh nauk* [Encyclopedia of military and naval sciences]. 8 vols. Saint Petersburg: V. Bezobrazova i komp., 1883–97.

———. "Generalnyi shtab i ego komplektovanie v Prussii i vo Frantsii" [General Staff and its recruitment in Prussia and France]. *Voennyi sbornik*, no. 11 (1868): 49–74.

———. *Opyt kritiko-istoricheskogo issledovaniia zakonov iskusstva vedeniia voiny (polozhitelnaia strategiia)* [The experience of historical-critical research into the laws of military art (positive strategy)]. Saint Petersburg: V. Golovin, 1869.

———. *Publichnye lektsii o voine 1870 mezhdu Frantsiei i Germaniei do Sedana vkliuchitelno* [Public lectures on the war of 1870 between France and Germany including Sedan]. Saint Petersburg: Obshchestvennaia polza, 1871.

———. *Zapiski strategii* [Notes on strategy]. Saint Petersburg: Obshchestvennaia Polza.

Leonhard, Wolfgang. *Was ist Kommunismus? Wandlungen einer Ideologie* [What is Communism? Transformations of an ideology]. Munich: C. Bertelsmann, 1976.

Levshin, V. I., A. V. Nedelin, and M. E. Sosnovskii, "O primenenii iadernogo oruzhiia dlia deeskalatsii voennykh deistvii" [On the use of nuclear weapons for the de-escalation of combat actions]. *Voennaia mysl*, no. 3 (1999): 34–37.

Lieven, Dominic. *Empire: The Russian Empire and Its Rivals*. London: John Murray, 2000.

———. *The End of Tsarist Russia: The March to World War I and Revolution*. New York: Viking, 2015.

———. *Russia and the Origins of the First World War*. London: Macmillan, 1983.

Longworth, Philip. *The Art of Victory: The Life and Achievements of Generalissimo Suvorov 1729–1800*. London, Constable, 1965.

Lopatin, V. S., ed. *A. V. Suvorov: Pisma* [A. V. Suvorov: Letters]. Moscow: Nauka, 1986.

Luttwak, Edward. *The Grand Strategy of the Soviet Union*. New York: St. Martin's, 1983.

MacMillan, Margaret. *War: How Conflict Shaped Us*. London: Profile Books, 2020.

Makarov, N. E. *Na sluzhbe Rossii* [In the service of Russia]. Moscow: Kuchkovo pole, 2017.

Matthews, Owen. *Overreach: The Inside Story of Putin's War against Ukraine*. London: Mudlark, 2022.

Mastny, Vojtech. "Imaging War in Europe." In *War Plans and Alliances in the Cold War: Threat Perceptions in the East and West*, edited by Vojtech Mastny, Sven G. Holtsmark, and Andreas Wenger, 15–45. London: Routledge, 2006.

McNeill, William H. *The Pursuit of Power: Technology, Armed Force, and Society since A.D. 1000*. Oxford: Basil Blackwell, 1982.

Medem, Nikolai. *Obozrenie izvestneishikh pravil i sistem strategii* [An overview of the most famous rules and systems of strategy]. Saint Petersburg: II Otdeleniia Sobstevennoi E. I. V. Kantseliarii, 1836.

Menning, Bruce. *Bayonets before Bullets: The Imperial Russian Army 1861–1914*. Bloomington: Indiana University Press, 1992.
Meretskov, Kirill. *Na sluzhbe narodu* [In the service of the people]. Moscow: Politizdat, 1968.
Meshcheriakov, G. P. *Russkaia voennaia mysl v XIX-om veke* [Russian military thought in the 19th century]. Moscow: Nauka, 1973.
Miakinkov, Eugene. "A Russian Way of War? Westernization of Russian Military Thought, 1757–1800." Master thesis in history, University of Waterloo, Ontario, 2009.
———. *War and Enlightenment in Russia: Military Culture in the Age of Catherine II*. Toronto: University of Toronto Press, 2020.
Mikhalev, S. N. *Liudskie poteri v Velikoi Otechestvennoi voine 1941–1945: Statisticheskoe issledovanie* [Losses of human life in the Great Patriotic War 1941–45: A statistical study]. 2nd ed. Krasnoiarsk: RIO KGPU, 2000.
———. *Voennaia strategiia: Podgotovka i vedenie voin Novogo i Noveishego vremeni* [Military strategy: Preparing for and waging wars in modern and contemporary history]. Moscow: Kuchkovo pole, 2003.
Mikhalev, Yuri. "Voenno-politicheskie vzgliady A. E. Snesareva i sovremennost: Avtoreferat dissertatsii" [The military-political views of A. E. Snesarev and contemporary times]. Diss. abstract, Military University, Moscow, 2008.
Mikhnevich, N. P. *Osnovy strategii* [The foundations of strategy]. Saint Petersburg: Tipografiia Trenke i Fiusno, 1913.
Miliutin, D. A. *Kriticheskoe issledovanie znacheniia voennoi geografii i voennoi statistiki* [A critical study of the significance of military geography and military statistics]. Saint Petersburg: Voennaia Tipografiia, 1846.
———. "Starcheskie razmyshleniia o sovremennom polozhenii voennogo dela v Rossii" [Elderly reflections on the current situation in Russian military affairs]. *Izvestiia Imperatorskoi Nikolaevskoi Voennoi Akademii*, no. 30 (1912): 833–58.
———. *Vospominaniia 1816–1843* [Memoirs 1816–43], edited by L. G. Zakharova. Moscow: Rossiiskii arkhiv, 1997.
———. *Vospominaniia 1843–1856* [Memoirs 1843–56]. Moscow: Rossiiskii arkhiv, 2000.
———. *Vospominaniia 1868–nachalo 1873* [Memoirs 1868–beginning of 1873]. Moscow: Rosspen, 2006).
Minic, Dimitri. *Pensée et culture stratégiques russes: Du contournement de la lutte armée à la guerre en Ukraine* [Russian strategic thought and culture: From bypassing armed struggle to war in Ukraine]. Condé-en-Normandie: Éditions de la Maison des science de l´homme, 2023.
Monaghan, Andrew, ed. *Russian Grand Strategy in the Era of Global Power Competition*. Manchester: Manchester University Press, 2022.
Moshes, Arkady, and András Rácz, eds. *What Has Remained of the USSR? Exploring the Erosion of the Post-Soviet Space*. FIIA Report no. 58. Helskini: Finnish Institute of International Affairs, 2019.
Nye, Joseph. *Soft Power: The Means to Success in World Politics*. New York: PublicAffairs, 2004.
Odom, William E. *The Collapse of the Soviet Military*. New Haven, CT: Yale University Press, 1998.
———. "Thoughts on the Future of the Soviet Military." *Defense Analysis* 7, nos. 2–3 (1991): 133–39.

Ogarkov, N. V. "Na strazhe mirnogo truda" [On guard for peaceful labor]. *Kommunist*, no. 10 (1981): 80–91.
———. *Istoriia uchit bditelnost* [History teaches vigilance]. Moscow: Voennoe izdatelstvo, 1985.
———, ed. *Sovetskaia voennaia entsiklopediia* [Soviet military encyclopedia]. 8 vols. Moscow: Voenizdat, 1976–80.
———. "Voennaia nauka i zashchita sotsialisticheskogo otechestva" [Military science and the protection of the fatherland]. *Kommunist*, no. 7 (1978): 110–21.
Paret, Peter, ed. *Makers of Modern Strategy: From Machiavelli to the Nuclear Age*. Princeton, NJ: Princeton University Press, 1986.
Persson, Gudrun. *Learning from Foreign Wars: Russian Military Thinking 1859–1873*. Solihull, UK: Helion, 2010.
———. "On War and Peace: Russian Security Policy and Military-Strategic Thinking." In *Putin's Russia: Economy, Defence and Foreign Policy*, edited by Steven Rosefielde, 347–77. Singapore: World Scientific, 2020.
———. "Russia and the Baltic Sea: A Background." In Dahl, *Strategic Challenges in the Baltic Sea Region*, 17–31.
———. "Vilka är vi? Rysk identitet och den nationella säkerheten" [Who are we? Russian identity and national security]. *Nordisk Østforum*, no. 3 (2014): 199–214.
Persson, Gudrun, Carolina Vendil Pallin, and Maria Engqvist, "Ryssland ändrar grundlagen: Innehåll och konsekvenser" [Russia changes the constitution: Content and consequences]. Memo 7091. Swedish Defence Research Agency. May 2020.
Peterson, Claes. *Peter the Great's Administrative and Judicial Reforms: Swedish Antecedents and the Process of Reception*. Stockholm: Nordiska bokhandeln, 1979.
Pipes, Richard. *The Formation of the Soviet Union: Communism and Nationalism 1917–1923*. Cambridge, MA: Harvard University Press, 1964.
———. *The Russian Revolution*. New York: Vintage Books, 1991.
———. *Survival Is Not Enough: Soviet Realities and America's Future*. New York: Simon & Schuster, 1984.
Plokhy, Serhii. *The Russo-Ukrainian War*. Dublin: Allen Lane, 2023.
Popov, Igor. "Voennaia mysl sovremennoi Rossii" [Military thought in contemporary Russia]. 2007. http://futurewarfare.narod.ru/theoryRF.html.
Popov, Igor, and Musa Khamzatov. *Voina budushchego: Kontseptualnye osnovy i prakticheskie vyvody; Ocherki strategicheskoi mysli* [The war of the future: A conceptual framework and practical conclusions; Essays on strategic thought]. Moscow: Kuchkovo pole, 2016.
Preston, R. A., S. F. Wise, and H. O. Werner. *Men in Arms: A History of Warfare and Its Interrelationships with Western Society*. London: Atlantic Press, 1956.
Putin, Vladimir. "Byt silnymi: Garantii natsionalnoi bezopasnosti dlia Rossii" [Be strong: National security guarantees for Russia]. *Rossiiskaia gazeta*, February 20, 2012.
Reach, Clint, Alyssa Demus, Michelle Grisé, Khrystyna Holynska, Christopher Lynch, Dara Massicot, and David Woodworth. *Russia's Evolution toward a Unified Strategic Operation: The Influence of Geography and Conventional Capacity*. Research Report. Santa Monica, CA: RAND Corp., 2023.
Rentola, Kimmo. *How Finland Survived Stalin: From Winter War to Cold War, 1939–1940*. Translated by Richard Robinson. New Haven, CT: Yale University Press, 2023.
Renz, Bettina. *Russia's Military Revival*. Cambridge, UK: Polity Press, 2018.

Rich, David A. *The Tsar's Colonels: Professionalism, Strategy, and Subversion in Late Imperial Russia.* Cambridge, MA: Harvard University Press, 1998.
Rogov, Sergei, ed. "Russian Defense Policy: Challenges and Developments." Occasional Papers, Institute of USA and Canada Studies and Center for Naval Analyses, February 1993.
Rose, Olaf. *Carl von Clausewitz: Wirkungsgeschichte seines Werkes in Russland und der Sowjetunion* [Carl von Clausewitz: History of the impact of his work in Russia and the Soviet Union]. Munich: R. Oldenbourg Verlag, 1995.
Rothenberg, Gunther. *The Army of Francis Joseph.* West Lafayette, IN: Purdue University Press, 1976.
Rowlands, Kevin, ed. *21st Century Gorshkov.* Annapolis, MD: Naval Institute Press, 2017.
Rumiantsev, Petr. "Mysl" [Thought]. In Goncharov, *Russkaia voennaia mysl XVIII vek*, 99–117.
———. "Obriad Sluzhby" [Customs of military service]. In Goncharov, *Russkaia voennaia mysl XVIII vek*, 118–38.
Sarotte, M. E. *Not One Inch: America, Russia, and the Making of the Post–Cold War Stalemate.* New Haven, CT: Yale University Press, 2021.
Savinkin, A. E., I. V. Domnin, and Iu. T. Belov, eds. *Kakaia armiia nuzhna Rossii? Vzgliad iz istorii* [What kind of army does Russia need? A view from history]. In *Rossiiskii voennyi sbornik* [Russian military collection], edited by A. E. Savinkin, vol. 9. Moscow: Voennyi universitet, 1995.
Savinkin, A. E., A. G. Kavtaradze, Iu. T. Belov, and I. V. Domnin, eds. *Postizhenie voennogo iskusstva: Ideinoe nasledie A. Svechina* [Understanding military art: The ideological heritage of A. Svechin]. In *Rossiiskii voennyi sbornik* [Russian military collection], edited by A. E. Savinkin, vol. 15. Moscow: Voennyi universitet, Russkii put, 2001.
Seaton, Albert, and Joan Seaton. *The Soviet Army: 1918 to the Present.* New York: Meridian, 1988.
Shaposhnikov, Boris. *Mozg armii* [The brain of the army]. 3 vols. Moscow: Voennyi vestnik, 1927–29.
Slipchenko, V. I. "K kakoi voine dolzhny gotovitsia vooruzhennye sily?" [What kind of war should the armed forces prepare for?]. *Otechestennye zapiski*, no. 8 (2002). http://www.strana-oz.ru/2002/8/k-kakoy-voyne-dolzhny-gotovitsya-vooruzhennye-sily.
———. *Voina budushchego* [Future war]. Moscow: Moskovskii Obshchestvennyi nauchnyi fond, 1999.
Snesarev, A. "Edinaia voennaia doktrina" [A unified military doctrine]. *Voennoe delo*, no. 8 (April 26, 1920): 225–334.
———. "Retsenziia na knigu A. Svechina 'Strategiia'" [Review of A. Svechin's book *Strategy*]. *Voina i revoliutsiia*, no. 4 (1927): 144–47.
———. *Vvedenie v voennuiu geografiiu* [Introduction to military geography]. Moscow: Tip. Voennaia akademiia R. K. K. A, 1924.
Snesarev, A. E. *Pisma s fronta 1914–1917* [Letters from the front 1914–17]. Moscow: Kuchkovo pole, 2012.
———. *Zhizn i trudy Klauzevitsa* [The life and work of Clausewitz]. Moscow: Kuchkovo pole, 2007.
Snesarev, Andrei. *Afganskie uroki* [Afghan lessons]. Moscow: Russkii Put, 2003.
———. *Filosofiia voiny* [The philosophy of war]. Moscow: Lomonosov, 2013.
Sokolovskiy, V. D. *Soviet Military Strategy.* 3rd ed. Edited and with an analysis and commentary by Harriet Fast Scott. London: Macdonald & Jane's, 1968.

Steinberg, John. *All the Tsar's Men: Russia's General Staff and the Fate of the Empire*. Baltimore: Johns Hopkins University Press, 2010.
Stevens, Carol B., *Russia's Wars of Emergence, 1460–1730*. London: Routledge, 2013.
———. *Soldiers on the Steppe: Army Reform and Social Change in Early Modern Russia*. DeKalb: Northern Illinois University Press, 1995.
Stone, John. *Military Strategy: The Politics and Technique of War*. London: Bloomsbury Academic, 2018.
Strachan, Hew. *European Armies and the Conduct of War*. London: Unwin Hyman, 1983.
Sukhotin, N. N. *Voina v istorii Russkago mira* [War in the history of the Russian world]. Saint Petersburg: Trenke i Fiusno, 1898.
Suvorov, Aleksandr. "Nauka pobezhdat" [The art of victory]. In Goncharov, *Russkaia voennaia mysl XVIII vek*, 302–16.
Svechin, A. "Shto takoe voennaia doktrina?" [What is a military doctrine?]. *Voennoe delo*, no. 2 (1920): 29–41.
———. *Evoliutsiia voennogo iskusstva* [The evolution of the art of war] 2 vols. Moscow: Gos. Izd. Otdel Voennoi Literatury, 1927–28.
———. "Opasnye illiuzii" [Dangerous illusions]. *Voennaia mysl i revoliutsiia*, no. 2 (1924): 44–55.
———. *Strategiia*. 2nd ed. Moscow: Voennyi vestnik, 1927.
Taylor, Brian D. *Politics and the Russian Army: Civil-Military Relations, 1689–2000*. Cambridge: Cambridge University Press, 2003.
Tiushkevich, S. A. "Razumnaia dostatochnost dlia oborony: Parametry i kriteriii" [Reasonable sufficiency for defense: Parameters and criteria]. *Voennaia mysl*, no. 5 (1989): 53–61.
Trenin, Dmitri. *Post-Imperium: A Eurasian Story*. Washington, DC: Carnegie Endowment for International Peace, 2011.
Trotskii, L. "Voennaia doktrina ili mimo-voennoe doktrinerstvo" [A military doctrine or a pseudo-military doctrinaire attitude]. *Voennoe delo*, no. 2 (1921): 204–34.
Tukhachevskii, M. *Voina klassov* [War of the classes] Moscow: Gosizdat, 1921.
Tumakov, O. G. "Osnovnye napravleniia sovershenstvovaniia voenno-politicheskoi raboty pri podgotovke operatsii" [The basic directions for improving military-political work in preparing for an operation]. *Voennaia mysl*, no. 2 (2023): 38–48.
Wahlde, Peter von. "Military Thought in Imperial Russia." PhD thesis, Indiana University, 1966.
Wirtschafter, Elise Kimerling. *From Serf to Russian Soldier*. Princeton, NJ: Princeton University Press, 1990.
Vladimirov, Aleksandr I. *Osnovy obshchei teorii voiny, chast I: Osnovy teorii voin* [Foundations of the general theory of war, volume 1: Foundations of the theory of war]. Moscow: Universitet Sinergiia, 2013.
Yudin, Stanislav. "General M. I. Dragomirov (1830–1905): Voennyi myslitel i praktik" [General M. I. Dragomirov (1830–1905): Military theorist and practitioner]. PhD diss., Moscow State University, 2020.
Zabrodskyi, Mykhaylo, Jack Watling, Oleksandr V. Danylyuk, and Nick Reynolds. *Preliminary Lessons in Conventional Warfighting from Russia's Invasion of Ukraine: February–July 2022*. RUSI Special Report. London: Royal United Services Institute, 2022.
Zaionchkovskii, P. A., ed. *Dnevnik D. A. Miliutina* [D. A. Miliutin's diary]. 4 vols. Moscow: Gosudarstvennaia ordena Lenina Biblioteka SSSR imeni V. I. Lenina. Otdel rukopisei, 1947–50.

———. *Samoderzhavie i russkaia armiia na rubezhe XIX–XX stoletii, 1881–1903* [Autocracy and the Russian army at the turn of the twentieth century, 1881–1903]. Moscow: Mysl, 1973.

———. *Voennye reformy 1860–70 godov v Rossii* [Military reforms of 1860–70 in Russia]. Moscow: Izdatelstvo Moskovskogo Universiteta, 1952.

Zhilin, P. A., ed. *Russkaia voennaia mysl konets XIX–nachalo XX v* [Russian military thought at the end of the 19th century and beginning of the 20th century]. Moscow: Nauka, 1982.

Zhukov, G. K. *Vospominaniia i razmyshleniia* [Memoirs and thoughts]. 3 vols. Moscow: Novosti, 1990.

Zisk, Kimberly Marten. *Engaging the Enemy: Organization Theory and Soviet Military Innovation*. Princeton, NJ: Princeton University Press, 1993.

Zolotarev, V. A., ed. *Istoriia voennoi strategii Rossii* [A history of Russia's military strategy] Moscow: Kuchkovo pole, 2000.

Zolotarev, V. A., and I. A. Kozlov. *Tri stoletiia Rossiiskogo flota: XIX–nachalo XX veka* [Three centuries of the Russian fleet: 19th century to the beginning of the 20th century]. Moscow: AST, 2004.

# INDEX

"action-reaction" paradigm, 170
Adamsky, Dima, 9
Afghanistan, 59, 65, 77, 104–5, 112–13, 116
Akhmatova, Anna, 82
Alexander II, 8, 24, 29, 34, 137
Alexander III, 35
Allison, Roy, 8
American-British imperialism, 12, 82
American Civil War, 34, 94
*Analyse militaire des différentes frontières en Europe* (Lloyd), 41
Andropov, Yuri Vladimirovich, 155
a-rationality, doctrine, 11
Arbatov, Alexei Georgievich, 115–16, 128
armed conflict, 150, 154; characterization of, 89; defining, 131–32; naval doctrine and, 95; potential escalation of, 88, 132, 141
armed masses, 37
armed struggle, 9, 96, 109–10, 133
*Armiia i politika*, 7
army: and art of winning, 167, 173, 178; connection between political system and, 40–43; conscript army, 32, 35; creating effective army, 46–48; debates on strategy/doctrine prior to World War I, 48–52; development of, 16–19; and general staff as brain of, 33; "golden age" of, 62; impressions of foreign wars, 53; indirect criticism of, 47; laying foundations for, 17; lessons taken from World War II, 96–99; mobilization army, 136, 155; and morale in nuclear war, 92; morale of, 53–54; navy and, 75, 94; position as founding part of Russian state, 174–75; relevance of, 51–54; Russian army, 2, 8–19, 21, 33–34, 36–38, 40–41, 53, 60, 167, 173; and state, 40–43, 65–68; as state builder, 66, 174–77; strategy and policy, 19–21; strategy as synthesis, 44; and unified military doctrine, 62; and universal military conscription, 35–36; between world wars, 60–62. *See also* military thought; Russia: army of
*Art of War: War and Military Thought, The* (Creveld), 10
art of winning: "action-reaction" paradigm, 170; considering influence from abroad, 171–72; factors influencing thought on strategy and doctrine, 169–71; key concerns in strategy debate, 167–68; overview, 177–78; pronounced constants, 168–70; and repressive political system, 170–71; Russia as geopolitical actor, 174–77; technology-morale balance, 172–74

193

asymmetrical warfare, 130, 135
Austria, 18, 23, 31, 33, 71; identifying as main threat, 38–40; investments in roads and railways, 42–43
Austrian Empire, 31, 42
Austro-Prussian War, 31
authority, doctrine, 11

Babchenko, Arkady, 93
backward, term, 53
Baev, Pavel Kimovich, 8, 125
Baikov, L. M., 47
balance (of technology-morale), 51–54
Baluevskii, Iurii Nikolaevich, 64
Bartosh, Aleksandr, 64, 145
"Basic Principles of the State Policy of the Russian Federation in the Domain of Nuclear Deterrence," 139–40
Batiushin, Nikolai Stepanovich, 147
Battle of Königgrätz, 47
Battle of Kursk, 115
Battle of Sedan, 31
bean counting, 98
Belarus, 124, 154
Belavezha Accords, 123
Berlin, Isaiah, 1
Beskrovnyi, L. G., 8
Betts, Richard, 5
Bismarck, Otto von, 31
"Blitzkrieg of the Twenty-First Century, The" (Khamzatov), 142–43
"blitzkrieg of the twenty-first century," term, 142–43, 155
Bloch, Ivan Stanislavovich, 66–67, 117
Bloch, Marc, 3, 64
Blok, Alesandr, 59
Bonaparte, Napoleon, 18
Braithwaite, Rodric, 104
Brezhnev, Leonid Ilich, 83, 155
Brezhnev Doctrine, 104, 114
Budapest Memorandum, 124
*Budushchaia voina* (Bloch), 117
Bukkvoll, Tor, 4
Bulganin, Nikolai Aleksandrovich, 133

Catherine II, 17–18, 19–20
CFE Treaty. *See* Treaty on Conventional Armed Forces in Europe
Chechnya, 13, 122, 128, 153
Chernyshevskii, Nikolai Gavrilovich, 36
Chief Political Administration, 92
China, 10, 105, 133, 172
Chvarkov, Sergei, 145–46
CIS. *See* Commonwealth of Independent States
Civil War, 12, 59, 61, 65–66, 68, 70, 99, 147, 167
Clausewitz, Carl von, 2, 5, 25, 40, 47, 85, 87, 99, 168–69, 172–73, 177–78; Clausewitzian statement, 20; emphasizing dictum of, 86; fascination with, 68–72; views on strategy, 44–46; writing about, 64–65
close-order infantry column, obsoletion of, 33–34
Coehoorn, Menno van, 22
Cold War, 104, 137, 143, 169; beginning of, 83–84; end of, 122–25; period of détente and, 103–5
*Collapse of the Soviet Military, The* (Odom), 8
Collective Security Treaty (CST), 124
color revolutions, 144–46
Commonwealth of Independent States (CIS), 123
conscript armies, skepticism of, 32–33
"Considerations on the Defense of Russia" (Obruchev), 38
Consultative Committee, 43
contactless battlefield, 116, 135, 177
contemporary wars, aims of, 50–51
controlled chaos, 144–46
Coordination of Military Cooperation, 123
counteroffensives, strategic level, 114–15
counterraids, strategy, 16–17
Creveld, Martin van, 10
Crimea, 2, 19, 128, 130, 175; annexation as example of soft power, 144–45; "correcting historical injustices,"

125–26; illegal annexation of, 90, 125, 150, 153; interpreting military aggressions in, 153
*Crime and Punishment* (Dostoevsky), 30
Crimean Tatars, 19
Crimean War, 11, 18, 94, 169
Crimean War, strategy and doctrine after: changes in warfare, 31–34; debates prior to WWI, 48–52; development of strategic thought, 36–37; friends and foes in wake of war, 37–38; historical background, 29–31; identifying Germany/Austria as main threat, 38–40; lessons from Crimea, 34–36; military system reflecting political system, 40–43; morale *versus* technology, 46–48; need for modern army, 51–54; views on strategy on, 43–46
CST. *See* Collective Security Treaty
Cuban Missile Crisis, 83
*Culture of Military Innovation The Impact of Cultural Factors on the Revolutions in Military Affairs in Russia, Russia, the US, and Israel, The* (Adamsky), 9
Curas, Hilmar, 22
current war, military thinking on, 130–34

Danilenko, Ignat Semenovich, 85
"Dannyia dlia otsenki Vooruzhennykh sil Rossii" (Obruchev), 37
Darwin, Charles, 30
*Das Kapital* (Marx), 30
Decembrists, 24, 175
Declaration of Saint Petersburg, 32
defense, strategic, 90
defense sufficiency, 116
defensive strategy, 12–13, 90, 95, 114, 168; future war and, 74–75; and strategic nuclear weapons, 107–10. *See also* offensive strategy
Demidov Prize, 24
Denikin, Anton Ivanovich, 147
*Der totale Krieg* (Ludendroff), 67

détente, period of, 103–5
deterrence, strategic, 139–42
*Deterrence and the Revolution in Soviet Military Doctrine* (Garthoff), 7
dialectical materialism, 84–85
*Die Philosophie des Rechts nach geschichtlicher Ansicht* (Stahl), 67
doctrine, 1–4; debates on, 48–52; defensive, 114, 153, 169–70; distinction between "military thinking" and, 131; Maritime Doctrine of 2022, 152–53; naval, 93–96; nuclear/nonnuclear deterrence, 139–42; offensive, 169–70; Soviet, 9, 71, 92, 95; soviet military doctrine after World War II, 87; state, 87; term, 6–7; unified military, 62–63; and view of war, 106–7. *See also* military doctrine
Donbas, 130
Donetsk, Ukraine, 125, 144, 153
DOSAAF (Volunteer Society for Cooperation with the Army, Aviation, and Fleet), 149
Dostoevsky, Fyodor, 30
Dragomirov, Mikhail Ivanovich, 24, 29, 37, 45, 50, 69–70, 99, 177; continuing in footsteps of, 62; interpretations of war, 42–43; morale *versus* technology, 46–48; views on strategy, 43–46; writings about past-future balance, 52–53
Duffy, Christopher, 20

Eideman, Robert Petrovich, 62, 75
*Einleitung zur Universalhistorie* (Curas), 22
Eitelhuber, Norbert, 9
*Empire: The Russian Empire and Its Rivals* (Lieven), 8
*End of Tsarist Russia, The* (Lieven), 8
enemy, cultivation of hatred of, 93
Engels, Friedrich, 86
*Entsiklopediia voennykh i morskikh nauk* (Leer), 44
*Esli zavtra voina?* (Gareev), 132

Eugene, Prince of Savoy, 23
*Evolution of Strategy: Thinking War from Antiquity to the Present, The* (Heuser), 10

"father of Russian military thought." *See* Rumiantsev, Petr Aleksandrovich
February Revolution, 60
Federal Security Service (FSB), 155
Feodorovna, Maria, 147
Field Regulations, 77
Field Regulations from 1936 (PU-36), 75
fifth columnists, combatting, 151–52
*Filosofiia voiny* (Snesarev), 65–66
firepower, improvement of, 34
First Five-Year Plan, 76
Fomin, Aleksandr, 144
foreign policy, military organization and, 41
Foreign Policy Concept, 144
"Foundations for Russia's Naval Activity for the Period up to 2030," 141
France, 19, 23, 30–31, 37–38, 54, 60–71
Franco-Prussian War, 29, 31, 38
Freedman, Lawrence, 5
French Revolutionary Wars, 32
Fridman, Ofer, 9
Frunze, Mikhail, 6, 63
Frunze Military Academy, 71, 84
FSB. *See* Federal Security Service
Fuller, William, 4, 8, 175
future war: "blitzkrieg of the twenty-first century," 142–43; impact of nuclear weapons on view of, 88–90; and military history, 134–35; military thinking on, 130–34; revolution in military affairs and, 110–12

Galeotti, Mark, 10
Gardie, Jacob Pontusson De la, 17
Gareev, Makhmut Akhmetovich, 13, 24, 97, 105, 115, 122, 125; criticizing sixth-generation warfare, 135; linking Crimean annexation to soft power, 144; military thinking on/current/future war, 132–33; nuclear/nonnuclear deterrence, 139–42
GARF. *See* State Archive of the Russian Federation
Garthoff, Raymond L., 7, 170
Gat, Azar, 10
general staff, rise of, 32–33, 131
General Staff Academy, 16, 18, 36, 50, 71, 74, 87, 145, 147; army-state connection, 40–42; and domestic military strategy, 64; Snesarev and, 64–65; strategy-politics connection, 68; and views on strategy, 43; war-state connection, 65
generational warfare ideas, 135
geography: indirect influence of, 169–70; role of, 51; strategic geography, 125–26
Georgia, 13, 122, 128, 131, 136, 153, 175
geography, role of, 72–74
Gerasimov, Valerii Vasilevich, 13, 24, 64, 90, 122, 129; "blitzkrieg" discussion, 143; military strategy, 149–52; outlining views on future war, 134–35
Gerasimov Doctrine, 130
Germany, 3, 36, 51, 72, 113, 116, 124, 168; holding up as example of "homogenous" state, 40; identifying as main threat, 38–40; peace treaty with, 60–61; Soviet-Germany military cooperation, 75–76; unification of, 31; World War II and, 98–99
Glantz, David, 9
Gneisenau, August von, 53
Goethe, Johann Wolfgang, 62
Golovin, Nikolai Nikolaevich, 50
Gorbachev, Mikhail Sergeevich, 105, 113–16, 139, 169, 174
Gorbatov, Aleksandr Vasilevich, 77
Gorchakov, Aleksandr Mikhailovich, 30
Gorshkov, Sergei Georgievich, 12–13, 82, 94
Grachev, Pavel Sergeevich, 123, 139

*Grand Strategy of the Soviet Union, The* (Luttwak), 9
Gray, Colin, 126
Great Northern War, 18–19
great-power status, Russian desire for, 175
Great Reforms, 34–36
Gromyko, Andreevich, 155
Guibert, Jacques Antoine Hippolyte, 21
Gulf War, 131, 134, 142–43

Hart, Basil Liddell, 89
Heine, Heinrich, 62
Herspring, Dale, 9
Heuser, Beatrice, 3, 10, 19
Higham, Robin, 9
*Histoire romaine depuis la fondation de Rome jusqu'à la bataille d'Actium* (Rollin), 23
historical materialism, 84–85
history (of early Russian strategic thought): developing strategic thought, 24–26; science of winning, 22–24; from steppe toward professionalization, 16–19; strategy and policy, 19–21
*History of Military Thought: From the Enlightenment to the Cold War, A* (Gat), 10
Høiback, Harald, 4, 11
Hübner, Johann, 22–23
hybrid war, 86, 130–31, 133, 144, 151

ICBMs. *See* intercontinental ballistic missiles
Ilyin, Ivan Aleksandrovich, 147
Immortal Regiment, concept, 149
imperialistic war, category, 86–87
Imperial Military Academy, 24
INF Treaty. *See* Intermediate-Range Nuclear Forces Treaty
intelligence briefs, focus of, 98–99
intercontinental ballistic missiles (ICBMs), 104, 112
Interim Agreement on Offensive Weapons, 104

Intermediate-Range Nuclear Forces Treaty (INF Treaty), 113
*Introduction to Military Geography* (Snesarev), 73
Iraq, 129, 131, 142–43, 150, 177
*Istoriia sovetskoi i voennoi mysli: Kratkii ocherk; 1917–iiun 1941* (Korotkov), 8
*Istoriia uchit bditelnost* (Ogarkov), 106, 109, 110
*Istoriia voennoi strategii*, 77
*Istoriia voennoi strategii Rossii*, 8
Iunarmiia (Youth Army), 149
Ivanovich, Vasilii, 22
Ivashov, Leonid Grigorevich, 17, 156

Jellinek, Georg, 67–68
Jomini, Antoine-Henri, 2, 5, 18, 25, 40, 44
Jonsson, Oscar, 9

Kagan, Frederick, 9
Kazakhstan, 124
Kersnovskii, Anton Antonovich, 167, 172, 178
key concepts, 5–7
Khamzatov, Musa Magomedovich, 117, 125, 142–43, 171
Khodarenok, Mikhail Mikhailovich, 156
Khrushchev, Nikita Sergeevich, 82, 83, 87, 103, 174
Khrushchev Thaw, 65, 87
Kiev, Ukraine, 19, 125
Kiev Military District, 35
Kipp, Jacob, 135
Kirill, Patriarch, 18
Kjellén, Rudolf, 67
Kliuchevskii, Vasilii Osipovich, 174
Kofman, Michael, 112
Kokoshin, Andrei Afanasevich, 7–8, 13, 61, 64, 105, 122, 137–38
Kolesnikov, Mikhail Petrovich, 64
Konyshev, Valerii, 4
Korotkov, I. A., 8
Kosovo, 127–28, 142, 177

Kuibyshev Military Engineering Academy, 105
Kulikov, Marshal Viktor Georgievich, 115
*Kurze Fragen aus der alten und neuen Geographie* (Hübner), 23

land organization *(zemelnoe ustroistvo)*, 37
"La Russie ne boude pas, mais se recueille" (Gorchakov), 30–31
"lawfulness" *(zakonnost)*. See Prussia
Law on Strategic Planning, 126
Leer, Genrikh Antonovich, 5, 29, 37, 40–41, 64; accusations against, 42; defining offensive war, 42; and views on strategy, 43–46
Lenin, Vladimir Ilich, 24
Leonhard, Wolfgang, 85
Libya, 131, 150
Lieven, Dominic, 8
Likhonosov, Aleksandr, 145–46
Lloyd, Henry, 2, 21, 25, 40, 44
Lomov, Nikolai, 87
Ludendorff, Erich, 67
Luttwak, Edward, 9

MacMillan, Margaret, 2
Main Staff, 36, 43, 48, 50, 55n20, 68
Makarov, Nikolai Egorovich, 13, 49, 98, 117–18, 122, 124, 136, 150, 170, 173
Marshall, Andrew, 3
Maritime Doctrine, 152–53
Marxism-Leninism: affecting military strategy and doctrine, 99; compromise with, 92; confrontation according to, 82–83; ideological "scientific law" of, 74–75; and offensive strategy, 90; scientific claims of, 85; sociohistorical phenomenon as defined by, 86
Matthews, Owen, 10
Medem, Nikolai Vasilevich, 24–26, 46
Medinskii, Vladimir, 143

megatheory, creating, 134
Meshcheriakov, G. P., 8
*Mes rêveries* (Saxe), 23
Messner, Evgenii Eduardovich, 167
Miakinkov, Eugene, 18
Middle East, 150
Mikhalev, Sergei Nikolaevich, 77
Mikhnevich, Nikolai, 50
Mikhnevich, Nikolai Petrovich, 29
military: conflict types, 131–32; cooperation, 75–76; council establishment, 17, 20; district creation, 35, 38, 137; doctrine after World War II, 87; future war and military history, 134–35; Gerasimov and military strategy, 149–52; specialists, 60, 65; thinking on current and future war, 130–34; reforming, 34–36, 135–38; revolution in military affairs, 110–12; science, 43–46, 137; Soviet military doctrine, 64, 91, 112–15, 172; unified military doctrine, 62–63; and view of war, 106–7. *See also* military thought
military doctrine, 3, 6–7, 12, 22; contributing to development of, 19–20; debates on, 48–52; Gorbachev and, 113–16; revolution in military affairs, 110–12; Soviet military doctrine, 64, 91, 112–15, 172; unified military doctrine, 62–63; and view of war, 106–7; between world wars, 61–62
Military Doctrine of 1993, 127, 139, 158n24
Military Doctrine of 2000, 129
Military Doctrine of 2014, 7, 127–32, 139, 141–42, 153
*Military History of Russia: From Ivan the Terrible to the War in Chechnya, A* (Stone), 9
*Military History of the Soviet Union, The* (Kagan), 9
*Military History of Tsarist Russia, The* (Kagan), 9

Military-Scientific Committee, 43
military strategy, 8, 11–12; Gerasimov and, 149–52; history of, 18; and legacy of World War II, 82, 84–85, 87, 89, 92, 94–95, 99; nuclear weapons and, 105–6, 108, 113, 115, 117; post-Soviet strategy, 131–32, 137–38, 145, 150; and unified military doctrine, 62–64
*Military Strategy of the Soviet Union: A History, The* (Glantz), 9
military theory, debate on, 43–46
military thought: brief history of early strategic thought, 16–28; Crimean War and, 29–58; crisis of, 134; distinction between "doctrine," 6–7; factors influencing development of, 3; following Soviet Union dissolution, 122–166; forming Soviet strategy, 59–81; importance of studying, 1–3; key concepts, 5–7; legacy of World War II, 82–102; limitations of analyzing, 10–11; outlining, 11–13; previous research on, 7–10; process of studying, 4–5; role of geography in, 72–74; sources, 7; Soviet Union-Civil War strategic thought development, 59–83; strategy beyond nuclear weapons, 103–21; thoughts on art of winning, 167–78
Miliutin, Dmitrii Alekseevich, 12, 24, 29, 34, 40, 49, 98, 137, 170
Minic, Dimitri, 9
modernists, 4
modernity (of warfare), 31–34
Mongols, 16, 54
morale: balancing act, 51–54; nuclear war and, 92–93; technology *versus*, 46–48
*Morskaia moshch gosudarstva* (Gorshkov), 94
Moscow University, 17

Napoleonic Wars, 18, 24, 32, 42, 60
Napoleon III, 31

*Na sluzhbe Rossii*, 117
nationalism, growth of, 36
nationality, question of, 175
national security, 126–30
National Security Concept 2000, 128–29
National Security Strategy (NSS), 126–30
nationalism, growth of, 37
national spirit *(narodnyi dukh)*, 43
NATO. *See* North Atlantic Treaty Organization
*Nauka pobezhdat* (Suvorov), 22, 24, 47
New Economic Policy, 61
"new Soviet man," creating, 93
new thoughts and theories, adapting to, 2–3
new-type warfare, 135
*Nezavisimoe voennoe obozrenie*, 7
Nicholas I, 18, 24, 30, 47
Nicholas II, 12, 48, 50, 174
Nikolaevich, Mikhail, 38
Nikolaevich, Nikolai, 48
"no-first-use" principle. *See* deterrence, strategic; nuclear weapons
nonlinear warfare, 64, 130, 171
nonmilitary means, discussing use of, 89–90
nonnuclear deterrence, 139–42
North Atlantic Treaty, 84
North Atlantic Treaty Organization (NATO), 84, 111, 124, 127–29, 133, 152
Northern Caucasus Military District, 65
NSS. *See* National Security Strategy
Nuclear Deterrence Policy, 141
nuclear war: and impact of nuclear weapons, 88–90; initial period of, 91–92; moral in, 92–93. *See also* nuclear weapons
nuclear weapons: deterrence, 139–42; and fall of Soviet Union, 124; Gorbachev and, 113–16; impact of, 88–90; initial period of war involving, 91–92; military doctrine and view of war,

nuclear weapons (*continued*)
106–7; moral in war involving, 92–93; offensive *versus* defensive, 107–10; and period of détente, 103–5; revolution in military affairs, 110–12; strategy and policy, 105–6

*Obozrenie izvestneishikh pravil i sistem strategii* (Medem), 25
*Obriad Sluzhby* (Customs of military service) (Rumiantsev), 19
Obruchev, Nikolai Nikolaevich, 30, 37, 53, 149; and Far East, 48; identifying Germany/Austria as main threat, 38–40
October Revolution, 149
Odom, William, 8, 175
offensive strategy, 12–13, 54, 83, 95, 168; *versus* defensive strategy, 90; and initial period of nuclear war, 91; regarding future war, 74–75; and strategic nuclear weapons, 107–10
offensive war, defining, 12, 18, 41–42, 64
Office of Net Assessment (Pentagon), 3
Ogarkov, Nikolai Vasilevich, 13, 98, 155, 170, 173; defining relationship between military strategy and policy, 105–6; legacy of, 116–18; nuclear/nonnuclear deterrence, 139–42; revolution in military affairs, 110–12; on use of strategic nuclear weapons, 107–10
Okudzhava, Bulat, 122
*One Soldier's War in Chechnya* (Babchenko), 93
*On the Origin of Species* (Darwin), 30
*On War* (Clausewitz), 44–45, 65
Operation Vesna, 76
*Opyt kritiko-istoricheskogo issledovaniia zakonov iskusstva vedeniia voiny* (Leer), 43–44
Orange Revolution, 145
Order No. 55, 76
*Osnovy strategii* (Mikhnevich), 50

Ottoman Empire, 19, 38
*Overreach: The Inside Story of Putin's War against Ukraine* (Matthews), 10

Panin, Nikita, 20, 21
Patriotic War of 1812, 53
patriotism, Russian history and, 146–49
Paul I, 23
peaceful coexistence, 103–5, 146
*Pensée et culture stratégiques russes: Du contournement de la lutte armée à la guerre en Ukraine* (Minic), 9
Peter I, 17
Peter the Great, 18, 93, 174
Pintner, Walter, 2
Pirogov, Nikolai Ivanovich, 46
Plokhy, Serhii, 10
Poland, past/potential wars with, 19, 39–40, 54, 60, 72, 104, 107, 111, 113, 175
policy: early foundations of, 19–21; foreign policy, 3, 6, 17, 41, 50, 54, 87, 103, 106, 113, 127, 142, 144, 154; history of early Russian strategic thought, 19–21; legacy of World War II, 84–87; military, 13, 41, 83, 104; no first-use, 107–9; nuclear weapons, 105–6; "peaceful coexistence," 71, 103–4, 146; security, 122, 126–27, 130, 139, 142; state, 85, 148; strategy beyond nuclear weapons, 105–6; World War II legacy, 84–87. *See also* doctrine; military thought
Polish-Lithuanian Commonwealth, 17
politics, strategy and, 68–72
*Politics and the Russian Army: Civil-Military Relations, 1689–2000*, 9
*Politologiia i sotsiologiia voennoi strategii*, 8
Popov, Igor Mikhailovich, 117–18, 142–43, 171
post-Soviet strategy: "blitzkrieg of the twenty-first century," 142–43; changing rules of war, 149–52; color

revolutions, 144–46; contradictions in invasion of Ukraine, 155–57; controlled chaos, 144–46; end of Cold War, 122–25; future warfare and military history, 134–35; illegal annexation of Ukraine, 153–55; military reform, 135–38; military thinking on current/future war, 130–34; national security, 126–30; nuclear/nonnuclear deterrence, 139–42; role of Russian history, 146–49; soft power, 144–46; strategic geography, 125–26; strategic planning, 135–38; threat assessment, 126–30; updated Maritime Doctrine, 152–53. *See also* Russia; Soviet strategy, forming; Soviet Union
Potemkin, Grigorii, 21
Preobrazhensky Life Guards Regiment, 19
Primakov, Evgenii Maksimovich, 127–28
primary/secondary education, introduction of, 17–18
professionalization, progress toward, 16–19
Prompt Global Strike, 140, 143, 151
Prussia, 18, 21, 29, 31–32, 37–38, 40–41, 43, 48, 53
public life, universal military service and, 41
Putin, Vladimir Vladimirovich, 113, 147, 149, 152; defining soft power, 144; and framing illegal annexation of Crimea, 125–26, 153–54; invading Ukraine, 155–57; patriotism and, 147–49; repressive political system under, 171; Russian identity as "national sport," 176; strategic geography, 125–26; thoughts exploited under leadership of, 133
*Putin's Wars: From Chechnya to Ukraine* (Galeotti), 10

racial connections, 37
raids, strategy, 16–17
rationality, doctrine, 11
recruitment system, devising, 17

Red Army, 9, 24, 60–61, 68, 136, 151; and consequences of repressions, 76–77; strategic offensive/defensive and, 74–76; strategy and politics, 70–72; "strong morale" of, 92; World War II and, 84
"Red Army man" *(krasnoarmeets)*, rank, 60
"Red commander" *(krasnyi komandir)*, rank, 60
Red Cross, 32
reform (of military), 135–38
Repin, Ilya, 42
*Reply of the Zoporozhian Cossacks to Sultan Mehmed IV of Turkey* (Repin), 42
repressions, consequences of, 76–77
revolutionaries, 4
revolution in military affairs, 110–12
RGVIA. *See* Russian Military History Archive
Rich, David, 8
Rogozin, Dmitrii, 143
Rokossovsky, Konstantinovich, 77
Rollin, Charles, 23
*Rossiiskii voennyi sbornik*, 7
Rozanov, Vasilii, 123
Rumiantsev, Petr Aleksandrovich, 16, 19–22
Russia: army of, 2, 8–19, 21, 33–34, 36–38, 40–41, 53, 60, 167, 173; brief history of early strategic thought, 16–28; color revolutions, 144–46; controlled chaos, 144–46; Crimean War changing, 29–58; existence as state, 1–2; fall of Soviet Union, 122–25; following Soviet Union dissolution, 122–66; Foreign Policy Concept, 144; forming Soviet strategy, 59–81; forming strategy following World War I, 60–62; formulating military policy for, 41–42; friends and foes in wake of Crimea, 37–38; geostrategic position of, 125–26;

Russia (*continued*)
  identifying Germany/Austria as main threat, 38–40; importance of studying strategic thought of, 1–3; key concepts, 5–7; legacy of World War II, 82–102; lessons learned/not learned from World War II, 96–99; limitations of analyzing, 10–11; military thinking on current/future war, 130–34; morale *versus* technology, 43–46; myth of "third Rome," 148; naval doctrine of, 93–96; and nuclear weapons, 91–93; nuclear/nonnuclear deterrence, 139–42; outlining, 11–13; perception of West attacking, 147; post-Soviet military strategy, 149–52; previous research on, 7–10; process of studying strategic thought of, 4–5; relevance of army of, 51–54; and role of geography, 72–74; Russo-Ukrainian War, 153–57; soft power, 144–46; sources, 7; Soviet-Germany military cooperation, 75–76; Soviet Union-Civil War strategic thought development, 59–83; strategy beyond nuclear weapons, 103–21; thoughts on art of winning, 167–78; views on strategy in, 43–46. *See also* post-Soviet strategy
*Russia, the West and Military Intervention* (Allison), 8
Russian Armed Forces, 22, 149; creation of, 122–25; development of, 150; domestic role of, 151–52; dualism of, 172–73; four kinds of military conflicts, 131; fundamental reform of, 136–37; patriotism and, 147; and strategic geography, 125; and war against Ukraine, 155–56. *See also* Russia: army of
*Russian Army in a Time of Troubles, The* (Baev), 8
Russian Criminal Code, 145
Russian doctrine, developing, 62–63

Russian Empire, 1, 17, 60, 174
Russian Federation, 1, 7–8, 13, 68, 104, 125–26, 129–30, 132, 136, 139–40, 142, 146, 148, 153
Russian history, role of, 146–49
*Russian "Hybrid Warfare": Resurgence and Politicization* (Fridman), 9
Russian Military-Historical Society, 143
Russian Military History Archive (RGVIA), 7
*Russian Nuclear Orthodoxy: Religion, Politics, and Strategy* (Adamsky), 9
Russian Orthodox Church, 9, 146, 148
Russian Revolution of 1905, 12, 48
Russian Sun Tzu. *See* Snesarev, Andrei Evgenevich
*Russian Understanding of War: Blurring the Lines between War and Peace, The* (Jonsson), 9
*Russian Way of Deterrence, The* (Adamsky), 10
*Russkaia voennaia mysl konets XIX-nachalo XX v.* (Zhilin), 8
*Russkaia voennaia mysl v XIX-om veke* (Meshcheriakov), 8
*Russkaia voenno-teoreticheskaia mysl XIX i nachala XX vekov* (Beskrovnyi), 8
*Russkii invalid*, 36
*Russland im 21. Jahrhundert: Reif für eine multipolare Welt?* (Eitelhuber), 9
Russo-Georgian War, 136
Russo-Japanese War, 12, 48, 62
Russo-Polish War, 65
Russo-Swedish War, 19
Russo-Turkish War, 42, 46
Russo-Ukrainian War, 13, 122; contradictions, 155–57; illegal annexation of Crimea, 153; interpreting military aggressions in, 153; preceding events, 153–54; threats against Russia, 154–55. *See also* Crimea; Ukraine

SALT I. *See* Strategic Arms Limitation Talks
SALT II. *See* Strategic Arms Limitation Treaty
Samsonov, Viktor Nikolaevich, 123
Savinkin, A. E., 7
Saxe, Maurice de, 23
Scharnhorst, Gerhard von, 44, 53
sea warfare, importance of, 93–96
sea warfare. *See* doctrine: naval
Second Army, 19, 21
security policy, defining, 127
Serbia, 131
Serdiukov, Anatolii Eduardovich, 136
Sergunin, Aleksandr, 4
Seven Years' War, 19
Shaposhnikov, Boris Mikhailovich, 12, 50, 84, 168
Shaposhnikov, Evgenii Ivanovich, 123
Shoigu, Sergei Kuzhugetovich, 145
Shuvalov, Petr, 18
Sivkov, Konstantin Valentinovich, 141
sixth-generation warfare, 134
Skopin-Shuisky, Mikhail, 17
SLBMs. *See* submarine-launched ballistic missiles
Slipchenko, Vladimir Ivanovich, 134–35, 177
"small wars," theory, 94–95
*smutnoe vremia*. See Time of Troubles
Snesarev, Andrei Evgenevich, 5, 12, 44, 59, 62, 96, 126; approach to war and state, 65–68; defining unified military doctrine, 62–63; fate of, 77; influence on strategic thought, 63–64; preoccupation with military geography, 73–74; rise and fall of, 64–65
soft power, 144–46
Sokolovsky, Vasily Danilovich, 6, 82, 84, 87, 91
sources, 7
Soviet-Germany military cooperation, 75–76

*Soviet Military Encyclopedia*, 108
*Soviet Military Strategy* (Sokolovsky), 6, 12, 82, 84, 85–86, 88, 92–93, 99, 108; naval doctrine, 93–96
*Soviet Military Thought*, 104
Soviet Strategic Rocket Forces, 88
*Soviet Strategic Thought, 1917–91* (Kokoshin), 7
Soviet strategy, forming: consequences of repressions, 76–77; overview, 59; role of geography, 72–74; Snesarev influence on strategic thought, 63–68; Soviet-German military cooperation, 75–76; strategic intelligence, 72–74; strategic offensive/defensive, 74–75; strategy and politics, 68–72; between two world wars, 59–62; unified military doctrine, 62–63. *See also* post-Soviet strategy
Soviet Union, 1, 3, 6, 13, 54, 69, 169–75; borders of, 73; crucial issues, 60–63; dissolution of, 122–25; fall of, 122–25; Gorbachev leading, 113–16; ignoring nationalities, 175–77; and legacy of World War II, 83–87, 90, 93–95, 99; likely enemy coalition against, 72; national security following end of, 126–30; nuclear weapons and, 103–5, 107–16, 118; possible use of strategic nuclear weapons, 107–10; post-Soviet strategy, 122–66; revolution in military affairs, 110–12; Soviet-Germany military cooperation, 75–76; strategic offensive/defensive of, 75. *See also* post–Soviet strategy; Soviet strategy, forming
"speed, assessment, attack," doctrine, 23–24
Stahl, Friedrich Julius, 67
Stalin, Joseph, 12, 22, 83
state: army and, 40–43; doctrine of, 87; essence of, 68; existence of, 68, 139–40, 156; goal of, 67–68; goals of,

state (*continued*)
  67–68; Maritime Doctrine of 2022, 152–53; military-state achievements, 6, 63; power of, 5, 94; relationship between war and, 67; security of, 52, 127, 152, 173; war and, 65–68. *See also under* army; Russia
State Archive of the Russian Federation (GARF), 7
State Armament Program 2011, 136
state-army connection, 40–43
State Defense Council, 48
*stavka*, establishing, 138
steppe, army evolving from, 16–19
Stone, David R., 9
Strategic Arms Limitation Talks (SALT I), 104
Strategic Arms Limitation Treaty (SALT II), 104
strategic culture, 9, 11, 107, 138, 170, 177
strategic deterrence, term, 138
strategic geography, 125–26
*Strategicheskoe upravlenie* (Kokoshin), 138
strategic intelligence, 72–74
strategic planning, 135–38; assessment of oneself, 138; passing law on, 137–38; political leadership, 138
strategic thought: brief history of, 16–28; and Crimean War, 29–58; developing, 24–26; development of, 36–37; factors influencing development of, 3; following Soviet Union dissolution, 122–66; forming Soviet strategy, 59–81; importance of studying, 1–3; key concepts, 5–7; legacy of World War II, 82–102; limitations of analyzing, 10–11; outlining, 11–13; previous research on, 7–10; process of studying, 4–5; role of geography in, 72–74; Snesarev influence on, 63–64; sources, 7; Soviet Union-Civil War strategic thought development, 59–83; strategy beyond nuclear weapons, 103–21; thoughts on

art of winning, 167–78. *See also under* Russia
*Strategiia* (Svechin), 66, 85
*Strategiya: The Foundations of the Russian Art of Strategy* (Fridman), 8–9
strategy: debates on, 48–52; early foundations of, 19–21; policy and, 84–87; politics and, 68–72; Snesarev on, 65–68; strategy beyond nuclear weapons, 105–6; term, 5–6; views on, 43–46. *See also* strategic thought
*Strategy and Power in Russia 1640–1914* (Fuller), 8
*Strategy of Indirect Approach, The* (Hart), 89
Struve, Petr Berngardovich, 174
submarine-launched ballistic missiles (SLBMs), 104
Sukhotin, Nikolai Nikolaevich, 18–19
*Summary of the Art of War* (Jomini), 5
Suvorov, Aleksandr, 150
Svechin, Aleksandr, 12, 21, 59, 62, 83, 96, 117, 171; on role of geography, 72–74; on strategic intelligence, 72–74; strategy of destruction, 74–75
Sweden, 17–18, 38, 42, 72
Swedish Academy of War Sciences, 40
Syria, 131, 143, 150, 153

Tashkent Treaty, 124
Taylor, Brian, 9
technology: balancing act, 51–54; morale *versus*, 46–48. *See also* morale
territorial expansion, Russia and, 175
Third Republic, 31
*Thought* (Rumiantsev), 19
threat, assessment of, 126–30
Time of Troubles (*smutnoe vremia*), 16–17
Tiushkevich, Stepan Andreevich, 115, 134
Tolstoy, Leo, 29, 30
traditionalists, 4, 174

trains, military use of, 33
Treaty of Brest-Litovsk, 65
Treaty of Paris, 31
Treaty of Rapallo, 75
Treaty on Conventional Armed Forces in Europe (CFE Treaty), 113
Treaty on the Limitations of Anti-Ballistic Missile Systems, 104
Triandafillov, Vladimir, 75
*Tsar's Colonels: Professionalism, Strategy, and Subversion in Late Imperial Russia, The* (Rich), 8
Tukhachevskii, Mikhail Nikolaevich, 12, 59, 61, 65, 68, 83; death of, 77; strategy and politics, 70–74; strategy of destruction, 74–75
Tumakov, Oleg, 156
Turenne, Henri de La Tour d'Auvergne de, 23
Turkistan Military District, 64

Uborevich, Ieronim, 75
Ukraine, 2, 10, 145, 147, 151, 171, 177; full-scale invasion of, 2, 18, 64, 90, 151, 153, 155–57, 169–70, 176; "nationality question," 72; nuclear weapons in, 124; Russo-Ukrainian War, 153–55; strategic geography, 125–26; strategy and policy, 19–21; surrendering, 60–61. *See also* Russo-Ukrainian War
unified military doctrine, defined, 62–63
United Nations Protection Force, 125
United Nations Security Council, 150
United States, 117, 154, 170–71, 175; assessing threat of, 128–29, 133; beginning of Cold War, 83–84; controlled chaos and, 145; and end of Cold War, 123–24; INF Treaty and, 113; nuclear war and, 91, 109, 112; period of détente and, 104; Prompt Global Strike and, 140; and revised Maritime Doctrine, 152; Russian patriotism and, 147–48; strategy and policy regarding, 105; "twenty-first-century blitzkrieg" and, 143. *See also* West
Universal Copyright Convention, 104
universal military service: as consequence of tendency toward public life, 41; creation of, 35–36
Ustinov, Dmitrii, 108, 133, 155
Ustinov, Dmitrii Fedorovich, 104

Valdai Discussion Club, 147
values, perceived attacking of, 146–49
Vauban, Sébastien Le Prestre de, 22
Versailles, King Wilhelm I of Prussia, 31
*Vestnik Akademii voennykh nauk* (Bulletin of the Academy of Military Sciences), 7
victory, concept, 177–78
Vladimirov, Aleksandr Ivanovich, 146, 178
*Voennaia mysl*, 7, 62, 114, 156
*Voennaia mysl i revoliutsiia*, 62
*Voennaia nauka i revoliutsiia*, 62
*Voennaia strategiia* (Kokoshin), 138
*Voennoe delo*, 62
*Voenno-promyshlennyi kurier*, 7
*Voennye reformy 1860–70 godov v Rossii*, 8
*Voennyi entsiklopedicheskii slovar*, 113
*Voennyi sbornik*, 36, 47, 62
Voide, Karl, 45
*Voina budushchego: Kontseptualnye osnovy i prakticheskie vyvody; Ocherki strategicheskoi mysli*, 117
*Voina i revoliutsiia*, 62
Voroshilov, Kliment, 133
Voroshilov, Kliment Efremovich, 65

Wahlde, Peter von, 4
war: basic categories of, 86–87; asymmetrical warfare, 130, 135; "blitzkrieg of the twenty-first century," 142–43; doctrine dualism, 85; future war

war (*continued*)
characteristics, 89; future warfare, 134–35; hybrid war, 86; impact of nuclear weapons on the view of future war, 88–90; kinds of military conflicts, 131–32; military doctrine and view of, 106–7; military thinking on current/future war, 130–34; modern war character, 88; "small wars" theory, 94–95; Snesarev on, 65–68. *See also* military thought
*War and Peace* (Tolstoy), 30, 46
warfare: becoming "modern," 31–32; changes in, 31–34; requirements leading to changes in, 49; role of geography in, 51
War Ministry, 35–36, 38, 48
War of Polish Succession, 19
Warsaw Pact, 107, 110–11, 114, 116
West, 1–2, 12, 21, 96, 118, 141, 150, 168, 170–71, 176, 178; assessing as threat, 127–30; color revolutions and, 144–46; controlled chaos and, 144–46; depicting as reactionary, 82–83; doctrines of, 6; and future war, 90, 130–34; impressing, 85; inspiration from, 53; intense confrontation in, 17; and Maritime Doctrine, 152; and military reform, 136; morale and, 93; Ogarkov infamy in, 105; patriotism and, 146–48; perceived attacks from, 147; and Russo-Ukrainian War, 153–54; soft power and, 144–46; as source of inspiration, 53; and strategy of attrition, 69–70. *See also* Cold War; nuclear weapons; Russia
Westernization of culture, 147–48
winning: science of, 22–24; thoughts on art of, 167–78

Witte, Sergei Iulevich, 174
world war, category, 86–87
World War I, forming Soviet strategy following, 12, 29, 43, 54, 89–91, 109, 138, 147, 149, 173; consequences of repressions, 76–77; debates on strategy and doctrine prior to World War I, 48–52; forming strategy following World War I, 60–62; overview, 59; role of geography, 72–74; Snesarev influence on strategic thought, 63–68; Soviet-German military cooperation, 75–76; strategic intelligence, 72–74; strategic offensive/defensive, 74–75; strategy and politics, 68–72; between two world wars, 59–62; unified military doctrine, 62–63. *See also* post-Soviet strategy
World War II, legacy of, 24, 60, 75; beginning of Cold War, 83–84; initial period of nuclear war, 91–92; lessons learned/not learned, 96–99; naval doctrine, 93–96; nuclear weapons, 88–90; overview, 82–83; Soviet military doctrine, 87; strategic offense/defense, 90; strategy and policy, 84–87
world wars, strategic thought development between, 60–62
writings, choosing, 4–5

Yakovlev, Aleksandr Nikolaevich, 175–76
Yanushkevich, Nikolai Nikolaevich, 50
Yazov, Dmitrii Timofeev, 114–15
Young Turks, 50

Zaionchkovskii, P. A., 8
Zeddeler, Loggin Logginovich, 47
Zhilin, P. A., 8
Zhukov, Georgii Konstantinovich, 77
Zolotarev, Vladimir Antonovich, 8, 172

# ABOUT THE AUTHOR

**DR. GUDRUN PERSSON** is an associate professor in Slavic studies at Stockholm University. She has published widely on Soviet and Russian affairs and is the author of *Det sovjetiska arvet* (The Soviet legacy; 2011), *Learning from Foreign Wars: Russian Military Thinking 1859–1873* (2010), *Varför föll Sovjetunionen?* (Why did the Soviet Union fall?; 2006), and *Gulag* (2005). In 2023 she was awarded His Majesty the King's Medal, 8th Size, "for outstanding research in the field of security policy."